Of Heroes and Villains

The Influence of the Psalmic Lament
on Synoptic Characterization

D. KEITH CAMPBELL

WIPF & STOCK · Eugene, Oregon

OF HEROES AND VILLAINS
The Influence of the Psalmic Lament on Synoptic Characterization

Copyright © 2013 D. Keith Campbell. All rights reserved. Except for brief quotations in critical publications or reviews, no part of this book may be reproduced in any manner without prior written permission from the publisher. Write: Permissions, Wipf and Stock Publishers, 199 W. 8th Ave., Suite 3, Eugene, OR 97401.

Scripture quotations are from The Holy Bible, English Standard Version® (ESV®), copyright © 2001 by Crossway, a publishing ministry of Good News Publishers. Used by permission. All rights reserved.

Wipf & Stock
An Imprint of Wipf and Stock Publishers
199 W. 8th Ave., Suite 3
Eugene, OR 97401

www.wipfandstock.com

ISBN 13: 978-1-62032-923-8

Manufactured in the U.S.A.

Dedicated to the Messiah who was human enough to lament

Contents

Acknowledgments | ix

List of Abbreviations | xi

1   Introduction | 1
2   Mark's Appropriation of the Psalmic Lament | 29
3   Matthew's Appropriation of the Psalmic Lament | 73
4   Luke's Appropriation of the Psalmic Lament? | 134
5   Conclusion | 173

Bibliography | 181

Acknowledgments

GEORGE COLMAN, AN EIGHTEENTH-CENTURY English dramatist, once quipped, "Praise the bridge that carried you." Journeys in writing are long—very long—with chasms that expand vast valleys. Many people carried me on this journey, often sacrificially building for me bridges over these chasms—so many, in fact, that it's impossible to mention them all. But certain people deserve a hearty "thank you" for selflessly supporting me along the way.

My thanks begin with the one who, for reasons that only grace can explain, chose me before the creation of the world (Eph 1:4); for, when all is said and done, it is from him and through him and to him that all things are (Rom 11:36). Beyond thanking Christ, I also thank Rick Hughes (along with the members at Cartledge Creek Baptist Church), who, in faithfulness to the call, introduced me to Jesus nearly twenty years ago, and his wife, Kathy, who modeled faithful discipleship in the complexities of everyday life. Noah Webster cannot produce enough words to adequately say "thank you" to my mom, Linda Cagle, for the exemplary life that she so sacrificially expends for others. Burney, your gifts and hospitality over the years cannot be repaid. Dad (Doug) and Nancy Campbell, thank you for so many contributions (both monetary and otherwise) over the years, including the PC that bore the five-year brunt of manuscript typing.

Chris Hawks, Roger Shuford, Bryan "Big Dog" Blackwell, Richard "Ricardo" Alexander, and Steven "Dr. Steve" Heatherly—the best friends a man could have—thank you for keeping me grounded and humbled and for always helping me see the forest while I too often focused on the trees. Luke Smith, a pastor, scholar, and friend, our long talks about every imaginable theological, philosophical, and political topic (not to mention your kind input on chapters 1–2 of this book) continue to shape

Acknowledgments

me. Centerville Baptist Church—a people I love and cherish—you were a wonderful congregation to shepherd while writing much of this work. Brian and Mendie Campbell, Angie and Jami Goldberg, Paul "P. J." and Mandy Reed, and Jennifer Griffin, thanks for being the brothers and sisters that every person should have and for making me "Uncle Keith" to the most wonderful seven-year-olds on earth: Ana "Banana", "Z-Dog" Zachary, Selah "Belālah," and "Action" Jaxon.

For those hard-to-find resources, Dougald McLaurin Jr., Tom Innes, and the SEBTS library staff, your work is stellar and your calling much appreciated. Michaella Johnson, thanks for making my nouns and verbs agree. Scott Gibson, thanks for being a mentor and friend. Andreas Köstenberger, Heath Thomas, and Alan Bandy, thank you for your rigorous scholarship, insightful guidance, and valuable input in helping this revised version of my 2011 Southeastern Baptist Theological Seminary PhD dissertation ("The Influence of the Psalmic Lament on the Synoptic Gospels: A Study in Characterization") see the light of day. And, especially thank you to Joel F. Williams; your selfless help, patient persistence (especially in so many e-mail correspondences with me), and timely encouragements in bringing this manuscript to publication, particularly amidst your own demanding teaching and writing schedule, reflects your admirable love for scholarship and faithfulness to the kingdom.

Finally, Rhonda (who moved from girlfriend to fiancée to wife while writing this manuscript—which alone deserves an award!), your patient and persistent encouragements and your genuine sweetness made the long days bearable and the good days magnificent.

Abbreviations

ABD	Anchor Bible Dictionary
ABR	Australian Biblical Review
ANE	Ancient Near East
ATR	Anglican Theological Review
AUSS	Andres University Seminary Studies
AYB	The Anchor Yale Bible
BASOR	Bulletin of the American Schools of Oriental Research
BBB	Bulletin de bibliographie biblique
BBR	Bulletin for Biblical Research
BDAG	A Greek-English Lexicon of the New Testament and Other Early Christian Literature (2001)
BECNT	Baker Exegetical Commentary on the New Testament
BET	Beiträge zur evangelischen Theologie
BETL	Bibliotheca ephemeridum theologicarum lovaniensium
BibInt	Biblical Interpretation
BL	The Bible Translator
BNTC	Black's New Testament Commentaries
BR	Biblical Research
BTB	Biblical Theology Bulletin
BZNW	Beihefte zur Zeitschrift für die neutestamentliche Wissenschaft und die Kunde der älteren Kirche
CBQ	Catholic Biblical Quarterly
CS	Chicago Studies

Abbreviations

DBCI	*Dictionary of Biblical Criticism and Interpretation*
EBC	*The Expositor's Bible Commentary*
EKKNT	Evangelisch-Katholischer Kommentar zum Neuen Testament
EQ	*Evangelical Quarterly*
ESV	English Standard Version
ET	English Translation
FB	Forschung zur Bibel
FOTL	The Forms of the Old Testament Literature
FRLANT	Forschungen zur Religion und Literature des Alten und Neuen Testaments
GBS	Guides to Biblical Scholarship
HBT	*Horizons in Biblical Theology*
HeyJ	*Heythrop Journal*
HKNT	Handkommentar zum Neuen Testament
HNT	Handbuch zum Neuen Testament
HTKNT	Herders Theologischer Kommentar zum Neuen Testament
HTR	*Harvard Theological Review*
ICC	International Critical Commentary
Int	*Interpretation*
IRT	Issues in Religion and Theology
ITQ	*Irish Theological Quarterly*
ITSS	Invitation to Theological Studies Series
JAAR	*Journal of the American Academy of Religion*
JAOS	*Journal of the American Oriental Society*
JBL	*Journal of Biblical Literature*
JBT	*Jahrbuch für Biblische Theologie*
JES	*Journal of Ecumenical Studies*
JETS	*Journal of the Evangelical Theological Society*
JSNT	*Journal for the Study of the New Testament*
JSNTSup	Journal for the Study of the New Testament Supplement Series

Abbreviations

JSOT	*Journal for the Study of the Old Testament*
JTS	*Journal of Theological Studies*
LHBOTS	Library of Hebrew Bible/Old Testament Studies
Lit.	Literally
LNTS	Library of New Testament Studies
LXX	Septuagint
MSS	Manuscripts
MT	Masoretic Text
NA^{27}	Novum Testamentum Graece (27th ed.)
NAC	New American Commentary
NAS	New American Standard
NASB	New American Standard Bible
NEB	New English Bible
NIB	The New Interpreters Bible
NIBC	New International Biblical Commentary
NICNT	The New International Commentary on the New Testament
NIGTC	New International Greek Testament Commentary
NIV	New International Version
NLT	New Living Translation
NovT	*Novum Testamentum*
NSBT	New Studies in Biblical Theology
NT	New Testament
NTS	*New Testament Studies*
NTSup	Novum Testamentum Supplement Series
NTT	New Testament Theology
NTTS	New Testament Tools and Studies
OBO	Orbis biblicus et orientalis
OT	Old Testament
OTG	Old Testament Guides
PNTC	The Pillar New Testament Commentary
PSPLC	Palgrave Studies in Pragmatics, Language and Cognition

Abbreviations

PTMS	Princeton Theological Monograph Series
Q	*Quelle* (German "Source")
Repr.	Reprinted
RSV	Revised Standard Version
SBEC	Studies in the Bible and Early Christianity
SGUA	Sammelbuch griechischer Urkunden aus Aegypten
SBJT	*Southern Baptist Journal of Theology*
SNT	Studien zum Neuen Testament
SBL	Society of Biblical Literature
SBLDS	Society of Biblical Literature Dissertation Series
SBLMS	Society of Biblical Literature Monograph Series
SHBC	Smyth & Helwys Bible Commentary
SJT	*Scottish Journal of Theology*
SNTG	Studies in New Testament Greek
SNTSMS	Society for New Testament Studies Monograph Series
SP	Sacra Pagina
ST	*Studia Theologica*
SupNT	Supplements to Novum Testamentum
TDNT	*Theological Dictionary of the New Testament*
THNT	Theologischer Handkommentar zum Neuen Testament
TPINTC	TPI New Testament Commentaries
TS	*Theological Studies*
v.	Verse
WBC	Word Biblical Commentary
WUNT	Wissenschaftliche Untersuchungen zum Neuen Testament
WW	*Word and World*
ZAW	*Zeitschrift für die Alttestamentliche Wissenschaft*
ZNW	*Zeitschrift für die Neutestamentliche Wissenschaft*

1

Introduction

THE INFLUENCE OF THE OT on the Synoptic Gospels, especially their passion accounts, can hardly be understated. The numerous, interlaced, OT threads, often detectable only via faint echoes, that weave through their narratives are quite difficult for modern exegetes to untangle, but, in order to understand them more accurately, attempts must be made. This book isolates and investigates one such thread—the Synoptists' appropriation of the psalmic lament, specifically in how they characterize their hero (Jesus) and his villians (Jesus' oppenents).

The following five introductory discussions in this chapter set the stage for this investigation: (1) A brief history of research on the psalmic lament provides the necessary background to discuss (2) my contributions to it. (3) Next, I delineate and define the psalmic lament in order to demarcate precisely what is under investigation. Then, in order to guard against anachronistically reading into the Synoptics something that is not there, (4) I explore to what degree the Synoptic writers recognize the core elements of the psalmic lament genre. Finally, before asking how Mark (chapter 2), Matthew (chapter 3), and Luke (chapter 4)[1] appropriate the

---

1. For the sake of simplicity, I use these names to refer to these respective gospels since, in keeping with the methodology outlined below, debates about gospel authorship do not impact my argument. Additionally, these names are used (instead of "implied author") while recognizing, as Howell notes, that there is a "distinction on the theoretical level between 'narrator' [and] 'author'" (*Matthew's Inclusive Story*, 1).

psalmic lament in establishing some of their characters, (5) I present a methodology for the task.

RESEARCH ON THE PSALMIC LAMENT

Old Testament

Hermann Gunkel, the founder of OT form criticism, was writing his groundbreaking *Einleitung in die Psalmen* when he died in 1932. Joachim Begrich completed Gunkel's work, publishing it in 1933, and it was translated into English in 1998.[2] Among Gunkel's many contributions was his demarcation of the lament genre in the Psalms, a key focus in much of his work. Gunkel identified common trends in certain psalms that he labeled as laments. This monumental (re)discovery laid the groundwork for eighty years of subsequent research.

Begrich (1934) and Sigmund Mowinckel (1951), among others,[3] continued exploring the psalmic lament, focusing especially on its *Sitz im Leben*. Begrich took interest in the lamenter's abrupt turn-to-praise that is common in many laments, while Mowinkel tried to explain what he thought was more central to interpreting them—namely, their cultic purposes.[4] Claus Westermann advanced the conversation in the 1960s and 1970s by establishing the structure, history, and role of the lament in OT theology.[5] He determined that structurally there are three determinate elements of the lament (discussed below in detail). Historically, the lament spanned three predominant periods: the primitive (unstructured), middle (most structured), and later years (wherein they fell into disuse).[6] Theologically, the lament gains its primary significance by giving a voice to the one who suffers.[7] Westermann's contributions triggered a theological conversation about the OT lament that has continued for forty years.

---

2. Gunkel and Begrich, *Introduction to Psalms*.

3. Because I focus primarily on the NT, it is unnecessary and (due to space limitations) impractical to give an exhaustive history of research on the OT psalmic lament. For a thorough bibliography, see Bouzard, *We Have Heard with Our Ears, O God*, 103n3.

4. See Begrich, "Das priesterliche Heilsorakel," 81–92, and Mowinckel, *Psalms in Israel's Worship*.

5. See Westermann, *Praise of God*; ibid., "Role of the Lament," 20–38.

6. Westermann, *Praise and Lament in the Psalms*, 165–213.

7. Ibid., 272.

Introduction

The late 1980s and 1990s saw an increased interest in the OT lament. Westermann, continuing his work, argued that the polarities "plea and praise" best describe the psalmic literature,[8] while Craig C. Broyles retorted that "plea and complaint" better describe it.[9] Paul Ferris explored the form, function, and motivations of the communal lament (1992),[10] while Walter Bouzard compared those of Mesopotamia and Israel and concluded that both share similar themes, motifs, and images (1991).[11] Patrick Miller, in a 1993 article, argued that the psalmic laments' rhetoric and form suggest that they are prayers for help; the petitioners, that is, seek to persuade God by motivating him to action.[12] Miller followed this article in 1994 by arguing at length that the psalmic petitioners authentically believed that prayer effects change in how God deals with his people.[13] Ingvar Fløysvik in 1997 wrote a monograph on the lament psalms arguing that God's wrath lies at the center of the lamenter's problem and the cause of their current distress.[14]

Inquiry into the psalmic lament in the twenty-first century has not abated. F. W. Dobbs-Allsopp investigated the generic evolution of the communal lament[15] while Carleen Mandolfo introduced the concept of a "didactic dialogic tension" (what she calls "multivoicing") in the lament psalms.[16] Richard Bautch continued Dobbs-Allsopp's interests in the generic evolution of the lament by comparing similar and dissimilar traits between post-exilic penitential prayers and the psalms of communal lament, suggesting that both interacted with the other in mutually transforming ways.[17] Then, in 2007 William Morrow, building on Westermann's work, argued that Israel's lament began informally (impromptu prayers), then developed into a formal stage (the height of the structured lament tradition), before falling out of use during the exiles.[18]

---

8. Ibid., 153–54.
9. Broyles, *Conflict of Faith and Experience in the Psalms*, 37.
10. Ferris, *Genre of Communal Lament*.
11. Bouzard, *We Have Heard with Our Ears, O God*.
12. Miller, "Prayer as Persuasion," 356–62.
13. Ibid., *They Cried to the Lord*.
14. Fløysvik, *When God Becomes My Enemy*.
15. Dobbs-Allsopp, "Darwinism, Genre Theory, and City Laments," 625–30.
16. Mandolfo, *God in the Dock*.
17. Bautch, *Developments in Genre*.
18. Morrow, *Protest Against God*. Cf. Westermann, *Praise and Lament*, 165–213.

These OT scholars provided the necessary groundwork for NT scholars to explore how NT writers appropriate the psalmic lament.

New Testament

As OT lament studies gained momentum after Gunkel, lament studies in the NT slowly began to appear. C. H. Dodd, for example, suggested that the lament psalms (which he called "psalms of the righteous sufferer") provide the plot for the gospel writers to understand Jesus' death and resurrection.[19] Barnabas Lindars argued that the lament psalms function apologetically for the gospel writers by showing that Jesus did not die as a result of God's displeasure and that they provide a category for understanding the suffering of Jesus.[20] Douglas Moo demarcated the gospel writers' intertextual dependence upon the lament psalms, concluding that it is best to view their use of this literature as typology.[21] Donald Juel explored how they used the lament psalms as midrash to explain Jesus' messiahship[22] while Joel Marcus, examining the trajectory of the interpretation of Psalm 22 in post-biblical Judaism, suggested that the lament psalms function in Mark eschatologically to depict Jesus as a warrior king who had to suffer as a righteous one.[23] Then, Adela Collins examined the lament psalms in Mark with an eye toward whether Mark accurately appropriated Jewish Scriptures.[24]

These scholars were primarily interested in the methods the gospel writers used in appropriating the OT (e.g., apologetically, midrash, typologically) and were less interested in each gospel writers' distinct narrative appropriation of the lament psalms, focusing more on issues "behind" these respective texts.[25] A common tendency of these NT scholars, especially after Lothar Ruppert's *Der leidende Gerechte*, was to collapse the Synoptists' clear allusions and quotations of the psalmic lament into their Isaianic Servant motifs,[26] subsuming the former under the

---

19. Dodd, *According to the Scriptures*, 102–3.
20. Lindars, *New Testament Apologetic*, 17–19.
21. Moo, *Old Testament in the Gospel Passion Narratives*, 298.
22. Juel, *Messianic Exegesis*, 31–57.
23. Marcus, *Way of the Lord*, 172–86.
24. Collins, "Appropriation of the Psalms of Individual Lament by Mark."
25. Collins's work, notwithstanding. Still, her focus is not on Mark as narrative.
26. It is beyond my scope to enter the longstanding debate about Isaianic authorship. For simplicity, the term "Isaiah" is used herein as a reference to the OT book of Isaiah.

latter.²⁷ Until Rebekah Eklund and Stephen P. Ahearne-Kroll (see below), Marcus was the sole exception, focusing on Mark's distinct christological appropriation of, among other things, the psalmic lament (like Dodd, calling them "psalms of the righteous sufferer"), emphasizing the way that Mark exegetes the OT.

More recently, an increased interest in the influence of the lament on the NT has surfaced in various professional societies, journals, and monographs,²⁸ two of which—Eklund and Ahearne-Kroll—are most pertinent for my focus on the Synoptics.²⁹ Eklund's insightful and groundbreaking 2012 Duke Divinity School dissertation "Lord, Teach Us How to Grieve: Jesus' Laments and Christian Hope," in traversing an impressive swath of primary and secondary literature (from pre-exilic Israel through the NT to Ambrose, Barth, and beyond!), explores the role and function of the lament in the NT, with a specific focus on Jesus as a lamenter and its theological and practical implications.³⁰ Although Eklund and I worked independently of one another, and although we draw some different conclusions that I will note and critique along the way, we agree substantially on broader interpretive issues about Jesus as a lamenter. Most important at this juncture is to note the different methodological and interpretive emphases that distinguish my trajectory from hers.

My primary goal is to advance more specifically the field of literary criticism within Synoptic studies via the Synoptists' appropriation of

---

27. Ruppert, *Der leidende Gerechte*. For a summary and discussion of this topic, see Ahearne-Kroll, *Psalms of Lament in Mark's Passion*, 13–16. See also chapter 2 below.

28. Simmons, "Apostle Paul and Lament"; Skaggs, "Apocalypse of John"; Crisler, "Paul's Use of Lament in Romans"; ibid., "Caring for Creation by Hearing Its Lament"; ibid., "'I' Who Laments"; Rindge, "Reconfiguring the Akedah and Recasting God"; ibid., "Theological, Religious, and Sociopolitical Aspects of Lament"; and my own work in the lament, "Matthew's Hermeneutic of Ps 22:1 and Jer 31:15"; "Psalmic Lament in the Synoptic Gospels"; "Mark's Appropriation of the Psalmic Lament in Relation to His Conflict Motif"; "NT Scholar's Use of OT Lament Terminology and Its Theological and Interdisciplinary Implications"; and Novello, "Jesus' Cry of Lament."

29. Markus Öhler also briefly engages the Synoptists' appropriation of the lament, but his failure to define what he means by lament, resulting essentially in a summary of grief, mourning, weeping, and despair in the gospels, makes a sustained interaction with him, beyond my discussion below on defining the lament, irrelevant to my argument. (Öhler, "To Mourn, Weep, Lament and Groan," 150–65). It is irrelevant because, as discussed below, sad emotions do not, in and of themselves, equate with biblical lament.

30. For works on theological and practical interests in the NT lament, subjects beyond the scope of this project, see Eklund's bibliography. See also Harasta and Brock, *Evoking Lament*.

the lament, with a tangential interest in theological implications; Eklund, conversely, advances the discussion more theologically than literarily.[31] In this way, our works complement one another well. Because of these different emphases, the primary focus herein is on Ahearne-Kroll's contributions, because it is his method and conclusions that I more specifically build upon.

Stephen P. Ahearne-Kroll

Ahearne-Kroll, Assistant Professor of New Testament at the Methodist Theological School in Ohio, entered the conversation of the lament's influence on the NT in 2007 by focusing on Mark's appropriation of the lament psalms in his published University of Chicago Divinity School 2005 dissertation. Unlike his predecessors, Ahearne-Kroll focuses on the Second Gospel as a narrative, wherein he explores how Mark appropriates the lament psalms to explain his main character and protagonist, Jesus. In essence, Ahearne-Kroll seeks to answer the question, "What does it mean for Jesus to die 'as it is written of him'" (Mark 14:21).[32] Within the Markan narrative, Ahearne-Kroll argues, Jesus dies "as it is written" by becoming the suffering David of the lament psalms.[33] This portrayal of a suffering Davidic messiah, Ahearne-Kroll continues, contravenes the militaristically and politically triumphant Davidic messiah that many Second Temple writers expected.[34] Thus, Mark, by characterizing Jesus in Davidic terms with respect to the lament psalms, presents "a progressive redefinition of messiahship with respect to David."[35] Mark, then, appropriates the psalmic lament in order to characterize Jesus as the Davidic psalmic lamenter par excellence who dies "as it is written" without the messianic militaristic expectations of the Second Temple era.

---

31. Note especially her delightfully engaging subsections in chapter 4 ("The Relationship of Lament to Power" and "Feminist Critiques of Submission") and her conclusion ("Lament as a Christian Practice").

32. Ahearne-Kroll, *Psalms of Lament in Mark's Passion*, 1.

33. Ibid., 168–69.

34. Concerning the messianic militaristic expectations during the Second Temple era, see Collins, *Mark*, 53–58.

35. Ahearne-Kroll, *Psalms of Lament in Mark's Passion*, 57.

CONTRIBUTION

My goal is to pick up where Ahearne-Kroll left off. Specifically, by building upon the works of OT and NT scholars from Gunkel to the present, I advance Ahearne-Kroll's work by, first, exploring how Mark appropriates the psalmic lament in relation to his use of other psalmic literature,[36] in relation to his characterization of Jesus' opponents, and in relation to his use of Isaiah's Servant motif (chapter 2).[37] Second, I advance Ahearne-Kroll's work by exploring the degree to which Matthew and Luke detect and appropriate Mark's use of the psalmic lament to characterize Jesus and Jesus' opponents, in relation to other psalmic literature, and in relation to Isaiah's Servant motif (chapters 3–4). As a result, I hope to paint a broader picture of the Synoptists' characterization of Jesus and his opponents as paradigmatic OT hero and villains.

These two advancements of Ahearne-Kroll's work reflect the general trajectory of my argument. Ancillary contributions made along the way include (1) an argument that Mark and Matthew understand how the psalmic lament functioned as prayer within the psalmic literature, (2) explorations into the similarities and distinctions between the Synoptists' use of Isaiah's Servant and psalmic lamenter motifs, (3) an argument for a way forward in the debate to understand how, and to what degree, the Synoptists unify their characterizations of Jesus' opposition, and (4) an examination into the narrative and rhetorical implications of the Synoptists' appropriations of these motifs.

Before presenting my methodology for exploring these contributions, I must address three background issues important to the discussions in chapters 2–4: The definition of a "psalmic lament" (in order to clarify the object of my investigation), the degree to which the Synoptic writers recognize the psalmic lament genre (in order to avoid anachronistically imposing it on their narratives), and a definition of "characterization" (since I primarily focus on the Synoptists' characterization of Jesus and his opponents).

---

36. Susan Gillingham suggests this need in her review of Ahearne-Kroll (Review of *The Psalms of Lament in Mark's Passion*, 199).

37. Watts suggests this need in his review of Ahearne-Kroll (Review of *The Psalms of Lament in Mark's Passion*, 161).

Of Heroes and Villains

DELINEATING AND DEFINING THE PSALMIC LAMENT

The label "lament"[38] (German: *Klage*) is a modern term that biblical interpreters apply to an ANE literary genre[39] of expressing grief and despair found predominantly, but not exclusively (Jer 14; Isa 63:7—64:12; Habakkuk 1), in the OT psalms and in other extant literature.[40] Since the ancient writers failed to leave behind official labels for this genre or any objective means by which to determine its presence, modern interpreters are left with the difficult task of delineating, classifying, and defining this amorphous literary corpus. The following attempts to define the psalmic lament and to demarcate its parts in light of data that the OT psalmists left behind. Defining and classifying the psalmic lament[41] requires a consideration of Herman Gunkel's and Claus Westermann's form-critical works that I mentioned above.[42] These two works provide the basis for a workable definition of lament.

In his groundbreaking work, *Introduction to Psalms*, Gunkel helps the modern readers to identify certain generic trends in the Psalmic

---

38. Some scholars use the word "complaint" (German: *Anklage*). See, e.g., Gunkel and Begrich, *Introduction to Psalms*, 82, 121, and Gerstenberger, *Psalms*, 10. For more information on the terminology of the lament, see Day, *Psalms*, 20. For simplicity and consistency, I use the term "lament."

39. Genre "serves as a shared pattern of communication by which speakers can make themselves understood to listeners" (Broyles, *Conflict of Faith and Experience in the Psalms*, 25). In proposing the following definition of the psalmic lament, I do not intended to suggest a static idea of genre as if the OT lament never changed or developed (cf. Westermann, *Praise and Lament*, 165–213 and Morrow, *Protest Against God*); rather, this definition represents a minimalist understanding of the psalmic lament as it is situated within a broadly evolving genre. That the lament genre was dynamic and flexible is in keeping with a key conclusion of modern genre theory. Concerning the adaptability and flexibility of the lament genre, see Dobbs-Allsopp, "Darwinism, Genre Theory, and City Laments," 625–30. For entrances into genre theory, consult Unger, *Genre, Relevance and Global Coherence*, Vanhoozer, *Is There a Meaning in this Text*, 335–50, and their respective bibliographies. For a succinct historical survey of genre theory and practice, see Brown, "Genre Criticism and the Bible," 111–50.

40. For information on the lament in other ANE literature, see Ferris, *Genre of Communal Lament in the Bible and the Ancient Near East*.

41. Unless otherwise noted, I use the term "lament" interchangeably with the phrase "psalmic lament."

42. Other scholars have contributed to the understanding of the lament, especially concerning its *Sitz-im-Leben*. These, however, primarily nuance the works of Gunkel and Westermann and are, therefore, beyond the scope of this book. Most notable are Mowinckel, *Psalms in Israel's Worship*, and Gerstenberger, *Psalms*. For a more thorough bibliography, see Bouzard, *We Have Heard with Our Ears, O God*, 103n3.

literature. Pioneering and relying upon form criticism, Gunkel demarcated the psalms into various genres, including the lament.[43] He further subdivided the lament into two genres, the communal and the individual laments, based primarily on their respective uses of first person plural and singular pronouns.[44] These two subgenres, although portraying marked differences, are related in form, content, and mood.[45]

Gunkel recognized and categorized the laments by noting the following generic trends. Typically, the first few words of this genre name YHWH in the vocative, and it commonly ends with a "certainty of being heard" (MT Ps 61:5). Additionally, the writer often asks God "Why?" or "How long?" (MT Ps 74:10–11) in relation to his distress, seeks to elicit a response from God via various pleas and rationales, reflects political concerns, and sometimes ends with a tone of rejoicing.[46] The structure, although flexible, is predictable: A summons precedes a complaint, which leads to a petition. The petition is the central aspect of the complaint and is often followed by an abrupt change in the complainer's mood—namely, a confidence that God has heard him.

Gunkel, then, defined and delineated the lament by observing consistent and recognizable generic patterns therein. Although subsequent scholars recognize the existence of this genre, its amorphous nature prevents a consensus about the precise classification of many apparent lament psalms. The abiding problem in classifying these psalms is that they often resist specific classification, since every literary trend is not found within each one. Scholars subsequent to Gunkel struggle with this indistinctness, which is evident in their differences in classifying particular psalms as laments.[47]

---

43. Gunkel used three criteria for establishing a "genre": (1) The psalms in question must belong to, or derive from, a specific occasion in the worship service, (2) they must share common thoughts and moods, and (3) they must share a common form (Gunkel and Begrich, *Introduction to Psalms*, 15–16).

44. See also Westermann, "Role of the Lament," 29. Mowinckel is more reluctant to see this distinction, suggesting that the "I" of the so-called individual laments represents the nation of Israel (*Psalms in Israel's Worship*, 225–26).

45. Ferris, *Genre of Communal Lament*, 5; cf. Westermann, *Praise and Lament*, 102.

46. For further common trends within these genres, see Gunkel and Begrich, *Introduction to Psalms*, 82–98.

47. See, e.g., the charts that identify how various scholars classify communal laments in Bouzard, *We Have Heard with Our Ears, O God*, 102, and Ferris, *Genre of Communal Lament*, 16.

Of Heroes and Villains

Claus Westermann sought to resolve this problem by specifically constructing criteria for delineating the lament that satisfactorily considers the fluidity of the form. Although he considerably furthered lament research, I only mention here two pertinent contributions to lament classification. First, almost in passing, Westermann demarcated two possibly confusing genres—namely, what he calls "the lament of distress" (the category he broadly classifies simply as "lament") and "the lament of the dead." He suggested:

> The essential characteristics of the lament of the dead in contrast to the lament of distress are:
>
> 1. The lament of the dead is not addressed to God; the name of Yahweh never occurs in it.
>
> 2. Characterizing the lament of the dead is the address to the dead, the call for lamentation, the announcement of death, and the description of suffering.
>
> 3. The lament of distress is combined with supplication, i.e., it looks to the future for the time of deliverance; the lament of the dead confronts the fact of death and looks to the past.[48]

In examining the psalmic material, then, a dirge and a lament are not synonymous.[49] This discovery is important in that it prevents one from defining the lament exclusively in terms of sadness. A lament is more than one's sorrow for particular circumstances, because it must include supplication to God.

Second, and most importantly, Westermann, refining Gunkel's work, suggests three determinant elements in classifying a lament: "the one who laments, God, and the others."[50] He further clarifies these elements by describing what he calls the "component parts of the lament": (1) the complaint against God (often asks "Why?" or "How long?"), (2)

---

48. Westermann, *Praise and Lament*, 168. See also Westermann, "Role of the Lament," 22. Gunkel calls these "public funeral services" (*Introduction to Psalms*, 85). Westermann's demarcation is correct. It is, however, less confusing to refer to the "lament of the dead" as a "dirge," a modern word that more succinctly describes this genre.

49. A logical connection between the two, however, may exist. See Ferris, *Genre of Communal Lament*, 73.

50. Westermann, *Praise and Lament*, 169. Although he reduces the lament to these determinant elements, Westermann still recognizes and modifies Gunkel's more pervasive lament elements, such as the address, lament, confession of trust, assurance of being heard, petition, and vow of praise. The "determinate elements" are what Westermann argues are the core elements of the lament.

the lament over personal suffering (which is dependent upon the "complaint against God"), and (3) the complaint about the enemy.

The delineation and the definition of the psalmic lament that I use depend upon Gunkel's and Westermann's work in the following ways. First, the lament exhibits an identifiable yet flexible structure. Second, the lament is more than the recitation of despair but must be a prayer directed toward God. Third, the lament must contain a nuanced version of Westermann's three determinant elements: the one who laments, God, and a real or perceived problem.[51] Fourth, the lamenter desires God to change his circumstances.[52]

Based on these contributions by Gunkel and Westermann, then, I use the following definition to identify the core elements of the OT psalmic lament: An OT psalmic lament is a distressful complaint/question/appeal directed toward God (a prayer) in order to bring about change for a real or perceived problem.[53]

---

51. Westermann's third determinate element is "the others." The nomenclature "real or perceived problem" more accurately represents the data, since sometimes the lamenter's problem may not specifically be "others" but may be inanimate ideas such as sickness (MT Pss 38; 41; 88).

52. That the lamenter desires a change is based on the assumption that prayer has "as a primary function the effort to persuade and motivate God to act in behalf of the petitioner who is in trouble and needs God's help" (Miller, "Prayer as Persuasion," 356). Broyles agrees: A lament psalm "does more than simply bemoan current hardship. It seeks change" (*Conflict of Faith and Experience*, 14).

53. Adapted from a conversation with Heath Thomas, associate professor of OT and Hebrew and director of PhD Studies at Southeastern Baptist Theological Seminary, April 8, 2008 (cf. Lee, *Lyrics of Lament*, 3). Eklund defines a lament as "a persistent cry for salvation to the God who promises to save, in a situation of suffering or sin, in the confident hope that this God hears and responds to cries, and acts *now* and *in the future* to make whole" ("Lord, Teach Us How to Grieve," 17, italics in original). Broyles eloquently portrays the complexity of the lament. He states, "A lament psalm relates an experience, so it conveys a narrative. It presents this within a metrical structure, so it is poetry. It asks for something from God, so it is prayer. It pleads a case, so it is argument. It expresses faith so it is theology. This list is but the beginning" (Broyles, *Conflict of Faith and Experience*, 13). Ferris, although recognizing predictable elements in the lament (namely, the invocation, the lament proper, and the appeal), refuses to force it into a predictable mold, but suggests that "it is the mood, purpose, and situation that dictate its presence" (Ferris, *Genre of Communal Lament*, 7).

DID THE SYNOPTIC WRITERS RECOGNIZE
HOW THE LAMENT FUNCTIONS?[54]

Delineating and defining the psalmic lament does not address whether the Synoptic writers understood how they function as prayers to bring about change for a given plight, a second background investigation that deserves lengthy attention for at least three reasons: (1) The Synoptists could have read the Psalms without any indication that Psalms 107 and 109[55] (cf. Mark 11:9–10; 12:10–11, 36) function any differently than Psalms 21 and 41/42[56] (cf. Mark 15:34; 14:34). (2) This question is especially pertinent in light of William Morrow's recent argument that, by the time of the NT, the lament genre had been eclipsed. He states: "The writers of the New Testament . . . had no knowledge of a living tradition of [the individual lament]."[57] (3) If the Synoptic writers did not recognize to a degree how the psalmic lament functions, then it is anachronistic for NT scholars to attach this label to their writings.

My focus in this section is not on the degree to which the Synoptic writers saw thematic parallels between Jesus and the lament, although this is a worthwhile undertaking and a fact that is assumed by most scholars (recall discussion above). Rather, the question I explore is, "Did the Synoptic writers understand the core elements of the lament genre in such a way that validates modern researchers' use of the phrase in relation to their works and that validates the subsequent examination of this book?"

In response to this question, I argue that, although there is no evidence to suggest that Mark and Matthew classified Psalms into generic categories such as "laments," nor is there any indication that they used the term or employed the genre in everyday worship,[58] their narratives indicate that they were aware of particular psalms (the ones labeled as "laments" by modern scholars) that functioned in distinct ways in the

---

54. This section is adapted from Campbell, "Psalmic Lament in the Synoptic Gospels."

55. Unless otherwise noted, all psalmic citations correspond to the LXX.

56. Most commentators rightly argue that Pss 41 and 42 originally comprised one psalm.

57. Morrow, *Protest Against God*, 211. To be fair to Morrow, he speaks of an awareness of a *living* tradition, that is, a cultic tradition of the lament that was present during the Synoptic era. However, while the Synoptists show no knowledge of a cultic lament tradition in vogue at the time of their writings, they do show knowledge of the lament tradition as found in the psalmic literature.

58. Cf. Morrow, *Protest Against God*, 211.

psalmic era.[59] By "function" I do not mean that Mark and Matthew knew the cultic ways that the lament served ancient Israel's worship (their *Sitz-im-Leben*), a topic that interested the early pioneers of lament studies; rather, I mean that they understood how the psalmic lament functioned as a particular type of prayer to God. Luke, on the other hand, with respect to his portrayal of Jesus, shows little-to-no awareness of the core elements of the psalmic lament. The following discussion focuses on establishing Mark's and Matthew's awareness of the lament in order to validate the investigations in chapters 2 and 3, while the discussion of Luke's gospel is postponed until chapter 4.

I substantiate this argument, which depends on Westermann's core elements of the lament discussed above, by exploring the Gethsemane and crucifixion accounts in the First and Second Gospels with an eye toward these core elements. I argue that Mark and Matthew detect these elements and appropriate them into their narratives toward certain literary ends. In a brief excursus, I glance at the core elements of the lament in Revelation 6:10 in order to provide an incremental degree of supporting evidence for these conclusions regarding Mark and Matthew. Revelation 6:10, in essence, provides a glimpse at a writer contemporary with Mark and Matthew who appropriates the core elements of the psalmic lament.

It is these core elements, and not only subsidiary thematic trends in general, that Mark and Matthew detect in the psalmic literature and appropriate in their respective Gethsemane and crucifixion accounts. When Mark and Matthew quote or allude to a psalmic lament in correlation with their use of these core elements, then the likelihood that they understand the lament's function increases.

Mark 14:32-42 (Gethsemane); 15:34 (Crucifixion)

Mark's Gethsemane scene (Mark 14:32-42) reflects the core elements of the lament. It contains a distressed petitioner (Mark 14:33: "He began to be very distressed and troubled") who, afflicted by opposition (Mark 14:41: "The Son of Man is betrayed into the hands of sinners"), prays to God (Mark 14:36: "Abba, Father") in order to bring about change for his present dilemma (Mark 14:36; "take this cup from me").

---

59. To the degree that this is true, modern interpreters can cautiously use the term "lament" in relation to NT writers without anachronism.

Aside from reflecting the core elements of the lament, Ahearne-Kroll rightly argues that Mark portrays Jesus as the embodiment of the lamenter via structural similarities to lament Psalm 41/42: Jesus' threefold prayer in Gethsemane parallels the same threefold refrain found in Psalms 41:6, 12 and 42:5 ("Why are you downcast, O my soul? Why so disturbed within me? Put your hope in God, for I will yet praise him, my Savior and my God").[60] In support of Ahearne-Kroll's argument, two further form-critical aspects of the lament are present in Mark's Gethsemane scene—namely, an address to God in the vocative case (Mark 14:36; αββα) and a turn-to-praise (Mark 14:36c; "yet not what I will but what you will").

Jesus' cry of dereliction (Mark 15:34) also reflects the core elements of the lament. It contains a distressed petitioner who prays to God (Mark 15:34c; "My God, my God") and is afflicted by enemies (Mark 15:24–30). His cry of dereliction (Mark 15:34c; "why have you forsaken me?") implies a desire for God to change his situation. If one charges God with forsaking him, then it can be assumed that he does not like the current situation and desires it to be different. This is explicitly evident in the context of Psalm 21:1: "Why are you so far off from saving me, so far from the words of my groaning?" (cf. Ps 21:3, 20–22).

Aside from reflecting the core elements of the lament, Mark's crucifixion scene portrays Jesus as the embodiment of the Psalm 21 lamenter. This is clear not only in that Jesus' prayer is the same as the psalmist's, but also in that Mark conflates portions of his narrative with that of Psalm 21 (Mark 15:24, 29; cf. the echo of lament Psalm 68 in Mark 15:36).

It seems reasonable, then, that Mark is aware of how laments function. He understands that certain psalms represent distraught petitioners who prayed to God in order to bring about change for a given plight. He then correlates this understanding of the lament's core function into his narrative toward specific literary ends.[61] Adding support to this conclusion is that Mark alludes to and/or quotes a psalmic lament in each respective narrative in which he shows awareness of the lament's core function. In essence, although William Morrow is correct that by the time of the NT the cultic use of the lament had been eclipsed, he is incorrect in insinuating that Mark shows no awareness of it.[62]

---

60. Ahearne-Kroll, *Psalms of Lament in Mark's Passion*, 179–86 (esp. 183–84).
61. See chapter 2 below.
62. Morrow, *Protest Against God*, 195–97, 211.

Introduction

Matthew 26:36–46 (Gethsemane); 27:46 (Crucifixion)

Since Matthew 26:36–46 and 27:46 parallel Mark 14:32–34 and 15:34 and contain the core elements of the lament discussed in the previous section, it is unnecessary to address these issues again. The issue that I must address here is whether or not *Matthew detects* Mark's awareness of the core elements of the lament or merely copies them unknowingly.

Since Matthew 26:28 copies Mark's evocation[63] of Psalm 41/42 verbatim ("my soul is overwhelmed with sorrow"), it is possible that Matthew did not detect it.[64] There is evidence, however, that Matthew did detect Mark's evocation. Specifically, the evidence revolves around Matthew's use of λυπέω ("I grieve") and περίλυπός ("excessive grief") in relation to Mark's use of the same terms. Matthew uses λυπέω six times (Matt 14:9; 17:23; 18:31; 19:22; 26:22, 37) and περίλυπός once (Matt 26:38; the evocation of Psalm 41/42). Matthew's predilection for λυπέω is well known, with Robert Gundry calling it a "Mattheanism."[65] Most notable is that prior to Matthew's possible evocation of Psalm 41/42 in 26:38, he only uses λυπέω to describe the grief and despair of his characters. At one point he replaces Mark's use of περίλυπός with λυπέω (Matt 14:9; cf. Mark 6:26), further revealing his predilection for λυπέω over περίλυπός. When Matthew comes to Mark's evocation of Psalm 41/42, instead of utilizing his preferred term λυπέω, he retains Mark's use of περίλυπός. This is Matthew's sole use of the term περίλυπός in his gospel and a key term in linking Mark's evocation to Psalm 41/42 (τί περίλυπος εἶ ψυχή). Matthew's unexpected sole use of the term περίλυπός in direct correspondence with Mark's use of the same term suggests that Matthew detects Mark's evocation of Psalm 41/42. In other words, if Matthew did not detect Mark's evocation of Psalm 41/42, one would expect Matthew to use the term λυπέω (or, more specifically λύπη) instead of περίλυπός in Matthew 26:38. That Matthew departs from his favored use of λυπέω at the precise point that Mark evokes Psalm 41/42 indicates that he intentionally follows Mark's evocation of Psalm 41/42.

---

63. See "Methodology" below for an explanation of the phrase "evocation."

64. Ahearne-Kroll notes that his argument for the detection of an evocation of Ps 41/42 in Mark 14:34 would be strengthened if it could be demonstrated that Matthew recognizes the same evocation (*Psalms of Lament in Mark's Passion*, 69). The goal here is to demonstrate this recognition.

65 Gundry, *Matthew: A Commentary on His Literary and Theological Art*, 354.

Of Heroes and Villains

There is further evidence that Matthew detects Mark's evocation of Psalm 41/42. First, περίλυπός is a rare word, both in the NT (four times: Matt 26:38; Mark 6:26; 14:34; and Luke 18:23) and in the LXX (eight times). The rarity of the word alone does not secure a Matthean recognition of Mark's evocation of Psalm 41/42, but when coupled with the previous and subsequent arguments, it increases the likelihood that Matthew intends to evoke the psalm. Second, Matthew expands Mark's account of Gethsemane by more specifically highlighting Jesus' threefold prayer refrain. He adds a second prayer to the narrative (Matt 26:42), one that repeats the first (Matt 26:39). Then, he notes a third prayer without repeating the refrain (Matt 26:44). Recall from the section above that Ahearne-Kroll argues that Mark's threefold prayer parallels the threefold refrain in Psalm 41/42. Matthew's expansion of Mark at this precise location suggests that he was likely aware of Mark's evocation of Psalm 41/42.

Concerning Matthew 27:46 (Jesus' cry of dereliction), no one disputes that Matthew realizes that Mark quotes Psalm 21:1. Aside from the numerous direct linguistic similarities between Matthew 27:46 and Psalm 21:1, Matthew changes Jesus' cry from Aramaic to Hebrew. Furthermore, Matthew adds to Mark's crucifixion narrative at least one more echo of Psalm 21 (Matt 27:42–43; cf. Matt 27:29; 27:35).[66] This addition, when read in concert with his Gethsemane account, makes it clear that Matthew understands and reinforces Mark's trend to embody Jesus as the lamenter par excellence.

In sum, Matthew retains Mark's evocations and narrative patterns in his Gethsemane and crucifixion accounts, which indicates an awareness of the core elements of the psalmic lament traditions. These elements, however, could have been retained unknowingly by Matthew. I argue here, however, that Matthew detects Mark's use of the lament tradition. Specifically, his use of λυπέω/περίλυπός and his expansions of Mark's account suggests that Matthew recognizes what Mark was doing in his narrative with the lament. It is reasonable, therefore, to conclude that, like Mark, Matthew is aware of how laments function. He understands that certain psalms represent distraught petitioners who prayed to God in order to bring about change for a given plight. He then correlates this understanding of the lament's core function into his narrative toward specific literary ends.[67] Adding support to this conclusion is that

---

66. Cf. Marcus, "Old Testament and the Death of Jesus," 210–11.
67. See chapter 3 below.

Matthew alludes to and/or quotes a psalmic lament in each respective narrative in which he shows awareness of the lament's core function. In essence, although William Morrow is correct that, by the time of the NT, the cultic use of the lament had been eclipsed, he is incorrect in insinuating that Matthew shows no awareness of it.[68]

Excursus: Revelation 6:10

This brief excursus on Revelation 6:10 notes a writer contemporary with Mark and Matthew who incorporated the core elements of the lament into his narrative.[69] This is not to suggest, of course, interdependence between the Synoptics and Revelation; rather, noting another NT author's use of the same core elements of the lament simply alerts us to the fact that Mark and Matthew do not represent isolated events and adds an incremental degree of supporting evidence for their awareness of it.[70]

In Revelation 6:9, Jesus opens the fifth seal, and John sees souls of those "under the altar . . . who had been slain for the word of God and for the witness they had borne." These martyred souls are then depicted praying to God about their plight: "How long, Sovereign Lord . . . until you judge the inhabitants of the earth and avenge our blood?" (Rev 6:10). Linguistically and contextually, this imprecatory prayer reflects the core elements of the lament.[71] Linguistically, the prayer begins ("how long") similarly to the psalmic lament prayers (e.g., MT Ps 74:10–11).[72] Contextually, the souls under the altar are in dire distress as they cry out to God. In essence, Revelation 6:10 represents petitioners who pray to God in a distressful situation, who ask God to bring about change for their given plight, and whose dilemma is directly related to their enemies (Rev 6:10c: "until you . . . avenge our blood").

---

68. Morrow, *Protest Against God*, 195–97, 211.

69. Heath Thomas first directed my attention to the fact that Rev 6:10 reflects the lament. Contrast with Donald Senior, who sees Jesus' prayer in Gethsemane as the "sole place in the New Testament where [a lament] prayer is retained" (*Passion of Jesus in the Gospel of Mark*, 72).

70. To the degree that Eklund is correct in seeing lament features in Heb 5:7 and Romans 8, her conclusions add incremental support to my argument beyond Rev 6:10. See Eklund, "Lord, Teach Us How to Grieve," 122–27; 185–91; cf. Crisler, "Lament in Romans."

71. On the imprecatory nature of this prayer, see Aune, *Revelation 6–16*, 407.

72. See Gunkel and Begrich, *Introduction to Psalms*, 89–90.

Of Heroes and Villains

Revelation 6:10, then, attests to a writer contemporary with Mark and Matthew who integrates the core elements of a lament into his narrative.

Summary

Mark understands the core elements of the psalmic lament and weaves this understanding into his narrative. Furthermore, Matthew detects Mark's understanding and capitalizes on it within his own narrative. This understanding of the lament genre runs deeper than (but not exclusively to) simply recognizing and utilizing themes therein (e.g., "wagging heads" [cf. Mark 15:29; Ps 21:8] and "casting lots for clothing" [cf. Mark 15:24; Ps 21:19]); rather, it reveals an understanding of how the psalmic lament functions theologically. In other words, Mark and Matthew appropriate the psalmic lament on a deeper theological level than just the surface detection of particular trends related to Jesus' life.

CHARACTERIZATION

Characterization is a final background discussion needed prior to turning attention to methodological matters, since it emcompasses the heart of each subsequent chapter. Literary characterization is a burgeoning subdiscipline of narrative criticism in Synoptic studies. Elizabeth Malbon rightly suggests that "characterization is an essential element of any critical theory of narrative."[73] According to Rhoads, characterization refers to how authors bring characters to life within a narrative by describing them or by revealing them through the things they say, the things they do, and how other characters perceive and react to them.[74] Anderson adds that authors also describe their characters via

> social identity (gender, marital status, nationality, occupation, etc.); physical or personality traits, emotional state; habits of speech and mannerisms; settings associated with a character; names, labels or allusions; a character's past; thoughts or actions

---

73. Malbon, *In the Company of Jesus*, 131, ix. See also Rhoads, "Narrative Criticism and the Gospel of Mark," 411–34; Powell, *What Is Narrative Criticism?*, 51; and Weeden, *Mark: Traditions in Conflict.*

74. Rhoads, "Narrative Criticism and the Gospel of Mark," 417. Cf. Malbon, *In the Company of Jesus*, ix; and Anderson, *Matthew's Narrative Web*, 78–83.

in specific situations; interactions with other characters and the responses evoked; a character's attitude toward him or herself; and the use of foils.[75]

Another aspect of characterization, especially for gospel studies, should be added to Rhoads' and Anderson's descriptions: Authors, as demonstrated in my argument in this book, can also describe and reveal their characters by evoking other texts.[76] In other words, one method that the Synoptists use to bring certain characters to life is by characterizing them as certain OT people or groups.

Understanding characterization in relation to certain OT people or groups is similar to, but also distinct from, typology. Ahearne-Kroll distinguishes sharply between Mark's characterization of Jesus as David and what Douglas Moo labels as typology.[77] Much of this distinction depends on how one defines typology. Ahearne-Kroll, following Alter and Frank Kermode, defines typology as "an Old Testament passage or character whose hidden sense is made plain only when fulfilled by the New Testament antitype: e.g., the high priest Melchizedek is a type of Christ."[78] Others, instead of defining it as "prefiguration," define it as historical "correspondence"—"a form of historical interpretation."[79] While Ahearne-Kroll is correct that Mark does not specify his understanding

---

75. Anderson, *Matthew's Narrative Web*, 79. For more theoretical discussions on characterization in the NT (e.g., whether characters in texts are persons or words), see Burnett, "Characterization and Reader Construction," 3–28.

76. Rhoads hints at, but does not elaborate on, the fact that Mark quotes from Scripture at times "to reveal character and define conflicts" ("Narrative Criticism and the Gospel of Mark," 425). Following Moo (*Old Testament in the Gospel Passion Narratives*, 21–22), Donald Senior refers to such intertextual references as "structural" elements of the story ("Lure of the Formula Quotations," 111–12). The following discussion advances Rhoads' and Senior's suggestions by examining how the Synoptics establish characters by evoking the Psalms, Isaiah's Servant motif, and, in Matthew and Luke, an OT rejected-prophet motif. Space is too limited to explore this within Malbon's recent methodological contribution that explores Mark's Christology via what his characters say and do in relation to Jesus and in relation to how Jesus responds to what they say and do (Malbon, *Mark's Jesus*). The focus here is simply on how the Synoptists subtly nuance their characterizations of Jesus and Jesus' opponents via their OT hermeneutic.

77. Moo, *Old Testament in the Gospel Passion Narratives*, 299–300.

78. Ahearne-Kroll, *Psalms of Lament in Mark's Passion*, 172, citing Alter and Kermode, *Literary Guide to the Bible*, 672. Cf. Alsup, "Typology," 682–83, and Knowles, *Jeremiah in Matthew's Gospel*, 223.

79. Baker, "Typology and the Christian Use of the Old Testament," 315.

of Jesus as "prefigured" by David, Mark's Jesus clearly historically "corresponds" to David.

My examination in subsequent chapters occurs at the intersection of typology (whether defined as prefiguration or correspondence) and characterization. Typology is interested in correspondences between certain NT entities (types) and certain OT entities (antitypes). Characterization is interested in how authors develop certain entities within their respective narratives. Thus, the characterization investigated in the following chapters explores how the Synoptists interconnectedly develop their characters within an OT matrix.

Narratives can contain an array of major and minor characters, ranging from single narrative appearances to a pervasive portrayal of them.[80] An author can portray characters as "round" (multidimensional, developing, and individual) or as "flat" (one dimensional, static, and stereotypical).[81] The Synoptists construct a plot full of characters (e.g., Jesus, disciples, religious leaders, crowds, demonic beings) that they progressively reveal and describe as they propel the narrative toward Jesus' climactic crucifixion. My specific interest is on the Synoptists' characterization of their hero (Jesus) and villains (Jesus' opponents).[82] Scholars study these characters via several methods. Many are interested in the history "behind" the text, emphasizing the nature of the historical Jesus' interactions with his historical opponents, the identity of the religious leaders, and parallels between the opponents in Mark's narrative and those in his community.[83] Narrative

---

80. Examples of major characters in Mark, for example, include Jesus and his disciples. Examples of minor characters include Simon's mother-in-law and Joseph of Arimathea. Cf. Rhoads, "Narrative Criticism and the Gospel of Mark," 417–19.

81. See Malbon, *In the Company of Jesus*, 191, referencing Forster, *Aspects of the Novel*. Cf. Powell, *What Is Narrative Criticism?*, 55.

82. One should keep in mind throughout my ensuing study that the Synoptists' characterization of Jesus' opponents is always a means to an end and never vice versa—namely, they always function to "reveal who Jesus is and what he is all about" (Le Donne, "Jewish Leaders," 199).

83. Albertz, *Die synoptische Streitgespräche*; Banks, *Jesus and the Law in the Synoptic Tradition*; Bock, "Jesus as Blasphemer," 76–94; Bowker, *Jesus and the Pharisees*; Borg, *Conflict, Holiness, and Politics*; Cook, "Jesus and the Pharisees" 441–60; ibid., *Mark's Treatment of the Jewish Leaders*; Lührmann, "Die Pharisäer und die Schriftgelehrten im Markusevangelium," 169–85; Efroymson, "Jesus: Opposition and Opponents"; Evans, *Jesus and His Contemporaries*; Goppelt, *Theology of the New Testament*, 1:84–105; Hultgren, *Jesus and His Adversaries*; Jeremias, *New Testament Theology*, 142–51; McKnight and Modica, *Who Do My Opponents Say that I Am?*; Merkel,

critics concern themselves with what is "in" the text, focusing on the role that characters play within Mark's narrative world. Some of these scholars examine the nature of Jesus' conflict with his opponents and his disciples, addressing, for example, whether Jesus' conflict with the Jews was over the Torah or over authority?[84] Others explore Mark's character portrayal and development of Jesus' opponents and the accompanying conflict within Mark's broader literary purposes, addressing, for example how it coincides with Mark's use of irony.[85]

As discussed in the following methodology, I enter the conversation of narrative critics as they explore characterization in the gospel narratives, focusing not on what is behind the text but with what is within it.

METHODOLOGY

N. T. Wright's and Andreas Köstenberger's "hermeneutical triad" (history, literature, and theology) methodologically governs my arguments in the subsequent chapters.[86] Within this triad, history, literature, and theology are not divorced from one another but are recognized as necessary, balanced, and interrelated disciplines within the study of biblical literature.[87] Thus, within this investigation of the Synoptists' appropriation of the psalmic lament to characterize Jesus and his opponents, although the gospels' literary features are emphasized more due to the nature of the investigation, no facet of the triad is favored over another.

"Opposition between Jesus and Judaism," 129–44; Mulholland, "Markan Opponents of Jesus," 166; Saldarini, "Social Class of the Pharisees in Mark," 69–77; Weeden, *Mark: Traditions in Conflict*, 159; ibid., "Conflict between Mark and His Opponents over Kingdom Theology," 203–41.

84. Jesus' conflict was over the Torah: Jeremias, *New Testament Theology*, 211; Merkel, "Opposition between Jesus and Judaism"; Pannenberg, *Jesus—God and Man*, 86; Perrin, *Rediscovering the Teaching of Jesus*, 97, 103. Jesus' conflict was over authority: Efroymson, "Jesus: Opposition and Opponents," 96; Gundry, *Mark*, 6; Kingsbury, *Conflict in Mark*, 67; ibid., "Religious Authorities in the Gospel of Mark," 54. Rhoads et al. suggest that Jesus' conflict concerns God's rule (*Mark as Story*, 78–82).

85. Dewey, *Markan Public Debate*; ibid., "Literary Structure of the Controversy Narratives in Mark," 394–401; Kelber, *Mark's Story of Jesus*; Kingsbury, *Conflict in Mark*; ibid., "Religious Authorities in the Gospel of Mark"; Malbon, *Mark's Jesus*; Smith, "Role of Jesus' Opponents in the Markan Drama," 161–82; Tannehill, "Gospel of Mark as Narrative Christology," 57–95; Webb, *Mark at the Threshold*, 207–8.

86. Wright, *New Testament and the People of God*, 6; Köstenberger and Patterson, *Invitation to Biblical Interpretation*.

87. Cf. Bockmuehl, *Seeing the Word*, 49.

Of Heroes and Villains

Within the broader application of this triad, following Graham Stanton, W. D. Davies, and Dale Allison, I utilize a methodological eclecticism that adheres to specific methods for specific tasks.[88] The method I use to isolate the Synoptists' use of the lament psalms is Ahearne-Kroll's concept of "simple evocation." A simple evocation (used herein synonymously with "evocation" and "evoke") is the "discernible [allusion] of *one and only one* text outside the narrative."[89] Limiting the discussion to the Synoptists' simple evocations of the lament psalms increases the probability that the original authors and readers (or listeners)[90] intended and recognized the respective allusions[91] by guarding against what Jonathan Pennington, in an analogy to Samuel Sandmel's famous article, calls "intertextomania."[92] With this in mind, I demonstrate and examine in

---

88. Stanton reviews the contributions of source, redaction, literary, and social criticisms and wisely argues that their integrated use within biblical studies is preferred (*Gospel for a New People*, 23–110). Likewise, Davies and Allison argue for a methodologically eclectic approach (*Critical and Exegetical Commentary on the Gospel According to Saint Matthew*, 1–4).

89. Ahearne-Kroll, *Psalms of Lament in Mark's Passion*, 24 (italics added). The more common terms "allusion" and "echo" insufficiently describe the nature of this exploration, since they do not distinguish the number of possible referents to which a NT text references. To substantiate a simple evocation, linguistic, thematic/contextual similarities between the evocation and the evoked text, and the broader use of the evoked text in Second Temple literature are examined, I also explore how the Synoptists appropriate the psalmic lament in relation to other OT motifs (e.g., Isaiah's Suffering Servant). The methods used for isolating these motifs are addressed as they are discussed in their respective chapters.

90. I use the terms "readers" and "listeners" interchangeably. Perhaps Geoff R. Webb's appellative "hearing-reader" is most accurate (*Mark at the Threshold*, 8–9). Unless otherwise noted, I use the term "reader" in correspondence to the term "implied reader" used in current literary critical parlance. The implied reader is the "reader created by the text" (Culpepper, *Anatomy of the Fourth Gospel*, 205). The implied reader, however, is not far removed from Matthew's original "real" reader; thus, I use "reader" as a synonym for both terms while recognizing the theoretical differences between them (Novakovic, *Messiah, The Healer of the Sick*, 9).

91. For the purposes of this book, allusion is "a literary device that makes reference to or attempts to conjure up in the memory of the reader a historical or literary event, object, or character" (Tate, *Interpreting the Bible*, 11; and Boda, "Quotation and Allusion," 1:296–98). Unlike a simple evocation, an allusion may refer to numerous texts.

92. Pennington, "Refractions of Daniel in the Gospel of Matthew," 68 (cf. Sandmel, "Parallalomania," 1–13). Juel suggests proceeding in a similar fashion: "It seems wisest to begin with the clearest allusions before proceeding to the less sure, making verbal identity with LXX the basic criterion" (*Messianic Exegesis*, 95). I think that Eklund's dissertation would be strengthened by closer attention to a similar methodology, since she often assumes but does not defend intertextual echoes to only one OT text.

Introduction

subsequent chapters the Synoptists' simple evocations of the following lament psalms.

- Psalm 6 (Matt 7:23; Luke 13:27): "I never knew you; depart from me, you workers of lawlessness."
- Psalm 21
    - Matt 27:35; Mark 15:24; Luke 23:34: "They divided his garments among them by casting lots."
    - Matt 27:39–40; Mark 15:28: Wagging heads.
    - Matt 27:42–43; Luke 23:35: "He saved others . . ."
    - Matt 27:46; Mark 15:34: "My God, my God, why have you forsaken me?"
- Psalm 30 (Luke 23:46): "Father, into your hands I commit my spirit!"
- Psalm 40 (Mark 14:18): "The one who is eating with me."
- Psalm 41/42 (Matt 26:38; Mark 14:34): "My soul is very sorrowful, even to death."
- Psalm 68 (Matt 27:34, 48; Mark 15:36): "They offered him wine to drink, mixed with gall."

Although as a control I emphasize the gospels' simple evocations of these texts, I also undertake auxiliary examinations of "supplementary data" that include *possible* psalmic allusions. These examinations test more broadly on each respective gospel the conclusions drawn from exploring the simple evocations. If, for example, as I argue in chapter 2, Mark characterizes Jesus and Jesus' opponents as the psalmic lamenter and as the opponents of the psalmic lamenter, respectively, via simple evocations *and* via most other supplementary data that alludes to the psalmic lament, then the validity of my argument substantially increases.

Beyond detecting these intertextual occurrences between the psalmic lament and the Synoptic Gospels, I also more broadly focus on examining what these occurrences mean within their respective

---

The degree to which the gospel readers would have detected certain evocations raises complex sociological and anthropological issues (see Hatina, *Biblical Interpretation in Early Christian Gospels*, 1:7). It is assumed in the subsequent discussions that these readers would have possessed varying degrees of literary and OT competence, resulting in various degrees of recognizing OT evocations. In other words, it is unlikely that all of the gospel readers would have detected each writer's evocations, but some, if not most, would have.

narratives. This is accomplished by employing narrative, redaction, and rhetorical criticisms towards specific interpretive ends. A brief glance at these criticisms more specifically clarifies my nuanced use of them.

In contrast to structural,[93] deconstructive,[94] and reader-response[95] approaches to the Synoptics, the narrative criticism that I employ focuses on the texts as complete literary narratives that contain plotline(s), characterizations, and meaning(s).[96] Within the unfolding of their narratives, the Synoptists unveil their respective literary intentions and theologies in relation to the psalmic lament.[97] My primary emphasis, then, lies upon what is "within" instead of what is "behind" the text.[98]

The redaction criticism I employ assumes that Mark wrote his gospel first and that Matthew and Luke later use Mark as a source to construct their respective gospels.[99] In light of the burgeoning field of narrative

---

93. See Patte, *Structural Exegesis for New Testament Critics*.

94. See Derrida, *Of Grammatology*. Cf. Detweiler, "Derrida and Biblical Studies," 1–97.

95. See Detweiler, "Reader-Response Approaches to Biblical and Secular Texts," 1–230; Fowler, *Let the Reader Understand*; Resseguie, "Reader-Response and the Synoptic Gospels," 307–34; Thiselton, *New Horizons in Hermeneutics*, 516–55.

96. See Powell, *What Is Narrative Criticism?* See also Turner, *Matthew*, 3, 7–8; Frei, *Eclipse of Biblical Narrative*; Rhoads et al., *Mark as Story*; Kingsbury, *Christology of Mark's Gospel*; Culpepper, *Anatomy of the Fourth Gospel*; Tannehill, *Narrative Unity of Luke-Acts*; and Malbon, *In the Company of Jesus*, 1–40; ibid., *Mark's Jesus*.

97. Bockmuehl has recently critiqued narrative critics for imposing on the gospels a higher literary acumen than do the gospel writers themselves (*Seeing the Word*, 48–49; cf. Rhoads' discussion on common critiques of narrative criticism in *Reading Mark, Engaging the Gospel*, 25–30). While I heed Bockmuehl's cautionary remarks, it is worth noting that the gospel writers did construct literary pieces that contain plots, characters, conflict, irony, narrative progression, and other literary techniques (cf. Moloney, "Markan Story," 5–13). Thus, the gospels remain worthy of study via the methods of narrative criticism.

98. Clearly these two spheres interact. For classic studies that emphasize what is "behind" the text, see Dibelius, *From Tradition to Gospel*, and Bultmann, *History of the Synoptic Tradition*.

99. For a definition and explanation of redaction criticism, see Perrin, *What Is Redaction Criticism?*, and Stanton, *Gospel for a New People*, 23–53. Stanton presents an insightful critique of redaction criticism that I take into consideration: Since modern researchers cannot know how many sources that Matthew and Luke possibly redacted and since they cannot be certain that every redaction reflects their theological interests, care should be taken not to overstate one's redactional conclusions (*Gospel for a New People*, 36–41; cf. Beaton, *Isaiah's Christ in Matthew's Gospel*, 11; contrast with Beare, *Matthew*, 15, 44). In light of this critique, I recognize that any one of the proposed redactions may not accurately represent Matthew's or Luke's theological

criticism, some recent scholars read Matthew and Luke only vertically and occasionally critique redaction criticism sharply.[100] Exclusively reading the evangelists vertically advances the understanding of the gospels in new and creative ways. In some respects, however, the pendulum can swing too far away from redaction criticism since the fact remains that Matthew and Luke depend significantly on Mark.[101]

Such significant dependence inherently means that reading Matthew's and Luke's gospel in light of Mark's gospel, especially under the assumption that one can to a degree detect authorial intent (see discussion below),[102] results in a more accurate narrative-critical understanding of the First and Third Gospels.[103] This more accurate narrative understand-

---

interests, but the overall pattern of the data confirms the accuracy of my respective arguments. Stanton affirms the methodological application of this type of redaction criticism (*Gospel for a New People*, 40–41). In light of the serious historical doubts surrounding the hypothesized "Q-document," I make no attempts to reconstruct this source in order to then deduce alleged redactions from it (cf. Rowe's methodology in *Early Narrative Christology*, 16). Additionally, entering the speculative enterprise of Markan redaction exceeds the boundaries of this work.

100. See Huizenga, *New Isaac*, 5–9. In light of Huizenga's method (following Eco, *Limits of Interpretation*) to include *all* "socio-linguistic cultural encyclopedia" (i.e., texts, interpretive traditions, ways of reading, etc.) (Huizenga, *New Isaac*, 24–29), it seems particularly odd to omit investigations into how the Synoptic Gospels interact, especially since they interact in such complex ways (cf. O'Leary's recent redactional-critical work, *Matthew's Judaization of Mark*).

101. Stanton noted this shift as early as 1992, when he posed the question, "Are we reaching the end of the redaction critical era?" (*Gospel for a New People*, 23; 54–59).

102. Huizenga argues that "the evangelists did not intend their Gospels to be read in a way that redaction critics read, with such scrupulous attention to their sources. [Matthew] did not pass out copies of Mark and Q to his congregation and insist that they take careful note of his editorial work. Rather, the evangelists composed wholes and intended their Gospels to be read and heard as such" (*New Isaac*, 8). Huizenga's arguments are correct; nevertheless, understanding how a particular evangelist understands and appropriates another evangelist sheds light on the intentions of his particular narrative, thus providing insights into what he expects his audience to understand from reading it.

103. Dale C. Allison applies a similar methodology to his examination of Matthew's foreshadowing of the passion (*Studies in Matthew*, 217–35; note esp. 219). Frank Thielman does likewise in articulating Matthew's theology (*Theology of the New Testament*, 84–110). Cf. Gundry, *Matthew: A Commentary on His Literary and Theological Art*, xii. Huizenga rightfully notes some questionable assumptions of redaction criticism: "(1) That objective, determinative interpretation necessitates discovering the intention of the evangelist as empirical author; (2) that discovering an evangelist's intention necessitates examining the significance of alterations to presumed sources; and (3) that the evangelist's intention concerns static, cognitive propositional theology" (*New Isaac*, 6). One does not have to make these assumptions, however, to employ

ing is especially acquired via redaction criticism when trying to confirm Matthew's or Luke's detection and communication of certain narrative motifs, especially when these motifs appear nearly verbatim with Mark. For my purposes, specifically in chapters 3 (concerning Matthew's gospel) and 4 (concerning Luke's gospel), redaction criticism serves as a handmaiden to narrative criticism.[104]

Rhetorical criticism, which Dennis Stamps simply defines as "the way discourses are constructed and operate to create certain effects,"[105] is most often employed in understanding Pauline literature via an examination of timeless/universal communicative devices or via communicative devices contemporary with Paul.[106] As Stamps notes, however, it is appropriate to employ rhetorical criticism in trying to understand the gospels—namely, via what Robert Tannehill calls "narrative rhetoric"; narratives tell a story and "the story is constructed in order to influence its readers and particular literary techniques are used for this purpose."[107] My specific narrative-rhetorical technique of interest is Mark Allen Powell's "evaluative point of view," which he defines as "the standards of judgment by which readers are led to evaluate the events, characters, and settings that comprise the story."[108] Still more specifically, the narrative-

---

redaction criticism. It is simply historically unwise for the modern gospel interpreter to exclude from examination a comparison between the Synoptic Gospels when intertextual dependency among the writers is demonstrably apparent.

104. Often this is actually the case, although not explicitly stated. For example, Turner notes that his commentary is narrative critical (*Matthew*, 3) but consistently employs redaction criticism to augment his arguments (see, e.g., 39–42; 495–96; 513–14). Stanton argues similarly: "The results of redaction criticism are more compelling when they are complemented by other methods" (*Gospel for a New People*, 23). Strauss argues for a similar methodology (*Davidic Messiah in Luke-Acts*, 31–33).

105. Stamps, "Rhetorical Criticism of the New Testament," 157. Cf. Black, "Rhetorical Criticism," 264; Rhoads, *Reading Mark, Engaging the Gospel*, 31–32; and Witherington, *New Testament Rhetoric*, ix–x.

106. Stamps, "Rhetorical Criticism of the New Testament," 135–41.

107. Ibid., 148, citing Tannehill, *Narrative Unity of Luke-Acts*, 1:8. This type of rhetorical criticism is closely linked to how narrative criticism has come to be defined (Rhoads, *Reading Mark, Engaging the Gospel*, 24). Cf. Tolbert, "How the Gospel of Mark Builds Character," 347, 349.

108. Powell, *What Is Narrative Criticism?*, 24; cf. 53–54, 60–61. Cf. Petersen, "'Point of View' in Mark's Narrative," 97–121; Rhoads, *Reading Mark, Engaging the Gospel*, 44–62; Smith, *Lion with Wings*, 167–68; Anderson, *Matthew's Narrative Web*, 53–77; Kingsbury, *Matthew as Story*, 31–37; Weaver, *Matthew's Missionary Discourse*, 31–57; Howell, *Matthew's Inclusive Story*, 161–203; and Culpepper, *Anatomy of the Fourth Gospel*, 32–34.

rhetorical focus applied below is the Synoptists' evaluative point of view of their characterization of Jesus and Jesus' opponents in relation to their appropriation of the psalmic lament and related literature.[109]

More specifically, I employ these four methodologies (simple evocations, narrative, redaction, and rhetorical criticisms) in the following ways. In chapter 2 ("Mark's Appropriation of the Psalmic Lament"), I delineate six of Mark's allusions to the psalmic lament as simple evocations. Delineating these evocations lays the foundation to explore Mark's literary appropriation of the psalmic lament in relation to his characterization of Jesus' opponents and in relation to other OT motifs (e.g., Isaiah's Suffering Servant). Finally, I explore some effects that Mark intends his literary appropriation of the psalmic lament to have on his early readers via rhetorical criticism.

In chapters 3 and 4 ("Matthew's and Luke's Appropriation of the Psalmic Lament," respectively), I use redaction criticism to determine the degree to which Matthew and Luke utilize Mark's appropriation of the psalmic lament and to explore specific narrative emphases in Matthew's and Luke's appropriation of the motif. Narrative and rhetorical criticisms are applied to Matthew and Luke in order to examine the broader literary influence in relation to other motifs and to explore the intended effect of the tradition on their respective readers.

The methodological foundation that provides a degree of control in the use of the foregoing methodologies and that provides the foundational grounds for methodologically conjoining narrative and redaction criticisms is authorial intent. Although some argue that recovering authorial intent is nothing more than a subjective enterprise cloaked in a facade of objectivity, Grant Osborne is correct that it is possible to "spiral" toward it.[110] As the modern reader spirals toward an understanding of the author's intended meaning of a text, he or she, although challenged by the critical engagement with it, can survive the encounter to speak cogently about it. This is what N. T. Wright, following Ben Meyer, calls Critical Realism.[111] Thus, I undertake this investigation of the Synoptists' appropriation of the psalmic lament for the purpose of determining to

---

109. I discuss this more fully in chapter 2, where I also explain the methodology employed to explore the characterization of Jesus' opponents.

110. Osborne, *Hermeneutical Spiral*.

111. Wright, *New Testament and the People of God*, 32–37. Cf. Meyer, *Critical Realism and the New Testament*.

a degree of probability the original authors' intentions in utilizing this tradition within their respective narratives.

In summary, Köstenberger's and Wright's hermeneutical triad provides my broad methodological framework, giving the necessary, holistic, and integrated balance for the work as a whole. Within this framework, Ahearne-Kroll's concept of "simple evocations" helps delineate the Synoptic data explored below. The data is then examined within three established methodologies. Within Mark, narrative and rhetorical criticisms are employed in order to explore his literary usage of the psalmic lament. Within Matthew and Luke, narrative and rhetorical criticisms are employed in concert with redaction criticism in order to explore their literary usage of the lament. The ultimate goal, then, is to "spiral" toward an understanding of how the Synoptic authors appropriate Israel's psalmic lament in characterizing Jesus (the hero of the gospels) and Jesus' opponents (the villains of the gospels).

2

Mark's Appropriation of the Psalmic Lament

INTRODUCTION

SINCE MARK MOST LIKELY wrote his gospel first, it is most prudent to begin with how he appropriates the psalmic lament, an endeavor that, as mentioned in chapter 1, Stephen P. Ahearne-Kroll has recently undertaken.[1] Ahearne-Kroll's monograph is in essence an exploration into a particular aspect of Mark's characterization of Jesus. Specifically, Ahearne-Kroll argues that Mark characterizes Jesus as the Davidic lamenter par excellence who shuns the militaristic expectations that traditionally accompanied Second Temple messianic claims. At the heart of Ahearne-Kroll's work is his exploration of Mark's characterization of Jesus just prior to (Mark 10–12) and in (Mark 14–16) the passion account.[2] In chapters 10–12 of the Second Gospel, Ahearne-Kroll correctly argues that Mark characterizes Jesus as a Davidic royal figure primarily via Blind Bartimaeus' two addresses to Jesus as "Son of David" (Mark 10:47–48), two references to Psalm 117 (Mark 11:9–10; 12:10), and one reference to

---

1. Ahearne-Kroll, *Psalms of Lament in Mark's Passion*.
2. Ibid., chapters 5 and 6, respectively.

Psalm 109 (Mark 12:36).³ This conclusion concerning Mark 10–12 sets the stage for Ahearne-Kroll's exploration into Mark's depiction of Jesus in the passion account, wherein Ahearne-Kroll concludes that Mark characterizes Jesus as the Davidic lamenter par excellence.

In this chapter, I advance Ahearne-Kroll's work, which solely focuses on how Mark appropriates the psalmic lament to characterize *Jesus*, by exploring how Mark appropriates it to characterize Jesus' *opponents*. Specifically, two of the following sections of this chapter ("Mark's Appropriation of Non-Lament Psalms 109 and 117 in Mark 11–12" and "Mark's Appropriation of the Psalmic Lament in Relation to His Characterization of Jesus' Opponents in the Passion," respectively) correspond to and advance chapters 5 and 6 of Ahearne-Kroll's monograph where he examines the use of two non-lament psalms in Mark 11–12 (Ahearne-Kroll, chapter 5) and the use of the lament psalms in Mark's passion account (Ahearne-Kroll, chapter 6). The final section of this chapter ("Mark's Appropriation of the Psalmic Lament in Relation to His Isaianic Servant Motif") advances Ahearne-Kroll's work by exploring how Mark appropriates the psalmic lament in relation to his Isaianic Servant motif.⁴

---

3. Cf. Watts, "Lord's House and David's Lord," 307–22. In light of Mark 12:35–37a (the scribes' questioning of Jesus about his Davidic sonship), Elizabeth Malbon challenges Ahearne-Kroll's position that Mark depicts Jesus as the "Son of David," arguing that in Mark, Jesus both ignores Bartimaeus's appellation "Jesus, Son of David" (Mark 11:47, 48) and overtly rejects it (Mark 12:36) (Malbon, *Mark's Jesus*, 159–69; cf. Marcus, *Way of the Lord*, 139–40; Hahn, *Titles of Jesus in Christology*, 105, 240–45). The degree to which Mark understands Jesus as the Son of David is less relevant for the argument of this chapter. More pertinent is the fact that Mark characterizes Jesus *as David*, especially via his depiction of Jesus as one who prays and speaks the Psalms; see, for example, Hays, who argues that early Christians employed an OT hermeneutic of Jesus speaking and praying the Psalms as David (Hays, "Christ Prays the Psalms"). Cf. Mark 14:18, 34; 15:34; see also discussion below and the discussions in chapters 3 and 4.

4. Note that the specificity of the explorations in these three sections does not negate the important fact that Mark evokes these OT passages for other possible reasons that coincide with his broader use of the OT: (1) To indicate that Jesus fulfilled Scripture in his death (Kee, "Function of Scriptural Quoatations and Allusions in Mark 11–16," contra Suhl, *Die Funktion der alttestamentlichen Zitate und Anspielungen im Markusevangelium*); (2) for apologetic purposes (Hashimoto, "Function of the Old Testament Quotations and Allusions in the Marcan Passion Narrative"; Marcus, "Old Testament and the Death of Jesus"; McCaffrey, "Psalm Quotations in the Passion Narratives of the Gospels"); (3) to substantiate a particular train of thought (Vorster, "Function of the Use of the Old Testament in Mark," 62–72); (4) as a catechesis (Schneck, *Isaiah in the Gospel of Mark*); (5) to re-present Isaiah's New Exodus theme (Watts, *Isaiah's New Exodus and Mark*).

Mark's Appropriation of the Psalmic Lament

In essence, I build on Ahearne-Kroll by concluding that Mark establishes a group of opponents to Jesus—namely, the religious leaders—in chapters 1–10 that is intended to incite a negative point of view for his first readers. In chapters 11–12, Mark begins a new narrative trend that gradually intensifies this negative point of view. Specifically, Mark uses Psalms 109, 117, Isaiah's Suffering Servant (crescendoing his narrative with the lament psalms) to characterize Jesus' opponents as the respective opponents of these OT passages and motifs. As a result, Mark, aside from inviting his readers to understand Jesus as the OT paradigmatic hero (Isaiah's Servant, David, etc.), invites them to understand Jesus' opponents as OT paradigmatic villains. Mark uses these depictions, as discussed in my conclusion at chapter's end, toward certain narrative and rhetorical ends.

Aside from advancing Ahearne-Kroll's work, the cumulative argument in this chapter, that Mark characterizes Jesus' opponents as paradigmatic OT villains, makes an ancillary contribution to the understanding of how Mark demarcates his characterization of Jesus' opponents. Specifically, this cumulative argument provides a way forward in understanding Mark's method in amalgamating Jesus' opponents into a unified force of opposition against Jesus. Before turning specifically to advancing Ahearne-Kroll's work, it is first necessary to explain this way forward, which I then substantiate in the advancements to Ahearne-Kroll's work in the subsequent three sections.

MARK'S CHARACTERIZATION OF JESUS' OPPONENTS: A WAY FORWARD

An array of Jesus' opponents surface in Mark's narrative. Some of these opponents appear pervasively as "main characters" and consistently oppose Jesus throughout the story: Pharisees, scribes, chief priests, and the elders.[5] Other opponents make their debut in the passion: Pilate, the

---

5. As Malbon and David Rhoads note, Theodore J. Weeden and Werner H. Kelber are incorrect in labeling the disciples as Jesus' opponents. Kelber, following Weeden (*Mark: Traditions in Conflict*), suggests that "Mark's story is essentially that of the conflict and break between Jesus and the Twelve" (Kelber, *Mark's Story of Jesus*, 88; cf. ibid., "Mark 14:32–42," 166–87). Kelber establishes this argument primarily based on Jesus' comment to his disciples that their hearts had become hardened (Mark 6:52) since it is the same phrase used in relation to Jesus' other opponents (Mark 3:5). The distinct difference, however, between the disciples and the religious leaders, according to Rhoads, is that the disciples are at least trying to follow and understand Jesus while the religious leaders take no interest in doing so, Joseph of Arimathea (Mark 15:12–47)

Soldiers, and an unnamed man who offers Jesus wine vinegar to drink.⁶ Another character group in Mark, the crowd, is portrayed prior to the passion as non-hostile to Jesus but makes a decisive change in the passion to oppose Jesus.

Scholars agree that Mark presents the crowd as a Markan character group who is amicable toward Jesus prior to the passion but opposes him when the passion begins.⁷ Scholars also agree that Mark presents Jesus' opponents as a unified character group, but they are divided on exactly which opponents are included in this group. For example, did Mark intend to include both the Jewish and the Gentile leaders in this group or simply the Jewish leaders? Rhoads, Dewey, and Michie argue that all the authori-

---

and the friendly scribe (Mark 12:28–34) notwithstanding (Rhoads, "Narrative Criticism and the Gospel of Mark," 416; concerning Joseph and the friendly scribe, see Kingsbury, "Religious Authorities in the Gospel of Mark,"" 47–50, who notes that these serve as ironic characters. Cf. Malbon, *In the Company of Jesus*, 158, who suggests that the key to their exceptional nature is how they respond to Jesus; although Jewish leaders are generally categorized as foes, they should not be automatically categorized as such). Similarly, Malbon rightly counters Kelber by noting the importance of distinguishing the differing levels of "opposition" between the disciples and the Jewish leaders (ibid., 150, cf. 135). For Malbon, then, the term "opponents" is "an extremely misleading label for [the disciples in Mark]" (ibid., 150; cf. Thielman, *Theology of the New Testament*, 80–82).

6. Relatively little is written on Mark's characterization of Jesus' non-human opponents (Satan, demons, and unclean spirits); see Collins, *Mark*, 384 (cf. 231–34); Edwards, *Mark*, 40; and Stuckenbruck, "Satan and Demons," 173–97. Cf. Hanson, *Endangered Promises*, 160; Malbon, *Mark's Jesus*, 80–83; Marcus, *Way of the Lord*, 136. Although more research into how Mark characterizes these opponents is needed, examining them exceeds my purposes, since Mark does not correlate them to Jesus via his use of the psalmic lament. See below for an argument that Mark portrays negatively and not positively the unnamed man who offers Jesus wine vinegar.

7. The "crowds," Jack Kingsbury argues, function uniquely in Mark in that they are "at once 'well disposed' toward Jesus and 'without faith' in him" (Mark 11:18, 32; 12:12, 37) (Kingsbury, *Conflict in Mark*, 24). By the end of the gospel, Kingsbury continues, "the crowd demonstrates its complete solidarity with [the] leaders" (ibid., 24; cf. Boomershine, "Mark, the Storyteller," 299–302, and Brown, *Death of the Messiah*, 2:1421). Thus, at the outset of Mark, the reader is unsure whether the crowds are in opposition to Jesus. In the passion account, however, the crowd, as demonstrated below, merges with the religious leaders who consistently oppose Jesus prior to the passion. Malbon argues that the crowd is portrayed in Mark as a compliment to the disciples where both exhibit positive and negative traits and both offer a composite portrait of Jesus' followers (*In the Company of Jesus*, 70–99). A marked distinction occurs between the disciples and the crowd, however, in the passion; the crowds participate in Jesus' crucifixion (Mark 14:43, 56; 15:8–15, 29), thus revealing their solidarity with Jesus' opponents, while the disciples do not. For a summary of the crowd in Mark, see Patten, "Thaumaturgical Element in the Gospel of Mark," 132–38.

ties in Mark, including Jews (scribes, elders, etc.) and Gentiles (high priest, the Sanhedrin, the Sadducees, the Gentile soldiers, and Pilate), constitute a single character group[8] while Malbon,[9] following Kingsbury,[10] argues that only the Jewish leaders (the Pharisees, Herodians, chief priests, scribes, elders, and Sadducees) represent a unified character group.[11] It is in relation to this scholarly dialogue that the cumulative argument of this chapter provides a way forward; but, first I introduce it here.

There is an explanation for Mark's portrayal of these character and character groups in his passion that clarifies more precisely his overarching interest in characterizing them in opposition to Jesus—namely, Mark's hermeneutic of the OT to depict Jesus' passion opponents as OT paradigmatic villains. This hermeneutic provides a category of characterization that represents the unity of opposition against Jesus that modern scholars sense in Mark's text and provides a fluidity that allows certain opponents to merge with others. In other words, Mark's characterization of Jesus' opponents as OT paradigmatic villains provides him a matrix in which to continue portraying characters individually (with their narratively unique attributes) and to introduce new opponents (e.g., the crowd and soldiers) while simultaneously providing a unifying force of opposition against Jesus. The thread of unification that Mark uses to bind these individual characters together is the concept that I call the OT paradigmatic villain.[12]

Establishing this way forward begins with exploring how Mark characterizes Jesus' opponents in relation to Psalms 109 and 117 and continues in the explorations of Mark's characterization of Jesus' opponents in the subsequent two sections.

8. Rhoads et al., *Mark as Story*, 117.

9. Malbon, *In the Company of Jesus*, 149–52; cf. Malbon's more recent work, *Mark's Jesus*, 110–17.

10. Kingsbury, "Religious Authorities in the Gospel of Mark,"' 44–47, 60.

11. Cf. Weber's 1966 article in which he argues for a break between the opponents of Jesus prior to the passion [chief priests, scribes, and Pharisees] and those that appear in the passion [the chief priests and the elders] ("Jesus' Opponents in the Gospel of Mark," 214–22). Contrast with Hanson who suggests that Mark probably does not intend a sharp distinction between the two groups (*Endangered Promises*, 160–65). Marcus groups them together collectively as "The Jewish Leaders in Mark" but examines them individually (*Mark 8–16*, 1099–103). Timothy Wiarda more recently cautions against focusing on Mark's characterization of groups to the exclusion of his characterization of individuals (*Interpreting Gospel Narratives*, 154–60).

12. Matthew's gospel, which significantly expands this type of characterization, and Luke's gospel, to a lesser degree, provides substantial validation for this technique of characterization (see chapters 3 and 4, respectively).

NON-LAMENT PSALMS 109 AND 117 IN MARK 11–12 IN CHARACTERIZING JESUS' OPPONENTS

Ahearne-Kroll rightly emphasizes the role that Mark 10–12 plays in Mark's characterization of Jesus as the Davidic lamenter par excellence.[13] In essence, Ahearne-Kroll demonstrates that Mark sets the stage in chapters 10–12 for his passion account by characterizing Jesus as the OT paragon King David—Jesus is the long awaited Davidic messiah.[14] Jesus, however, secures this position not by military force, as a Second Temple Jew might expect, but by suffering and death. Ahearne-Kroll establishes this characterization of Jesus by examining Bartimaeus' appellative for Jesus, "Son of David" (Mark 10:47, 48), and by examining Mark's three quotations of the following non-lament psalms: (1) Mark 11:9–10: "Those who went before and those who followed were shouting, 'Hosanna! Blessed is he who comes in the name of the Lord! Blessed is the coming kingdom of our father David! Hosanna in the highest!'" (cf. Ps 117:25–26); (2) Mark 12:10–11: "The stone that the builders rejected has become the cornerstone" (cf. Ps 117:22–23); and (3) Mark 12:36: "The Lord said to my Lord, Sit at my right hand, until I put your enemies under your feet" (cf. Ps 109:1; see also Mark 14:62).[15]

Although Ahearne-Kroll is correct in his assessment of Mark's characterization of Jesus, there is more to Mark's story that deserves attention.[16] Mark is not only concerned with characterizing Jesus as

---

13. Ahearne-Kroll, *Psalms of Lament in Mark's Passion*, 137–67.

14. Cf. Mark 1:1: "The beginning of the gospel of Jesus Christ (χριστοῦ [i.e., "messiah"]), the Son of God."

15. Methodologically, this section follows Ahearne-Kroll in focusing on Mark's appropriation of Psalms 109 and 117. Adding support to the arguments below, however, is data collected from Watts' commentary on Mark in *Commentary on the New Testament Use of the Old Testament* and in the NA[27] (as an aside, the NA[28] came out too late for me to use in this book). These two sources suggest five further possible Markan allusions to non-lament psalms. Four of these five (excluding Mark 8:37 [cf. Ps 48:8–10]: "In exchange for one's life"), to the degree that they represent allusions to their respective OT psalmic texts, confirm Mark's tendency to characterize Jesus as the Davidic psalmist; each allusion either portrays Jesus reliving an aspect of David's life as depicted in the Psalms or records God addressing Jesus in the same way that he addresses the Davidic psalmist: (1) Mark 1:11 (cf. Ps 2:7): "You are my Son"; (2) Mark 1:13 (cf. Ps 90:11): "Angels attended him"; (3) Mark 4:39 (cf. Ps 105:9): "He . . . rebuked the wind and the sea"; (4) Mark 9:7 (cf. Ps 2:7): "This is my Son."

16. In her review of Ahearne-Kroll's work, Susan Gillingham suggests that his work needs to be advanced by examining more closely Mark's integration of lament and non-lament psalms (Gillingham, Review of *The Psalms of Lament in Mark's Passion*,

David, but he is also concerned with characterizing Jesus' opponents as David's opponents.[17] I attempt to demonstrate in this chapter that Mark overtly initiates a trend in chapters 11–12 that continues throughout his narrative: As Mark characterizes Jesus with certain OT heroes, he also characterizes Jesus' opponents as certain, unnamed OT villains, which he intends, among other things, to have a rhetorical affect on Mark's readers.

Succinctly, this unfolds in Mark's narrative in the following way. In chapters 11–12, Mark characterizes Jesus as the victorious King David of Psalms 109 and 117 while, simultaneously, he characterizes Jesus' opponents as King David's conquered enemies.[18] In the passion, Mark characterizes Jesus as the lamenting King David while, simultaneously, he characterizes Jesus' opponents as the paradigmatic lamenters' opponents, who torment, mock, and kill the lamenter. The focus of the present section is on Psalms 109 and 117 in Mark 11–12, which sets the stage for focusing in the next section on the lament psalms in the passion.

In focusing on the characterization of Jesus' opponents via his use of Psalms 109 and 117 in Mark 11–12, the following two steps are needed. First, in order to understand how Mark characterizes Jesus' opponents prior to Mark 11–12 and in order to set the stage for this section (and the next one), I give a brief glance at Mark's characterization of Jesus' opponents and the crowd (who become Jesus' opponents in the passion) prior to chapter 11. Second, I look at Mark's characterization of Jesus' opponents via his use of Psalms 109 and 117 in chapters 11–12.

Jesus' Opponents and the Crowd in Chapters 1–10

Mark's characterization of Jesus' opponents is rooted in his conflict theme wherein Jesus is in constant struggle with the religious leaders.[19] Kings-

---

199). This section represents an initial step in this direction.

17. Mark's use of Psalms 109 and 117 in this way is subsidiary to his larger eschatological purposes in using these psalms (see Evans, "Praise and Prophecy in the Psalter and in the New Testament," 568; Subramanian, *Synoptic Gospels and the Psalms as Prophecy*). For exhaustive studies of the use of Psalms 109 and 117 in early Christianity, see Hay, *Glory at the Right Hand*; Loader, "Christ at the Right Hand," 199–217; Marcus, *Way of the Lord*, 111–52; Moyise and Menken, *Psalms in the New Testament*; and Juel, *Messianic Exegesis*, 89–117, 135–50.

18. It is unnecessary to argue for a Markan dependence on these psalms since there is a universal consensus that Mark quotes Ps 117:25–26 in Mark 11:9–10, Ps 117:22–23 in Mark 12:10–11, and Ps 109:1 in Mark 12:36.

19. Mark's conflict motif, which begins in 1:21–22, is well known, with modern

bury is correct that this theme is what propels the narrative forward.[20] A hint of this conflict surfaces as early as Mark 1:22 where Mark notes, "[The people] were astonished at his teaching, for he taught them as one who had authority, and *not as the scribes*" (italics added). This subtle hint quickly gives way to a sustained deluge of conflict stories between Jesus and the religious leaders (Mark 2:1—3:6). At the climax of these conflict stories, the Pharisees "plot with the Herodians how they might kill Jesus" (Mark 3:6). As the narrative continues through the next seven chapters, Mark sustains this conflict (Mark 3:20–30; 7:1–23; 8:11–13; 10:1–12) and, more importantly, uses the murderous plot of these religious leaders at three crucial narrative junctures to build anticipation toward the passion (Mark 8:31; 9:31; 10:33–34). Thus, in Mark 1–10, the primary plot of the story centers on religious leaders who are unified in their conflict with, and plan to kill, Jesus.

Mark establishes another character group concurrently with the religious leaders—namely, the "crowd" (variously referred to as "they," "many," "all," "multitude," "people").[21] Mark's depiction of the crowd is markedly different in chapters 1–10 than his depiction of the religious leaders. The crowd is amazed with Jesus' teaching (Mark 1:22; 6:1–5), marvel at his healings (Mark 2:12; 5:20; 7:36–37), and are obsessively attracted to his popularity (Mark 1:45; 2:2, 13; 3:7–10; 3:20; 4:1; 5:21, 24, 31; 6:31–34, 54–56; 8:1; 9:14–15, 25; 10:1, 46). Thus, unlike the religious leaders, the crowd in Mark 1–10 is well-disposed toward Jesus.

For my purposes here, it is important simply to note that prior to chapter 11, Mark characterizes the religious leaders as opponents of Jesus bent on killing him, and he characterizes the crowd as admirers of Jesus. It is also important to note that, prior to chapter 11, Mark does not clearly characterize either the crowd or Jesus' opponents in relation to any OT figures.[22] This changes in chapter 11.

---

scholarly contributions spanning over fifty years. For entries into this discussion, see Kingsbury, *Conflict in Mark*, 28, 63; Malbon, *In the Company of Jesus*, 17; and Keith and Hurtado, *Jesus Among Friends and Enemies*, 172–288.

20. Kingsbury, *Conflict in Mark*, 28, 63.

21. Mark 1:22, 27, 33, 45; 2:2, 12, 13; 3:7–10, 20, 32; etc. Cf. Patten, "Thaumaturgical Element in the Gospel of Mark."

22. There are two potential exceptions: (1) The possible echo of the common OT statement "sheep without a shepherd" (cf. Num 27:17; 1 Kings 22:17) in Mark 6:34 that Mark uses to describe the crowd; and (2) the possible echo of Ps 36:32 (ζητεῖ τοῦ θανατῶσαι αὐτόν) in Mark 14:55 ("The chief priests and the whole Council were seeking . . . to put [Jesus] to death [ἐζήτουν . . . τὸ θανατῶσαι αὐτόν]") that Mark uses

Jesus' Opponents and the Crowd in Chapters 11–12

Mark's method of characterizing Jesus' opponents and the crowd changes in chapter 11, Jesus' entry into Jerusalem—the beginning of Passion Week. For the first time, Mark explicitly characterizes the crowd as the worshippers of Psalm 117 (Mark 11:9–10) and Jesus' opponents as the villains of Psalms 117 and 109 (Mark 12:1–11 and 12:36, respectively).[23] In discussing Mark's use of these psalms, researchers primarily focus on Mark's characterization of Jesus as the Davidic messiah.[24] Mark, however, is doing more than this; he also characterizes Jesus' opponents and the crowd as those of Psalms 117 and 109, initiating a new Markan trend that continues throughout the rest of his narrative and that ultimately crescendos with his use of the lament psalms.

Beginning with the crowd, Mark characterizes them as those who celebrate the coronation of King David (Mark 11:1–11).[25] Mark does this by placing on their lips a quote from Psalm 117:25–26: "Hosanna! Blessed is he who comes in the name of the Lord!" Psalm 117 is a hymn of thanksgiving for the deliverance from enemies[26] and, in Mark's era, was thought to have been written by David.[27] At the end of the psalm, after "David" recounts God's protection from his many opponents, there is a shift from the singular to the plural (Ps 117:23–26) wherein the

---

to describe the actions of the chief priests and the Sanhedrin (Cf. O'Brien, *Use of Scripture in the Markan Passion Narrative*, 104–5).

23. Watts suggests that Mark may implicitly characterize Jesus' opponents as those of Ps 2:7 in Mark 1:11 ("Psalms in Mark's Gospel," 28, 30; cf. Watts, "Lord's House and David's Lord," 309–13; and Juel, *Messianic Exegesis*, 68–69), especially since the thrust of Psalm 2 is about enemy opposition. This, however, is quite speculative since Mark references the psalm only to identify Jesus as God's son and does not cite it explicitly in reference to Jesus' opponents.

24. Ibid., 135–50; Watts, "Psalms in Mark's Gospel," 36–39; ibid., "Lord's House and David's Lord"; Hay, *Glory at the Right Hand*; Ahearne-Kroll, *Psalms of Lament in Mark's Passion*, 137–67; Evans, "Praise and Prophecy," 553–65; Stein, *Mark*, 506, 537–38; Edwards, *Mark*, 336–37, 360–61; Marcus, *Way of the Lord*, 111–29, 130–52.

25. Stein and Hooker correctly note Jesus' kingship by arguing that a donkey, on which Jesus rode, was fit for a king and not a symbol of lowliness and meekness (Stein, *Mark*, 506; Hooker, *Gospel According to Saint Mark*, 257).

26. Allen, *Psalms 101–150*, 122–25.

27. It was commonplace among NT writers to attribute the Psalms to David, an historical assessment assumed throughout the rest of this book. See Collins, *Mark*, 520. Cf. Acts 4:25 where Psalm 2—which in the OT does not have a titular superscription—is attributed to David.

worshippers celebrate King David's victory. Similarly, when Jesus enters Jerusalem as David, the crowd receives him as a king and speaks in unison with the voices of those in the psalmic community of Psalm 117. Thus, as Mark characterizes Jesus as King David, he also characterizes the crowd as the community of worshippers of Psalm 117. Based on how the crowds relate to Jesus in Mark 1–10, their exuberantly positive response in Mark 11:9–10 is expected. Within Mark's narrative logic, then, Jesus is characterized as, among other things, King David, and the crowds are those who accept him as such.[28] As will be seen in the next section, however, the crowd's position towards Jesus changes after Gethsemane, and Mark notes this change via allusions to the psalmic lament.

Mark also uses Psalm 117 to characterize Jesus' opponents. After entering Jerusalem (Mark 11:1–11), clearing the temple (Mark 11:12–19), and cursing a fig tree (Mark 11:20–26), Jesus' conflict with the religious leaders resumes in Mark 11:27—12:40. When they question Jesus about his authority (Mark 11:27–33), he tells a parable (Mark 12:1–12), echoing Isaiah 5:1–7,[29] about tenants who beat and kill an array of servants sent by the vineyard owner. The vineyard owner finally sends his son, assuming that the tenants will respect him. The tenants, instead of respecting the son, kill him and throw him out of the vineyard. Mark changes metaphors from vineyard and tenants to builders as he appends an explanatory note to Jesus' parable via a quote of Psalm 117:22–23: "[Jesus said] have you not read this Scripture: 'The stone that the builders rejected has become the cornerstone; this was the Lord's doing, and it is marvelous in our eyes'?"

Collins is correct that Jesus identifies these builders as the religious leaders. She argues:

> In the context of Mark as a whole, it is clear that the stone that the builders rejected (ἀπεδοκιμάζειν) is Jesus, the Son of Man, who must be rejected (ἀπεδοκιμάζειν) by the elders, chief priests, and scribes, according to 8:31. This textual link makes clear also that the "builders" of the psalm are the leaders to whom the parable is addressed.[30]

---

28. Concerning the shouts of the crowd, Collins notes, "Although here Jesus is not hailed explicitly as king or as Son of David, the context suggests that he is both. Such an inference is supported by the address of Jesus by Bartimaeus as son of David" (*Mark*, 520). The crowd, however, is still ignorant about Jesus' true identity (Stein, *Mark*, 506; Edwards, *Mark*, 336–37).

29. Collins, *Mark*, 544–49.

30. Ibid., 548. Cf. Evans, "Praise and Prophecy," 560.

Mark's Appropriation of the Psalmic Lament

For the first time in his narrative, Mark clearly characterizes Jesus' opponents as the OT villains of Psalm 117, who "surround David on every side like bees" (Ps 117:10–12).[31] While Jesus, within Mark's narrative, is the Davidic king, his opponents are those of Psalm 117 who reject his kingship. As I demonstrate in the rest of this section and the next one, this Markan hermeneutic of characterization continues throughout his narrative, climaxing with his use of the psalmic lament.

In the final and climactic pericope (Mark 12:35–40) of these conflict stories (Mark 11:27—12:40), only a few verses after his quote of Psalm 117, Mark again characterizes Jesus as King David and the religious leaders as the opponents of David via Jesus' quote of Psalm 109:1:[32] "'David himself, speaking by the Holy Spirit, declared: 'The Lord said to my Lord: Sit at my right hand until I put your enemies under your feet'" (Mark 12:36). It exceeds my purposes here to enter into the longstanding and complicated discussions concerning the interpretations of this passage.[33] Rather, I simply note that in quoting Psalm 109, Jesus references his opponents as those of David; Mark characterizes both Jesus and Jesus' opponents in tandem with the protagonist and the antagonists of Psalm 109. This is significant since the primary purpose of the passage centers on Jesus' identity as David's son. In other words, Mark could have simply omitted Jesus' statement about "enemies" without altering the primary trust of Jesus' argument.

Summary

In the span of two chapters, at a crucial juncture in the gospel (Jesus' entry into Jerusalem), Mark characterizes Jesus as King David (*pace* Ahearne-Kroll), the crowd as the worshipping community of Psalm 117, and Jesus' opponents (namely, the religious leaders) as David's opponents

---

31. There are subtle hints of a similar trend in Mark's characterization prior to 12:10–11 via his appropriation of Isaiah's Servant motif (see "Mark's Appropriation of the Psalmic Lament in Relation to His Isaianic Servant Motif" below).

32. Hay suggests that "the primary interest motivating [Ps 109's] usage lay *not* in identifying Jesus' foes or the time of their defeat but in stressing the absoluteness of his exaltation and the utter security of those he willed to save" (*Glory at the Right Hand*, 129, italics in original). This may be the *primary* usage of Psalm 109 in early Christianity but, as the Markan context reveals, this is not his *only* usage.

33. For entries into the discussion, see Holladay, *Psalms through Three Thousand Years*, 117–19; Watts, "Psalms in Mark's Gospel," 36–41; Evans, "Praise and Prophecy," 560–65; and Gourgues, *À la droite de Dieu*.

of Psalms 109 and 117. Mark's characterization of the religious leaders as the villains of Psalms 109 and 117 is the first step in providing a way forward concerning the narrative-critical debate about how best to understand Mark's characterization of Jesus' opponents. As demonstrated in the next section, Mark continues to characterize Jesus with paradigmatic OT heroes and to characterize Jesus' opponents and the crowd with paradigmatic OT villains—namely, those of the psalmic lamenter.

THE PSALMIC LAMENT AND JESUS' OPPONENTS IN THE PASSION

Mark's characterization of Jesus, Jesus' opponents, and the crowd in chapters 11–12 sets the stage for the passion in chapters 14–15, where Jesus' anticipated (cf. Mark 8:31; 9:31; 10:33–34) suffering and death is realized. Mark's characterization of Jesus as King David continues (Mark 14:62: "Son of Man seated at the right hand"; cf. Ps 109:1), but, as Ahearne-Kroll astutely notes, Mark overlays on Jesus another OT character, the Davidic lamenter.[34] Whereas Ahearne-Kroll focuses on how the protagonist of Mark's story relates to the psalmic lament, this section focuses on how the antagonists of Mark's story, Jesus' opponents, relate to the psalmic lament. Ahearne-Kroll is correct that Mark uses the lament psalms to describe Jesus' suffering and Davidic kingship, but, as with his appropriation of Psalms 109 and 117, this is not Mark's sole focus. Instead, Mark appropriates the lament psalms more complexly by reading *both* Jesus and his opponents in tandem with the lament psalms.

To anticipate the discussion below, out of Mark's six simple evocations of the lament, he uses four to identify/describe Jesus' opponents, and he uses two to portray Jesus as one who prays the lament psalms. Thus, Mark *simultaneously* characterizes Jesus as the paradigmatic psalmic lamenter who challenges God *and* characterizes Jesus' opponents as the paradigmatic opponents of the lamenter. Viewing Mark's use of the lament psalms in such a way advances Ahearne-Kroll's work by seeing more broadly how Mark complexly uses this OT tradition.[35] This

---

34. Ahearne-Kroll, *Psalms of Lament in Mark's Passion*, 168–214.

35. This section also advances O'Brien's idea that Mark's use of the OT goes beyond, but does not exclude, Christology by functioning "to interpret the narrative *as a narrative*, to define characters and to foreshadow and give meaning to events," a pioneering move in this regard (*Use of Scripture in the Markan Passion Narrative*, 16, italics in original; cf. Watts, "Psalms in Mark's Gospel," 42, who briefly suggests

characterization, as noted in a brief excursus below, is both similar to and distinct from how Mark characterizes Jesus' opponents with Psalms 109 and 117.

This discussion on Mark's characterization is divided into four subsections. First, delineating Mark's lament evocations provides the working data to, second, explore Mark's characterization of Jesus' opponents as the villains of the psalmic lamenter. The third subsection, examining some supplementary data, substantiates the arguments in the first two subsections. Finally, by way on an excursus, I compare Mark's use of the lament and non-lament psalms in his characterization of Jesus' opponents.

Delineating Mark's Lament Evocations

In the previous section, it was unnecessary to establish Mark's references to Psalms 109 and 117 since scholars universally agree that Mark quotes these texts. Delineating Mark's lament evocations, however, is necessary, since suggested parallels abound, especially in his passion account.[36] Recall from the methodology discussed in chapter 1 that in assessing Mark's appropriation of the lament psalms, focus is placed on his simple evocations, those intertextual echoes in Mark that refer to one, and only one, text. Ahearne-Kroll has done a superb job at delineating Mark's simple

---

something similar but focuses on the specific influence of Psalm 21, especially its climactic, victorious conclusion). It further advances O'Brien's conclusion that Mark appropriates the OT in his passion account to, among other things, condemn Jesus' enemies (*Use of Scripture in the Markan Passion Narrative*, 192–93, 200). Boomershine, portending a similar endeavor, made a comment in passing thirty-five years ago in relation to Mark's use of Psalm 21: "The allusion reinforces the *characterization* of Jesus as the righteous sufferer *and* the soldiers as his enemies" ("Mark, the Storyteller," 218, italics added; cf. 222–23). More recently, O'Brien recognizes that many of Mark's scriptural allusions enhance his characterization of Jesus' opponents (*Use of Scripture in the Markan Passion Narrative*, 192, see discussion below). This endeavor to engage intertextuality as a mode of characterization has recently been applied to the book of Acts by O'Day, "Citation of Scripture as a Key to Characterization in Acts," 207–21.

36. See, for example, Marcus, who lists 14 possible echoes/allusions (*Way of the Lord*, 174–75). Ahearne-Kroll rightly critiques Marcus for offering no methodology for delineating these echoes/allusions (*Psalms of Lament in Mark's Passion*, 61–63). O'Brien presents a chart that summarizes 270 suggested allusions to the OT in Mark's passion narrative by mainstream commentaries, monographs, and articles (*Use of Scripture in the Markan Passion Narrative*, 68–74)! See also Juel, *Messianic Exegesis*, 95n7; Collins, "Appropriation of the Psalms of Individual Lament by Mark," 227n21; and Ahearne-Kroll, *Psalms of Lament in Mark's Passion*, 59–63.

evocations of Psalms 21, 40, 41/42, and 68 by noting lexical and thematic parallels between the Markan and psalmic texts and by noting general awareness of these respective psalms in Second Temple literature, especially in the Qumran texts.[37] It is unnecessary to repeat Ahearne-Kroll's arguments here. Rather, I will simply list his conclusions and, at a couple of points via footnotes, further substantiate his detection of these simple evocations. Mark evokes:

1. Psalm 40:10 in Mark 14:18 ("the one eating with me")

2. Psalms 41:6, 12, and 42:5 in Mark 14:34 ("my soul is very sorrowful")[38]

3. Psalm 21:19 in Mark 15:24 ("divided his garments . . . casting lots for them")

4. Psalm 21:8 in Mark 15:29 ("those who passed by derided him, wagging their heads")[39]

---

37. Ahearne-Kroll, *Psalms of Lament in Mark's Passion*, 59–81. O'Brien recently confirms Ahearne-Kroll's delineation of Mark's evocations of these psalmic passages, disagreeing with Ahearne-Kroll (although failing to interact with his arguments) only concerning Mark 14:18 ("one who is eating with me") as an evocation of Ps 40:10 (O'Brien, *Use of Scripture in the Markan Passion Narrative*, 91).

38. Ahearne-Kroll notes that support for a Markan evocation of Ps 41/42 in Mark 14:34 would increase if there was evidence that Matthew detects the same evocation in 26:38 instead of blindly copying Mark. In essence, Ahearne-Kroll notes that if Matthew had slightly changed Mark's evocation, then modern readers might be able to detect Matthew's knowledge of it. Instead, one is left to speculate the degree to which Matthew indeed detected it. There is evidence, however, that Matthew detects Mark's evocation, as I argued in chapter 1 above. Recall that the evidence specifically revolves around Matthew's use of λυπέω and περίλυπός. Matthew uses λυπέω six times (Matt 14:9; 17:23; 18:31; 19:22; 26:22, 37) and περίλυπός once (Mat 26:38: περίλυπός ἐστιν ἡ ψυχή). Since Matthew apparently has a predilection for the word λυπέω when explaining a character's grief/sadness, it is notable that he uses περίλυπός to explain Jesus' grief/sadness at the specific location in the narrative where he copies Mark's allusion to the psalmic refrain. When this is coupled with the fact that Matthew enhances Mark's Gethsemane account by expanding the refrain of Psalm 41/42, then the likelihood increases that Matthew detects and capitalizes on Mark's evocation of Psalm 41/42. These facts further substantiate Ahearne-Kroll's argument for a Markan evocation of Psalm 41/42 in Mark 14:34.

39. In light of two other possible referents (Lam 2:15 and Ps 108:25–26), Ahearne-Kroll rightly notes that this simple evocation is more difficult to secure than the other ones. Beyond Ahearne-Kroll's argument, Hashimoto offers another piece of evidence in support of a Markan evocation of Ps 21:8. Luke evokes the same passage as does Mark but with different words. Whereas Mark mentions the onlookers who shake their heads, Luke mentions the people and rulers who look (θεωρῶν) and scoff (ἐξεμυκτήριζον) at him (Luke 23:35; cf. Ps 21:8: πάντες οἱ θεωρῦντές με ἐξεμυκτήρισάν

5. Psalm 21:1 in Mark 15:34 ("My God, my God, why have you forsaken me?")
6. Psalm 68:22 in Mark 15:36 ("sponge with sour wine")

The following discussion is based on these evocations.

Characterization of Jesus' Opponents in the Passion

Mark's portrayal of Jesus' passion opponents in tandem with the opponents of the psalmic lamenter begins in Mark 14:18, the pericope of the Last Supper, and increasingly becomes clearer throughout the passion with each evocation of the lament. I demonstrate this by examining each of Mark's six evocations of the psalmic lament.

Mark's evocation of Psalm 40:10 in 14:18 portrays Judas in tandem with the opponents of the psalmic lamenter. During the Last Supper, Jesus relates to his disciples that one of them will betray him. In predicting his betrayal and in identifying his betrayer, Jesus evokes Psalm 40:10, "the one who is eating with me." Psalm 40 recounts a lamenter who is tormented by enemies (Ps 40:6, 8, 12), one of which is a "close friend" with whom the lamenter shares table fellowship (Ps 40:10). Similar to the lamenter of Psalm 40, Jesus is betrayed by a close friend, one of the Twelve (Mark 14:17). Immediately following the evocation of Psalm 40:10, Mark presents the disciples' response to Jesus' prediction via a discussion about the identity of the betrayer. Note that Ahearne-Kroll's argument that Mark portrays Jesus as the lamenter par excellence in Mark 14:18 is correct, since Jesus actually speaks the evocation, and since the larger Markan focus is on the protagonist of the story,[40] but this focus does not adequately capture every hue of Mark's portrait. Mark uses Psalm 40 to paint a portrait not just of Jesus but also of Judas. Mark simultaneously portrays Jesus as the lamenter and Judas as the lamenter's opponent.

με) (cf. Bock, *Luke 9:51—24:53*, 1147). Hashimoto concludes, "This fact indicates that the Psalm was commonly appealed to for the story of the people's derision at Jesus on the cross in the different streams of the tradition" ("Function of the Old Testament Quotations and Allusions in the Marcan Passion Narrative," 265). Hashimoto further notes that this trend continued with later Christian authors who used Ps 21:8: *1 Clement*, 16; Justin, *Dialogue*, 101; Justin, *Apology*, I.26. Thus, Hashimoto concludes that "such broad use of the Psalm suggests that in Mk 15:29, reference to Ps 21:8 should be considered primary in spite of the literary affinity of the verse to Lamentations" (ibid.).

40. Ahearne-Kroll, *Psalms of Lament in Mark's Passion*, 173–78.

Of Heroes and Villains

This dual focus continues in Mark's Gethsemane account. As argued in chapter 1, Ahearne-Kroll rightly notes that Mark portrays Jesus in Gethsemane as a psalmic lamenter.[41] Although Mark's spotlight is squarely on Jesus as the lamenter who imbibes the attributes of the psalmist of Psalm 41/42, Mark also portrays Jesus' opponents in tandem with those of the psalmic lamenter's. As Jesus' lament draws to an end, Mark transitions the reader in 14:41–43 to Jesus' arrest, a crucial turn of narrative events in relation to Mark's portrayal of Jesus' opponents.[42] Mark makes clear the significance of this turn of events at three critical moments prior to 14:41–43, where three times Jesus predicts his death and resurrection, each time disclosing the identity of those who will kill him. In Mark 8:31, Jesus predicts that he will suffer at the hands of "the elders, chief priests, scribes." A chapter later in Mark 9:31, Jesus predicts that he will be "betrayed [παραδίδοται] into the hands of men." Finally, in Mark 10:33–34, Jesus predicts that he will be "betrayed [παραδοθήσεται] to the chief priests and scribes" who in turn "will hand him over [παραδώσουσιν] to the Gentiles."

These predictions that Jesus will be betrayed / handed over are finally fulfilled at the transition between Jesus' lament in Gethsemane and his arrest in Mark 14:41–43. In Mark 14:41, Jesus is "betrayed [παραδίδοται] into the hands of sinners." These sinners (ἁμαρτωλῶν) are identified in Mark 14:43—namely, as Judas, the crowd, the chief priests, the scribes, and the elders.[43] When Mark 14:41–43 is read within its immediate Gethsemane context and within Mark's use of the lament psalms in the broader context of his passion, it becomes clear that Mark intends his reader to understand these opponents in tandem with the psalmic lamenters' opponents. Brief attention is now turned to demonstrating this.

Mark's reader, who understands that he presents Jesus as a psalmic lamenter in Gethsemane (*pace* Ahearne-Kroll) and who was familiar with the pervasive role that opponents play in the psalmic laments,[44] would

---

41. Ibid., 179–91.

42. On the close link between Mark's Gethsemane account and his arrest scene, see Collins, *Mark*, 683–84, and Stein, *Mark*, 668–69.

43. Robert G. Bratcher erroneously identifies these "sinners" as the Roman authorities by comparing Jesus' prediction that he will be handed over to the "Gentiles" in Mark 10:33–34 to the prediction's fulfillment in Mark 14:41 ("Unusual Sinners," 335–37). Mark, however, clearly identifies these "sinners" in 14:43—namely, as Judas Iscariot and the crowd who were under orders from the chief priests, teachers of the law, and the elders.

44. Dhanaraj, *Theological Significance of the Motif of Enemies*.

naturally see a parallel between Jesus, who is praying in Gethsemane as a lamenter, and his opponents, who appear at the end of his lament (Mark 14:41). In other words, if Jesus, a lamenter (Mark 14:32–41a), experiences opposition and betrayal by sinners (ἁμαρτωλῶν; Mark 14:41b) in a passage where he evokes a psalmic lament (Mark 14:34), a genre in which protagonists constantly face hostile opponents, it is quite reasonable to conclude that Mark intentionally portrays Judas, the crowd, chief priests, the scribes, and the elders (Mark 14:43) in tandem with those of the psalmic lamenter. Strengthening this argument is the fact that the plural form ἁμαρτωλῶν appears in the LXX almost exclusively in the Psalms (twenty-two times; the only other occurrences are in Num 17:3; 32:14; Amos 9:8; Isa 14:5). This increases the likelihood that Mark's readers, who are already thinking of Jesus as the psalmic lamenter, would have thought of the "sinners" in Mark 14:41 within a psalmic matrix. This argument is also strengthened when one examines how Mark continues to evoke the lament in his passion.

Mark continues to portray Jesus' opponents in tandem with the lamenter's opponents in the evocations of Psalm 21 in 15:24–34, where Mark masterfully weaves together a tapestry that simultaneously depicts Jesus as the lamenter par excellence and Jesus' opponents as those of the psalmic lamenter. In Mark 15:24, the soldiers who crucify Jesus are described with the words of Psalm 21:19. Just as the psalmists' opponents cast lots for the protagonist's clothing, the soldiers do the same thing. Similarly, in Mark 15:29, the passerby (οἱ παραπορευόμενοι) are described with words from Psalm 21:8–9.[45] Just as the lamenters' opponents shake their heads mockingly and insultingly, the passerby do the same thing. In Mark 15:34, while dying at the hands of his opponents, Jesus, depicted once again as the lamenter par excellence, quotes Psalm 21:1. Thus, while

---

45. Mark leaves the identity of these passerby obscure. Some commentators refer to them as random people (Collins, *Mark*, 749), Jews from the city (Taylor, *Mark*, 591), members of the Sanhedrin (based on their remarks about the destruction of the temple [cf. Mark 14:51]) (Lane, *Mark*, 569), or as newcomers to the rejection of Jesus (Moloney, *Mark*, 322), suggesting that they "knew little about Jesus" (Donahue and Harrington, *Gospel of Mark*, 443). In light of the passerby's comment in Mark 15:29b ("You who would destroy the temple and rebuild it in three days"), however, it is unlikely that they "knew little about Jesus." Interestingly, one of Mark's earliest interpreters understand the passerby as "the crowd/people" (ὁ λαός [Luke 23:35]; concerning Luke's conflation of the crowd and people into a unified character group, see chapter 4).

the lamenter laments (Mark 15:34), his antagonists mock and insult him (Mark 15:29) while vying for his clothing (Mark 15:24).

After Jesus' cry from the cross, some bystanders think that he is calling Elijah (Mark 15:35) while an unnamed man offers Jesus wine vinegar to drink (Mark 15:36). In describing this man's actions, Mark evokes Psalm 68:22: "They . . . gave me vinegar for my thirst." In the same way that Mark merges Judas (Mark 14:18), the "sinners" (including Judas, the crowd, the chief priests, scribes, and elders; Mark 14:41), the soldiers (Mark 15:24), and the passerby (Mark 15:29) with the psalmic lamenters' opponents, he does the same thing with this unnamed man. Substantiating this argument requires an excursion into long-debated questions concerning this man: Does Mark depict him as Jesus' friend or opponent? Is his act humane or one of mockery? It is important to take this lengthy excursion since Mark's depiction of this man is intricately tied to the overall argument of this section; if Mark portrays this man's act as humane, then it contravenes Mark's prior uses of the lament psalms. I argue here that Mark depicts this man as an opponent to Jesus whose action is inhumane and one of mockery.

This issue has been debated for decades, with most scholars concluding that the man's act is one of mockery or torture.[46] Thomas Boomershine and William Lane represent well the argument that the man's act was one of sympathy. Boomershine offers four pieces of internal evidence from Mark 15:36 to support this argument: (1) The adversative δέ conjunction that introduces the man's action is best understood contextually as a break with the negatively depicted scene of Jesus' crucifixion; (2) the pronoun τις implies a distinction between the man and the "bystanders" of Mark 15:35; (3) the verb "to give a drink" (ποτίζω) used to describe the man's action is the same verb used in a positive way in Mark 9:41, and the soldiers' offering of wine to Jesus in Mark 15:23 has no implication

---

46. These scholars include: Brown, *Death of the Messiah*, 2:1063–65; France, *Gospel of Mark*, 654–55; Donahue and Harrington, *Gospel of Mark*, 448; Hashimoto, "Function of the Old Testament Quotations and Allusions in the Marcan Passion Narrative," 298–99, 306; Klostermann, *Das Markusevangelium erklärt*, 167; Linnemann, *Studien zur Passionsgeschichte*, 149–51; Gnilka, *Das Evangelium nach Markus*, 2:323; Matera, *Kingship of Jesus*, 124; Senior, *Passion of Jesus in the Gospel of Mark*, 124–25; Lührmann, *Das Markusevangelium*, 263; Hooker, *Gospel According to Saint Mark*, 377; Brown, *Death of the Messiah*, 2:1063–64; Evans, *Mark 8:27–16:20*, 508; Marcus, *Mark 8–16*, 1065. Those that view the man's act as one of sympathy include: Blinzler, *Trial of Jesus*, 255; Brooks, *Mark*, 261n97; Boomershine, "Mark, the Storyteller," 229–30; Dodd, *Historical Tradition in the Fourth Gospel*, 123; Lane, *Mark*, 573–74; Witherington, *Mark*, 2001. Collins calls the man's act "dramatic irony" (*Mark*, 757).

of mockery or torture; and (4) Mark's use of the circumstantial participle (δραμών) to introduce the man's action indicates a positive gesture in light of Mark's only other use of the circumstantial participle in Mark 14:3b (σθντρίψασα), where it is used to describe the actions of an unnamed woman who pours nard on Jesus' head.[47] Lane adds a fifth piece of external evidence: (5) In the OT (Num 6:13; Ruth 2:14) and Greek literature (Plutarch, *Cato Major* I.13; Papyrus London 1245, 9), wine vinegar is mentioned as a refreshing drink; there are no examples of its use as a hostile gesture.[48]

Boomershine's internal evidence that Mark portrays the man positively is weak for the following reasons. First, Mark uses δέ over 160 times in various ways, both in an adversative sense as "but" (cf. Mark 1:8, 45; 2:18) and in a transitional sense as "now" (cf. Mark 1:14, 30; 2:6). Daniel Wallace rightly notes that δέ is most commonly used transitionally, while it is only used adversatively when the context clearly indicates it.[49] There is no clear contextual evidence that Mark intends the δέ in 15:36 to be adversative.[50] Thus, the man's action is best understood contextually as a continuation of the negatively depicted scene that precedes it. Second, Mark's use of τις might indicate a distinction between the man and those who crucify Jesus, but it does not indicate the quality of the distinction. It is a non sequitur to suggest that the man's action is negative simply because Mark delineates him from the others. Third, it is too limiting to suggest that Mark could not use the very common verb ποτίζω both negatively and positively in the same gospel. Mark simply does not use this term enough (only twice) to present the reader with a predictable pattern by which to judge qualitative traits in relation to it. The same holds true, fourth, for Mark's two uses of the circumstantial participle; Mark simply does not use the circumstantial participal enough to present the reader with a predictable pattern by which to judge qualitative traits in relation to it.

Lane's external observations about OT and Greek literature should be tempered with Stein's observation that Luke recounts a similar scene

47. Boomershine, "Mark, the Storyteller," 229–32.
48. Lane, *Mark*, 573–74.
49. Wallace, *Greek Grammar Beyond the Basics*, 671–72, 674.
50. Note, for example, the clear adversative use of δέ in Mark 1:8: "I have baptized you with water, but (δέ) he will baptize you with the Holy Spirit." Also note that all the major translators of Mark either interpret δέ transitionally (cf. ESV, NASB, RSV) or leave it untranslated (cf. NIV, NLT).

where soldiers offer Jesus wine vinegar (ὄξος; cf. Mark's use ὄξους of in 15:36) as they "mocked" him (Luke 23:36). Furthermore, at least two church fathers interpreted the man's act as torture: Cyril of Jerusalem (*Catechetical Lectures* 13.28) and Augustine (*Harmony of the Gospels* 3.11).[51] Finally, O'Brien notes two extra-Markan evocations of Psalm 68 that Second Temple writers used negatively: (1) Paul uses Psalm 68:11 with respect to insults and mockery (Rom 15:3); and (2) 1QHxii 8:22 relates it to one who is despised, ridiculed, and mocked.[52]

Aside from this convincing external evidence, there is strong internal evidence that Mark intends the man's act to be viewed negatively as one of torture and/or mockery. The most persuasive pieces of evidence lie in Mark's evocation of Psalm 68 and in his established use of the lament psalms prior to Mark 15:36. Hooker is correct that although the offering of wine was often seen as a humane act, in light of Psalm 68, it was a gesture of mockery.[53] It is unlikely that Mark would portray this man positively by evoking the negative actions of those in Psalm 68. Furthermore, at this juncture in the narrative, Mark has already evoked the psalmic lament four times in order to portray certain characters negatively. It is more likely that Mark continues this trend instead of diverting from it. Stein adds another piece of internal evidence, based on the man's identity, that suggests his act is one of mockery: If he was a soldier, then they are consistently described as mocking Jesus (Mark 15:16–20a); If he is a member of the crowd, they have also just been described as mocking Jesus (Mark 15:29–30).[54]

Mark, then, portrays this man's act as one of mockery and/or torture. In light of this portrayal, Mark continues his trend to evoke the lament psalms to characterize Jesus' opponents, in this case either a soldier or a member of the crowd. Just as the antagonists of Psalm 68 mockingly give the lamenter wine vinegar to drink, Jesus' antagonists do the same thing.

---

51. Koskenniemi et al., "Wine Mixed with Myrrh," 380.

52. O'Brien, *Use of Scripture in the Markan Passion Narrative*, 146.

53. Hooker, *Mark*, 377. Cf. O'Brien, *Use of Scripture in the Markan Passion Narrative*, 146.

54. Stein, *Mark*, 716.

Supplementary Data

Although the inquiry above focuses on Mark's simple evocations in characterizing Jesus' opponents as those of the psalmic lamenter, it is interesting to note the plethora of Markan citations that *possibly* echo the psalmic lament.[55] This data substantially supports the foregoing argument that Mark characterizes Jesus' opponents as those of the psalmic lamenter, since, in all but two (Mark 14:54 [cf. Ps 37:12] and Mark 15:40 [cf. Ps 37:12]) of these possible echoes, Mark focuses on characterizing Jesus (three times) and especially his opponents (ten times) in tandem with the psalmic lament. In other words, to the degree that any one or more of these references echo the psalmic lament is to the same degree that it substantiates the preceding argument. Space does not permit a detailed analysis of each of these references and/or how they might echo the lament psalms, which is aptly undertaken by most major commentators.[56] Instead, the possible echoes are listed and briefly explained with a specific focus on how they provide supplementary support for the foregoing thesis that Mark characterizes Jesus and his opponents as the psalmic lamenter and the psalmic lamenter's opponents, respectively.

Methodologically, these texts were chosen from O'Brien's helpful chart where she collates suggested OT allusions from twenty-one influential commentaries, monographs, and articles.[57] She categorizes the suggested allusions into three categories: correspondence greater than one common word, correspondence of a single common word, and no significant words corresponding. The supplementary data below represents psalmic lament literature taken from her first two categories (correspondence greater than one common word and correspondence of a single common word).[58]

---

55. As non-simple evocations, one should remember that more than one OT / Second Temple referent may lie behind these possible intertextual occurrences (see O'Brien, *Use of Scripture in the Markan Passion Narrative*, 68–74, 203–89).

56. See Ahearne-Kroll, *Psalms of Lament in Mark's Passion*, 61–77; Evans, "Praise and Prophecy," 565–66; Shires, *Finding the Old Testament in the New*, 202–6; and Moo, *Old Testament in the Gospel Passion Narratives*, 285–86.

57. O'Brien, *Use of Scripture in the Markan Passion Narrative*, 67n1. Cf. O'Brien's three very helpful appendices where she textually analyzes every possible Markan quotation, allusion, and/or echo in relation to their OT/ANE referents (ibid., 203–89).

58. O'Brien focuses only on Mark 14–15. I further accessed the NA[27] and Watts' Mark commentary in Beale's and Carson's *Commentary on the New Testament Use of the Old Testament* for psalmic lament allusions in Mark 1–13 and 16, which revealed

Of Heroes and Villains

Supplementary Data Used to Characterize Jesus' Opponents

- Mark 14:1: The narrator states that the chief priest and the scribes "were seeking how to arrest him by stealth (ἐν δόλῳ; cf. Ps 9:28: δόλου), and kill him."

- Mark 14:55: "The chief priests and the whole Sanhedrin were seeking (ἐζήτουν) for evidence against Jesus so that they could put him to death (εἰς τὸ θανατῶσαι αὐτόν)" (cf. Ps 36:32: ζητεῖ τοῦ θανατῶσαι αὐτόν).

- Mark 14:56: "Many testified falsely (ἐψευδομαρτύρουν) against him, but their statements did not agree" (cf. Ps 26:12 [μάρτυρες . . . ἐψεύσατο]).

- Mark 14:57: The narrator states that many of those present at Jesus' trial before the Sanhedrin "stood up (ἀναστάντες) and gave . . . false testimony against him (ἐψευδομαρπύρουν κατ' αὐτοῦ; cf. Pss 26:12 [παραδῷς . . . μάρτυρες ἄδικοι καὶ ἐψεύσατο] and 34:11 [ἀναστάντες μάρτυρες])."

- Mark 14:61b: The high priest asks Jesus, "Are you the Christ, the Son (υἱός; cf. Ps 85:16: υἱός) of the Blessed One?"

- Mark 15:1: The religious leaders bind Jesus and "hand him over (παρέδωκαν; cf. Pss 26:12; 73:19: παραδῷς) to Pilate."

- Mark 15:13: The crowd "cries out (ἔκραξαν; cf. Ps 21:6: ἐκέκραξαν)" for Jesus' crucifixion.

- Mark 15:14: Pilate asks the crowd, "What crime (κακόν; cf. Pss 37:21 and 108:5: κακά) has [Jesus] committed?"

- Mark 15:23: The narrator states that the soldiers "offered (ἐδίδουν) [Jesus] wine mixed with myrrh (οἶνον; cf. Ps 68:22: ἔδωκαν . . . ὄξος)" while he hangs on the cross.

- Mark 15:30–31: The passersby at Jesus' crucifixion exclaim, "Come down from the cross and save (σῶσον) yourself," while the chief priests and scribes similarly state, "He saved (ἔσωσεν) others . . . but he can't save (σῶσαι) himself" (cf. Ps 21:9: σωσάτω).

---

four more possible echoes: Mark 1:13 (Ps 9:12); 3:21 (Ps 68:10); 4:39 (Ps 64:9); 9:12 (Ps 21:8). These possible echoes are considered to correspond to O'Brien's third category "no significant words corresponding," thus, are not included in the list below. Interestingly, with the exception of Mark 3:21, these passages support the arguments of this section.

- Mark 15:32: Those crucified with Jesus "reviled him (ὠνείδιζον αὐτόν; cf. Pss 41:11 [ὠνείδισάν με] and 68:10 [ὀνειδιζόντων σε])."

Supplementary Data Used to Characterize Jesus

- Mark 14:38: Jesus, who is praying in Gethsemane and who returns to find his disciples sleeping, warns them that "the spirit is willing (τὸ μὲν πνεῦμα πρόθυμον; cf. MT Ps 51:14:ורוח נדיבה), but the body is weak."
- Mark 14:61a: When the Sanhedrin questions Jesus, he "remained silent (ἐσιώπα; cf. MT Pss 38:14: אלמתי 39:10; כאלם) and gave no answer."
- Mark 15:37: At his death, Jesus "with a loud cry (φωνήν; cf. Ps 30:23: φωνῆς)" takes his final breath.

Summary

Mark appropriates six simple evocations of the psalmic lament to characterize Jesus and Jesus' opponents as the hero and as the villains of the psalmic lament. While Jesus, as Ahearne-Kroll establishes, is characterized as the Davidic lamenter par excellence, the crowd, the religious leaders (both Jewish and Gentile), Judas Iscariot, and the soldiers are characterized as the villains of the Davidic lamenter. Adding substantial support to this Markan method of characterization is the fact that nearly all of Mark's possible allusions to the psalmic lament (the "Supplementary Data") also depict Jesus and/or Jesus' opponents as the psalmic lamenter and as the lamenter's opponents, respectively. Mark's characterization of these various opponents to Jesus in tandem with those of the psalmic lamenter is the second step in providing a way forward concerning the narrative-critical debate about how best to categorize Mark's characterization of Jesus' opponents; while Mark retains the distinct identity of each opponent to Jesus, they all possess the common trait of opposing Jesus as the OT paradigmatic villain.

EXCURSUS: COMPARING MARK'S USE OF LAMENT AND NON-LAMENT PSALMS IN CHARACTERIZING JESUS' OPPONENTS

The similarity between Mark's use of Psalms 109 and 117 and the psalmic lament to characterize Jesus' opponents are clear: Mark appropriates both sets of psalms to characterize Jesus' opponents as those of David's opponents. There is, however, a notable distinction between Mark's appropriation of Psalms 109 and 117 and the psalmic lament in his characterization of Jesus' opponents; Mark uses the non-lament psalms to emphasize Jesus' conquest of his enemies while he uses the lament psalms to narratively describe their attacks on Jesus. Note, for example, that in each quote of Psalms 109 (Mark 12:36) and 117 (Mark 12:10–11), Jesus explicitly states his victory over his opponents: "The stone... has become the capstone" (Mark 12:10) and "Sit at my right hand until I put your enemies under your feet" (Mark 12:36).[59]

As Jesus becomes the lamenter par excellence, however, Mark depicts Jesus' opponents as those who apparently gain the advantage over Jesus. The irony is thick as Mark highlights the distinctions between Psalms 109 and 117 and the lament psalms: As the Davidic king, Jesus is victorious over his opponents—an expected outcome from reading Psalms 109 and 117. As the lamenting David, Jesus succumbs to the murderous plot of his opponents—an expected outcome from reading Psalms 40, 41/42, 21, and 68. The irony is that the Davidic king conquers his opponents by becoming a rejected lamenter. In isolation, neither the non-lament nor the lament psalms offer Mark the necessary OT background to deliver the narrative goods that portray Jesus' opponents as those who are simultaneously *conquering* and those who are *conquered*.

THE PSALMIC LAMENT IN RELATION TO THE ISAIANIC SERVANT MOTIF

In the previous two sections, I advance Ahearne-Kroll's work by examining how Mark characterizes Jesus' opponents in relation to Psalms 109, 117, and the psalmic lament. In this section I turn attention to advancing Ahearne-Kroll's work by exploring Mark's appropriation of the lament in

---

59. Cf. Mark 14:62 ("You will see the Son of Man seated at the right hand of Power"), where Jesus implicitly refers to his triumph over his opponents via another allusion to Ps 110:1 (Marcus, *Mark 8–16*, 1007).

concert with his Isaianic Servant motif.[60] This is precisely the need Watts suggests in his review of Ahearne-Kroll's monograph:

> One wonders... if it might not have been more helpful and consistent [for Ahearne-Kroll] to explore Mark's rational in integrating [both Mark's Isaianic Suffering Servant and lamenter motifs], showing how the one informs and locates the other.[61]

Although Watts is correct, he demands too much of Ahearne-Kroll given the scope of his work.[62] Ahearne-Kroll's singular focus on Mark's psalmic lament motif is necessary in order to pave the way for later interpreters to pursue a more integrated approach. In a preliminary way, this section represents an answer to Watts's critique of Ahearne-Kroll by stepping beyond Ahearne-Kroll's work toward a more integrative understanding of Mark's use of the psalmic lament, specifically in relation to his Suffering Servant motif. This section, however, falls short of complete integration due to necessary space limitations. For example, it is beyond my scope in this section to explore how Mark integrates his psalmic lament motif with his Danielic Son of Man motif (cf. Mark 10:45). Thus, this section heeds Watts's advice to Ahearne-Kroll while recognizing that this attempt at integration is incomplete and ultimately needs further research.

By isolating Mark's tandem use of these two themes, I do not intend to suggest that Mark *only* has these motifs in mind; he writes much

---

60. This section also advances Bock's brief investigation into Mark's integration of Isaiah's Servant with, what he calls, the righteous-sufferer motif ("Function of Scripture," 8–17; see Ahearne-Kroll, "Challenging the Divine," 144–45, for a discussion on the inadequacies of the label "righteous suffer" used in relation to the Markan Jesus). Bock recognizes the need to investigate Mark's integration of these motifs but, as he states, does not do so due to the limited scope of his work. This section represents a step in this direction. On a different note, what Richard Beaton suggests about Matthew is applicable to Mark and Luke: It is difficult to determine whether they had in mind the Christological title "Servant" when characterizing Jesus (*Isaiah's Christ in Matthew's Gospel*, 175). It is perhaps better to suggest that they had in mind a descriptive task in appropriating Isaiah's Servant. As argued below, it is clear, however, that these writers at least had in mind an image from Isaiah that they use to characterize Jesus. For simplicity, I retain the title "Servant" in this book.

61. Watts, Review of *The Psalms of Lament in Mark's Passion*, JETS 52, 161. Cf. Watts, Review of *The Psalms of Lament in Mark's Passion*, TS 70, where he suggests that a more "integrative approach would have been more faithful to Mark" (500–501).

62. Indeed, Ahearne-Kroll recognizes that Mark retains a subtle Isaianic Suffering Servant motif in chapters 14–15: The psalmic lament "offers a model for Jesus' suffering that exists *alongside* that of the Servant from Isaiah" (*Psalms of Lament in Mark's Passion*, 171, italics added).

more complexly than that. Instead, Mark weaves many themes together in portraying his understanding of Jesus.[63] The reason that I isolate and investigate these two motifs in tandem, aside from adding support to my foregoing argument about Mark's characterization of Jesus and Jesus' opponents, is because, as noted in chapter 1, modern scholars consistently conflate the two into one and because of the close connection they share in scholastic dialogue. Marcus, for example, argues:

> The Gospel passion narratives interweave [these] two motifs, and it is sometimes difficult to tell whether a particular feature derives from the one or the other; it is, in any case, doubtful that the readers of the Gospels would have thought of the Righteous Sufferer and the Suffering Servant as two separate figures.[64]

Contrary to Marcus, as argued in chapter 1 and as further demonstrated below, although Mark conflates certain aspects of these motifs, he is also aware of, and narratively capitalizes on, their distinct aspects.

In order to explore Mark's appropriation of his Servant motif in relation to his lament motif, first I must establish the Servant motif in Mark, since some scholars contest its presence therein. Second, I explore Mark's appropriation of Isaiah's Servant motif, which provides the framework for, third, how Mark appropriates the two themes together. Finally, I examine some similarities and differences between them within the Markan narrative. From this exploration, I conclude that Mark characterizes Jesus distinctly as, among other things, Isaiah's Servant and the psalmic lamenter, utilizing both their similarities and distinctions towards specific literary ends.

Establishing the Motif in Mark

Before investigating Mark's tandem use of the Servant and lament motifs, it is first necessary to address a long-debated issue concerning Isaiah's Servant in Mark—namely, is the motif actually present in Mark's

---

63. See Culpepper, *Mark*, 349; Watts, *Isaiah's New Exodus and Mark*, 286–87; Maurer, "Knecht Gottes und Sohn Gottes im Passionsbericht des Markusevangeliums," 1–38; Bock, "Function of Scripture," 8–17; Hatina, "Embedded Scripture Texts and the Plurality of Meaning," 81–99; Moloney, *Mark*, 213–14; Lindars, *Jesus Son of Man*, 101–4. O'Brien is correct that "no single backdrop is sufficient for the Markan portrayal of Jesus" (*Use of Scripture in the Markan Passion Narratives*, 15, citing Best, *Temptation and the Passion*, lxxiv).

64. Marcus, "Old Testament and the Death of Jesus," 214.

narrative or do later interpreters, reading the Second Gospel through the lens of Matthew's gospel, anachronistically find it there? The initial underpinnings of this debate began in 1892 when D. B. Duhm first demarcated the Servant Songs in Isaiah, resulting in a watershed discovery in both OT and NT studies.[65] His influence on NT studies surfaced in investigations on how NT writers appropriate the Servant motif in their respective Christologies. Many mid-twentieth-century scholars, including Dibelius, Taylor, Lindars, Perrin, France, and Jeremias, deduced a pervasive Servant influence on the historical Jesus and/or on NT Christology.[66] This influence did not go unchallenged. Moule, Barrett, Kee, and Juel were led by Hooker's argument against a pervasive Isaianic Servant influence on the NT.[67]

Aside from arguments that address the role of Isaiah's Servant on the historical Jesus and/or on the NT as a whole, which are beyond the scope of the present section, it is more challenging to deduce its influence specifically on Mark's gospel in light of the alleged tenuous nature of his allusions to it. These allusions are allegedly tenuous because connections between Mark and the respective Isaianic Servant passages are based on

65. Duhm, *Das Buch Jesaja*, 285. Thielman is correct in reminding modern readers that "the exact boundaries of the Servant Songs ... are matters of scholarly dispute" (*Theology of the New Testament*, 71n65; cf. France, *Jesus and the Old Testament*, 110–11n102). Hooker is correct that it is anachronistic to isolate the servant passages from their Isaianic context (*Jesus and the Servant*, 25–30). As Moo argues, however, "as long as it is not attempted to understand the Servant apart from the total message of Isaiah, it is valid to continue speaking of four 'Servant Songs' in which the nature and mission of this enigmatic figure are the central themes" (*Old Testament in the Gospel Passion Narratives*, 79–80).

66. Dibelius, *From Tradition to Gospel*, 184–85, 187; Taylor, *Mark*, 378; Lindars, *New Testament Apologetic*, 77, 80; Perrin, *What Is Redaction Criticism?*, 56; France, *Jesus and the Old Testament*, 116–21 (cf. ibid., "Servant of Yahweh," 1:744–47); Jeremias, "Παῖς θεου," 5:677–717. Cf. Juel, *Messianic Exegesis*, 120; Moulder, "Old Testament Background and the Interpretation of Mark x.45," 120–27; Hengel, *Atonement*, 49–65; Pesch, *Das Markusevangelium*, 163–64; Davies and Allison, *Matthew*, 3:95–100; Hagner, *Matthew 14–28*, 582–83; Evans, *Mark 8:27–16:20*, 120–23; Torrey, "Influence of Second Isaiah in the Gospels and Acts," 24–36.

67 Hooker, *Jesus and the Servant*. In 1998, Hooker reconfirmed her 1956 argument: "Did the Use of Isaiah 53 to Interpret His Mission Begin with Jesus," 88–103; Barrett, "Background of Mark 10:45"; Kee, "Function of Scriptural Quotations"; Juel, *Messianic Exegesis*, 59–60; and, more recently, Huizenga, *New Isaac*, 189–208. Dunn, *Jesus Remembered*, 809–18, explores the degree to which the historical Jesus was influenced by Isaiah 52–53 (cf. Bellinger and Farmer, *Jesus and the Suffering Servant*).

Of Heroes and Villains

thin, albeit present, linguistic evidence.[68] Emphasis, therefore, is usually placed on thematic parallels between Mark and Isaiah's Servant (indeed, in concert with the thin linguistic connections) in order to substantiate an intertextual dependence. This is the basic methodology of Watts, Marcus, Moo, and most contemporary commentators.[69]

These contemporary commentators, contrary to Hooker and most recently O'Brien,[70] are correct that Mark's numerous thematic parallels between his narrative and Isaiah's Servant combined with the available linguistic evidence that connect the two is beyond coincidental,[71] especially since Mark composes his narrative with Isaiah in mind (Mark 1:1–3)[72] and in light of the pervasive use of Isaiah's Servant in Markan

---

68. For succinct summaries on why many argue that Isaiah's Servant is absent from Mark, see Moyise, *Old Testament in the New*, 29–30, and O'Brien, *Use of Scripture in the Markan Passion Narrative*, 76–87.

69. Watts, *Isaiah's New Exodus and Mark*; Marcus, *Way of the Lord*; Stuhlmacher, "Der messianische Gottesknecht," 143–44; Evans, *Mark 8:27–16:20*, 120–23; Collins, *Mark*, 500–501; Edwards, *Mark*, 326–28; Pesch, *Das Markusevangelium*, 2:163–64; Lane, *Mark*, 383–85; Culpepper, *Mark*, 349–50; Bock, "Function of Scripture," 8–12; La-Grange, *Évangile selon Saint Marc*, 264–65; Grundmann, *Das Evangelium nach Markus*, 219–20; Jeremias, *New Testament Theology*, 271–72; Gnilka, *Das Evangelium nach Markus*, 2:104; and Boring, *Mark*, 277; Marcus, *Mark 8–16*, 746. Contrast with Perkins, *Mark*, 654; Stein, *Mark*, 59; Gundry, *Mark*, 993.

70. O'Brien, *Use of Scripture in the Markan Passion Narrative*, 76–87. O'Brien rightly provides a caution for scholars who argue for an Isaianic Servant influence on Mark, but her methodology for substantiating an allusion to this motif is too rigid (see 20–46). In essence, she considers each possible allusion independently, searching for both linguistic and thematic parallels, and emphatically concludes, "if there is no verbal correspondence, there is no allusion" (46). She then applies this methodology too myopically to Mark 14–15. This approach is too rigid when addressing Mark's use of Isaiah's Servant because it fails to consider the impact that Mark's narrative as a whole (prior to chapters 14–15) has on these tenuous (but not altogether absent) linguistic connections to Isaiah's Servant because it fails to consider the impact that Mark's narrative as whole (prior to chapters 14–15) has only tenuous (but not altogether absent) linguistic connections to Isaiah's Servant. In other words, pervasive thematic trends in Mark, such as the fact that Isaiah significantly impacted the general tenor of Mark's gospel (Mark 1:1–3, 11; cf. Watts, *Isaiah's New Exodus and Mark*), increases the likelihood that Isaiah's Servant influenced a particular passage when linguistic echoes, although present, are fainter.

71. Concerning thematic parallels between Mark and the Servant, see Culpepper, *Mark*, 349–50.

72. Watts, *Isaiah's New Exodus and Mark*. Although Watts too rigidly forces an Isaianic matrix on a few parts of Mark's gospel (Marcus, Review of *Isaiah's New Exodus in Mark*, 222–25), his overall thesis that Isaiah broadly influences the general tenor of Mark is valid (cf. Marcus, "Old Testament and the Death of Jesus," 20–21). For others

contemporary Judaism.[73] It is, in essence, the cumulative evidence that is most convincing.[74]

Delineating the exact junctures at which Mark alludes to Isaiah's Servant, however, is often complex, and, as Moo rightly suggests, certainty exists on a continuum.[75] Entering the complexities of this discussion far exceeds the scope of this section. For the purposes of this exploration, Moo's delineation of Mark's allusions to Isaiah's Servant is used to frame the discussion below.[76] These allusions include Mark 1:11; the "betrayal / handing over motif" (παραδίδωμι) (Mark 3:19; 9:31; 10:33;

---

who see an Isaianic Servant motif in Mark, note Betz, "Jesus and Isaiah 53," 83–87; Donahue and Harrington, *Gospel of Mark*, 35, 439; Moo, *Old Testament in the Gospel Passion Narratives*, 107–9, 131–32, 148, 162; Marcus, *Way of the Lord*, 193–96; Watts, *Isaiah's New Exodus*, 365.

73. Page, for example, concludes concerning the historical Jesus that "given the diversity in the interpretation of the Servant Songs in the intertestamental period, and the possibility that some segments of Judaism were well disposed towards a messianic interpretation, it is completely credible that someone possessed with a messianic consciousness could have interpreted his career, and especially his death, in the light of the songs. So far as we know no one prior to Jesus did so, but the raw materials for such a development were already present in late Judaism" ("Suffering Servant Between the Testaments," 493). The same sentiments can be applied to Mark's gospel (see Marcus, *Way of the Lord*, 186–93; ibid., "Old Testament and the Death of Jesus," 217; Carroll and Green, *Death of Jesus*, 168). For the use of the Suffering Servant in intertestamental Judaism, see Brownlee, "Servant of the Lord in the Qumran Scrolls I," 8–15; ibid., "Servant of the Lord in the Qumran Scrolls II," 33–38; Cullmann, *Christology of the New Testament*, 52–60; Bruce, *Biblical Exegesis in the Qumran Texts*, 50–58. Contrast with Juel, *Messianic Exegesis*, 121–27, who argues that the use of the Servant Image in Intertestamental Judaism did not provide an adequate basis to influence the gospel writers' Christology.

74. Jeremias draws a similar conclusion in his review of Hooker's work: "She treats the New Testament like a mosaic and examines each stone separately" (Jeremias, Review of *Jesus and the Servant*, 140–44).

75. Moo, *Old Testament in the Gospel Passion Narratives*, 79.

76. A methodological caveat concerning the following investigation is needed in light of Moo's proposed Isaianic Servant allusions. This caveat comes in the form of appropriate hedging in regards to these allusions. To the degree that Hooker is correct that Mark never intends to allude to the Servant motif is to the same degree that Ahearne-Kroll's argument is strengthened—namely, that Mark's use of the psalmic lament is more central to his narrative than his use of Isaiah's Servant. Appropriate historical inquiry, when faced with a less-than-certain task, should consider several possible conclusions. This section explores Mark's evocations of the lament within the traditional conclusion that he also portrays Jesus as Isaiah's Servant. Subsequent researchers will have to consider the ramifications of Mark's use of the lament if he does not intend to echo Isaiah's Servant motif.

14:10, 11, 18, 21, 41, 42, 44; 15:1, 10, 15); and Mark 10:33–34; 45; 14:24, 61, 65; 15:5, 19.[77] Omitted from this list is Mark's general references to the fulfillment of Scripture (Mark 9:12–13; 14:21, 48–49[78]), which Mark likely intends to link with various OT motifs (e.g., Son of Man) instead of singularly to his Servant motif.[79]

Appropriation of the Motif

Attention is now turned to two explorations concerning Mark's appropriation of Isaiah's Servant motif: How previous scholars have understood it in Mark and his literary understanding of it.[80] These two explorations lay the foundation for my discussion in the next two sections concerning Mark's tandem use of Isaiah's Servant and the psalmic lament.

---

77. Ibid., 79–172. Moo does not necessarily detect a Servant influence at every Markan "betrayal/handing over" citation (see, for example, 92). Cf. Marcus, *Way of the Lord*, 186–93; Watts, *Isaiah's New Exodus*, 257–90. Influential on Moo, Marcus, and Watts is Maurer's 1953 article "Knecht Gottes und Sohn Gottes im Passionsbericht," 1–38, who sees far more allusions to Isaiah's Servant in Mark than later scholars do. For a good augmenting argument that Mark's παραδίδωμι motif reflects Isaiah's Suffering Servant, see Marcus, "Old Testament and the Death of Jesus," 216n16, and Bock, "Function of Scripture," 9–10. For a broader inclusion of Isaianic Servant motifs in Mark that is speculative and that offers little evidence for intertextual dependence, see Edwards, "Servant of the Lord and the Gospel of Mark," 36–49. For an insightful caution about too myopically detecting *only* Isaiah's Servant in these passages, see Hatina, "Embedded Scripture Texts and Plurality of Meaning," 81–99.

78. Also omitted is Mark 15:28: "And the Scripture was fulfilled which says, 'And He was numbered with transgressors'" (NAS), which is unlikely original to Mark (see Collins, *Mark*, 730). Contrast with the minority position of P. Rodgers who argues that Mark 15:28 is original to Mark ("Mark 15:28," 81–84).

79. See Evans, *Mark 8:27–16:20*, 44, 377, 426; Stein, *Mark*, 426, 648.

80. The purpose of this section, in keeping with the narrative-critical methodology spelled out in chapter 1, is not to explore, as most scholars do, the historical Jesus' possible self-perception as the Servant or to paint a picture of Jesus as the Servant from a synthesis of gospel narratives. For entries into these explorations, see Moo, *Old Testament in the Gospel Passion Narratives*; Bellinger and Farmer, *Jesus and the Suffering Servant*; and, most recently, Dunn, *Jesus Remembered*, 809–18. See also, Elbogen, *Der jüdische Gottesdienst in seiner geschichtlichen Entwicklung*; Black, "Servant of the Lord and Son of Man," 4–8; Maurer, "Knecht Gottes und Sohn Gottes im Passionsbericht des Markusevangeliums," 1–38; Buse, "Markan Account of the Baptism of Jesus and Isaiah LXIII" 74–75; Kee, "Function of Scriptural Quotations," 165–88; Guelich, "Beginning of the Gospels," 5–15; Chilton, *Galilean Rabbi and His Bible*; Matera, "Prologue as the Interpretive Key to Mark's Gospel," 3–20; and Marcus, *Way of the Lord*.

Most scholars rightly conclude that Mark Christologically uses the Isaianic Servant motif toward explanatory and eschatological ends:[81] Mark, in essence, uses it to explain why Jesus eschatologically died as a ransom for others. In his 1997 detailed study on Mark's use of Isaiah, for example, Watts argues that "Mark 10:45b functions as the final *explanatory* capstone to Mark's 'Way' section."[82] Similarly, Marcus, in his influential 1993 work on Mark's Christological exegesis, suggests that Mark's Servant "accomplishes a salvific purpose and thus wins an *eschatological* victory."[83]

Although the general tenor of these arguments is correct (and, thus, are not pursued further), their shortcoming is that they fail to consider specific distinctions between Mark's use of Isaiah's Servant and his use of the lament psalms. This oversight leads to an incomplete understanding of Mark's depiction of Jesus, his main character. Watts, Marcus, and others are right that Mark's Jesus *is* the eschatological sacrifice for others; but Jesus is more than that. Mark understands and applies the lament psalms in ways that complement, enhance, and depict Jesus in similar *and* distinct ways in relation to his understanding and application of Isaiah's Servant. Another shortcoming is their failure to explore how Mark appropriates the Servant motif in characterizing Jesus' opponents—namely, as the villains of Isaiah's Servant Songs.

In essence, I argue here that, in understanding how the Scriptures are to be fulfilled (Mark 14:49; cf. Mark 14:21), Mark sees in Jesus and his opponents the identity and attributes of two distinct OT figures that possess overlapping but discrete attributes. Mark presents these distinct figures by gradually fading the lamenter motif into the Servant motif. Mark depicts Jesus and his opponents within the matrix of Isaiah's Servant at the beginning of the gospel and sustains this depiction throughout. As the passion commences, Mark merges the psalmic lamenter motif with his Servant motif. At Jesus' crucifixion and death, the Servant motif, although still present, slips into the background as the lamenter motif

---

81. Ruppert, *Jesus als der leidende Gerechte?*, 177; Hurtado, *Mark*, 21; Donahue and Harrington, *Gospel of Mark*, 315; Marcus, *Way of the Lord*, 194–95; Thielman, *Theology of the New Testament*, 71 (one of the few NT theologies that addresses Mark's isolated use of Isaiah's Servant); Bock, "Function of Scripture," 17. Within the rubric of these two larger Markan uses of Isaiah's Servant motif (explanatory and eschatological), others suggest that the motif serves as an example of humility and servanthood to the Twelve (cf. Lane, *Mark*, 385; Culpepper, *Mark*, 349).

82. Watts, *Isaiah's New Exodus and Mark*, 270 (italics added).

83. Marcus, *Way of the Lord*, 194 (italics added), referencing Kee, "Function of Scriptural Quotations," 182–83. Cf. Marcus, "Old Testament and the Death of Jesus."

shifts to the foreground. Through this literary unveiling of Jesus, Mark understands the OT similarities and distinctions between these two figures and skillfully incorporates them into his narrative. The remainder of this section demonstrates this by sequentially examining Mark's allusions to Isaiah's Servant.[84]

After setting his narrative in the larger context of Isaiah in 1:1–3 by quoting Isaiah 40:1, thus indicating Mark's pervasive narrative interest in Isaiah,[85] Mark at the outset of his gospel taps into Isaiah's Servant passages by identifying Jesus via a conflated allusion to Psalm 2:7; Genesis 22:2, 12, 16; and Isaiah 42:1. In Mark 1:11, he writes, "And a voice came from heaven: 'You are my Son (σὺ εἶ ὁ υἱός μού; cf. Ps 2:7: με υἱός μου εἶ σύ),[86] whom I love; with you I am well pleased (ἐν σοὶ εὐδόκησα; cf. LXX Gen 22:2, 12, 16: υἱόν σου τὸν σου τὸν ἀγαπητόν ὅν ἠγάπησας).'"[87] Mark's reader does not have to guess at Jesus' identity; according to the logic of Mark's narrative, Jesus is a royal messiah (Mark 1:1, 11; cf. Ps 2:7), God's son (Mark 1:1, 11), Isaac's paragon (Mark 1:11; cf. Gen 22:2, 12, 16), and Isaiah's Servant (Mark 1:11; cf. Isa 42:1).[88] In the first few verses of the Second Gospel, then, the reader quickly realizes that Mark's depiction of Jesus is creatively complex and multifaceted, a trend that Mark continues

---

84. Examining Mark's narrative sequentially requires a methodological presupposition that focuses on the "freshness" of the narrative for the reader. This insinuates that Mark intentionally and progressively unveils his story in order to, among other things, elicit surprise and suspense. The converse methodological presupposition is that Mark intends, and the readers approach, the narrative as a "repeated performance" that was already well known. These two presuppositions represent current emergent issues in narrative criticism. Concerning these issues, see Hatina, *Biblical Interpretation in Early Christian Gospels*, vol. 2, esp. 7.

85. Watts, *Isaiah's New Exodus and Mark*, 53–90; Marcus, *Way of the Lord*, 17–45.

86. On the differences between Mark's use of υἱός in relation to the LXX's use of παῖς, see Jeremias, "Παῖς θεου," 5:677–717; cf. Watts, *Isaiah's New Exodus and Mark*, 108–12.

87. For an argument that Mark conflates allusions to both Ps 2:7 and Isa 42:1 in Mark 1:11, see Marshall, "Son," 326–36. Maurer, "Knecht Gottes und Sohn Gottes im Passionsbericht," 32 (cf. 28–36), depending on Jeremias' argument for a linguistic connection between υἱός and עבד (Jeremias, "Παῖς θεου," 5:677–717), too myopically concludes that *only* Isaiah's Servant influenced Mark 1:11." As a correction to Maurer, see Hatina, who also demonstrates Mark's echo of Genesis 22 in Mark 1:11 ("Embedded Scripture Texts and Plurality of Meaning," 81–99, esp. 88–93). On the importance of Mark 1:11 in relation to the rest of his gospel, see Lane, who notes that it "marks the high point of revelation in the prologue to Mark's Gospel and provides the indispensable background for all that follows" (*Mark*, 58).

88. Guelich, *Mark 1—8:26*, 35; Collins, *Mark*, 150–51; Hurtado, *Mark*, 21.

as he adds other OT descriptive images to Jesus as the narrative unfolds (e.g., Daniel's Son of Man [Mark 2:10, 28] and the psalmic lamenter [Mark 14:32-40; 15:34]). The following brief survey focuses on Mark's continued depiction of Jesus as Isaiah's Servant.

A couple of chapters later, Mark introduces a theme that subtly echoes the Servant motif and that resurfaces throughout the rest of the narrative. Judas Iscariot is introduced to the reader as one who betrays (παρέδωκεν) Jesus (Mark 3:19; cf. Isa 53:6 [καὶ κύριος παρέδωκεν αὐτὸν ταῖς ἁμαρτίαις ἡμῶν], Isaiah 53:12 [two times: ἀνθ' ὧν παρεδόθη εἰς θάνατον ἡ ψυχὴ αὐτοῦ ... καὶ διὰ τὰς ἁμαρτίας αὐτῶν παρεδόθη]). This theme of betrayal / handing over is significant in Mark, driving the narrative forward at crucial junctures.[89] After Mark identifies the betrayer in 3:19, Jesus twice reminds his disciples of it in his important passion predictions (Mark 9:31; 10:33). At the Last Supper, Mark updates the reader on Judas' betrayal (Mark 14:10-11), and Jesus, reminiscent of his passion predictions in 9:31 and 10:33, predicts his betrayal once again by identifying the betrayer to the rest of the disciples (Mark 14:18). The prediction is fulfilled immediately after Gethsemane, when the betrayer enacts his treason (Mark 14:41, 42, 44). The betrayal / handing over theme continues as the religious leaders hand Jesus over to Pilate (Mark 15:1) who, in turn, hands Jesus over to be crucified (Mark 15:15). In these allusions, Judas, and the rest of Jesus' opponents, are depicted as the means by which Jesus, Isaiah's Servant, is betrayed / handed over to die (note especially Isa 53:12b: παρεδόθη εἰς θάνατον ἡ ψυχὴ αὐτοῦ).

Mark alludes to Isaiah's Servant again in 10:33-34 and 10:45. Prior to these passages, the attentive reader knows that God has identified Jesus as the Servant and that Jesus' opponents who betray and hand him over coincide with the events of this Isaianic figure. In Mark 10:33-34, Jesus predicts the events of his death by telling the Twelve that the chief priests and scribes "will mock (μαστιγώσουσιν) him and spit (ἐμπτύσουσιν) on him" (cf. Isa 50:6). A few verses later in 10:45, Mark introduces through the words of his protagonist and via an allusion to Isaiah's Servant that Jesus will "give his life as a ransom for many" (cf. Isa 53:10-12), thus introducing the idea of a messiah's vicarious death for others. Mark reiterates this Isaianic theme again by recording Jesus' statement at the Last Supper: "This is my blood of the covenant, which is poured out for many" (Mark 14:24).

---

89. Collins, *Mark*, 441. Bolt, *Cross from a Distance*, 52-53. Collins and Bolt are correct that this phrase subtly alludes to Isaiah's Servant each time it is mentioned.

As the events finally unfold in the passion wherein Jesus undergoes the process of suffering for others, Mark alludes four times to Isaiah's Servant passages. Twice he depicts Jesus' opponents as those of the Servant's: In Mark 14:65, those present at Jesus' trial before the Sanhedrin spit on and beat him, and in Mark 15:19 the soldiers repeat the debacle (cf. Isa 50:65).[90] In both instances, Mark uses the Servant's opponents to characterize Jesus' opponents (cf. Mark 10:34: "And they will mock him and spit on him, and flog him and kill him"). This characterization resonates with how Mark's Jesus has already utilized Isaiah in relation to his opponents: He states that Isaiah prophesied about the hypocrisy of the Pharisees and scribes (Mark 7:6; cf. Isa 29:13), and he relates a parable about them from Isaiah 5:1–7 (Mark 12:1–12). Mark also twice depicts Jesus as Isaiah's Servant: In Mark 14:61, Jesus, like the Servant, remains silent before the High Priest, and in Mark 15:5, Jesus remains silent before Pilate (cf. Isa 53:7).

In summary, Mark uses Isaiah's Servant motif multifariously. Primarily, as mentioned in the previous section and as suggested by prior researchers, Mark descriptively portrays Jesus as Isaiah's eschatological, silent Servant who suffers beatings, mocking, and death as a ransom on behalf of others. Secondarily, Mark uses it to characterize Jesus' opponents as those of Isaiah's Servant. Judas, the chief priests, the scribes, the Gentiles, the elders, and Pilate betray / hand Jesus over to die on behalf of others (albeit ironically unbeknownst to them). Additionally, Mark uses it to characterize the soldiers and some Sanhedrin members similarly to those who spit on and beat Isaiah's Servant. Mark's characterization of these various opponents to Jesus in tandem with those of Isaiah's Servant is the third step in providing a way forward concerning the narrative-critical debate about how best to categorize Mark's characterization of Jesus' opponents; the trait that unifies Jesus' opponents is Mark's depiction of them as OT paradigmatic villains.

Isaiah's Servant and the Psalmic Lamenter: The Merging of Two Motifs

With an understanding of Mark's appropriation of Isaiah's Servant motif in place, I now shift focus to exploring it in relation to his lamenter motif. Explorations of other distinct Markan themes in relation to one

---

90. A third is added if one includes the prediction that the Gentiles will "spit" on Jesus at the crucifixion (Mark 10:34).

another are common (e.g., Jesus as Son of Man and Son of David; Jesus as royal king and Isaiah's Servant[91]); however, no one has yet considered Mark's Servant and lamenter motifs as distinct and then explored their narrative interaction. I demonstrate here that, after introducing Jesus as Isaiah's Servant at the beginning of his gospel, Mark merges the two motifs together in the passion, and then foregrounds the lamenter motif at Jesus' crucifixion and death via a sustained explication of Psalm 21. After demonstrating this, I explore in the next subsection similarities and distinctions in Mark's narrative appropriation of the two motifs, providing a glimpse into the unique contributions of each to his story.

Prior to the passion, the image of Isaiah's Servant, as demonstrated in the previous subsection, was fixed firmly in the minds of Mark's attuned readers. At the Last Supper, Mark subtly introduces another OT motif; in an evocation of Psalm 40:10, Mark identifies Judas with the lamenter's opponent and Jesus with the lamenter (Mark 14:18: "the one eating with me"). Also at this juncture, Mark mentions for the ninth time Jesus' betrayal (παραδίδωμι), this time in relation to Judas Iscariot (cf. Mark 3:19; 14:10, 11). Recall from above that Mark's παραδίδωμι theme is one of several ways that Mark manifests his Isaianic Servant motif. Also in the same context, Mark's Jesus reminds his disciples, in the tradition of the Servant, that his blood will be poured out for others (Mark 14:24).

For thirteen chapters, the attentive reader has visualized Jesus as, among other things, Isaiah's Servant protagonist and Judas as the Servant's antagonist. In 14:18c, Mark's first simple evocation of the psalmic lament, two similar OT motifs intersect within Mark's narrative, initiating a new trend in his story. Jesus, for the first time, speaks as the psalmic lamenter, and in so doing, identifies one of his antagonists. As Mark 14:18b ("one of you will betray me") and 14:24 ("this is my blood . . . which is poured out for many") reveal, however, he does not only speak as the lamenter, but he also speaks as the Servant who identifies his antagonist within Isaiah's framework (Mark 14:8b). Thus, Mark now imbues Jesus and Judas with character traits from both Isaiah and the lament psalms. At this point in Mark's narrative, these two motifs are similar, and, if interpreted in isolation from the rest of the passion, bear little interpretive difference as independent motifs. This changes fourteen verses later in Gethsemane.

---

91. Watts, *Isaiah's New Exodus*, 257; Ladd, *Theology of the New Testament*, 155; Black, "Servant of the Lord and Son of Man"; Culpepper, *Mark*, 349; Thielman, *Theology of the New Testament*, 71; and Maurer, "Knecht Gottes und Sohn Gottes im Passionsbericht."

The lament motif that Mark subtly introduces at Jesus' Last Supper becomes overt in Gethsemane, where Jesus evokes Psalm 41/42 and embodies many of the attributes of the psalmic lamenter (recall Ahearne-Kroll's argument from chapter 1 above that Jesus imbibes the psalmic lamenter in Gethsemane). Here the reader clearly realizes that Jesus, aside from imbibing the traits of Isaiah's Servant, is now also the psalmic lamenter par excellence. This new depiction of the lamenter does not signify a break with Mark's depiction of the Servant, since the Servant trend continues at the end of Gethsemane with a recurrence of the betrayal / handing over motif in Mark 14:41–44. The astute reader draws a connection between Jesus' opponents, to whom he is betrayed, and the opponents of Isaiah's Servant. Simultaneously, however, they would naturally have in mind the psalmic lamenter; recall from above that the "sinners" who surround Jesus at the end of his lament in Gethsemane (Mark 14:41) would resonate in the minds of Mark's OT-attuned readers as those of the psalmic lamenter. Thus, after the Gethsemane account, the reader understands Jesus to be simultaneously Isaiah's Servant and the psalmic lamenter and understands Jesus' opponents to be simultaneously those of the Servant and those of the psalmic lamenter.

After Gethsemane and prior to the crucifixion, Mark characterizes Jesus twice as Isaiah's Servant, focusing on Jesus' silence before his antagonists (Mark 14:61; 15:5). Mark also characterizes Jesus' opponents twice as those of Isaiah's Servants, focusing on their spitting and mocking of Isaiah's Servant (Mark 14:65; 15:19).

As the climax of Mark's gospel unfolds—that is, Jesus' crucifixion and death—Mark reenters the world of the psalmic lamenter by bringing it to center stage, depicting Jesus and his opponents within the framework of Psalms 21 (Mark 15:24, 29, 34) and 69 (Mark 15:36).[92] Mark's focus on the lamenter and his opponents in these scenes is more distinct than his prior focus on Isaiah's Servant. This distinction is evidenced in various ways. First, the literary location coupled with a sustained explication of one OT text (Psalm 21) indicates Mark's foregrounding of his lamenter motif. Mark directs his entire gospel toward Jesus' crucifixion and death (Mark 8:31; 9:31; 10:33–34), the climax of Jesus' conflict with

---

92. Mark 15:28 ("And the Scripture was fulfilled which says, 'And He was numbered with transgressors'" [NAS]) is not considered by Moo to be an allusion to Isa 53:12 (*Old Testament in the Gospel Passion Narratives*, 154–55; contrast with Watts, *Isaiah's New Exodus*, 362–63; cf. late MSS [L, 083, etc.] that added Mark 15:28 [see NA^{27}]).

his opponents that originates as early as Mark 1:22.⁹³ When the climax of his gospel arrives, Mark's primary OT interest is in Israel's lament, which is especially evidenced by Mark's sustained explication of Psalm 21 and Jesus' direct quote of Psalm 21:1 (Mark 15:34). It is unnecessary to enter the vast and complicated field of foregrounding⁹⁴ to realize that Jesus' crucifixion and death in Mark is central to his narrative.⁹⁵ Simply stated, Mark's focus on Psalm 21 at this juncture in his gospel, the juncture to which the entire gospel points, indicates its importance relative to his appropriation of the psalmic lamenter motif.

Mark, furthermore, evokes the lament more explicitly at Jesus' crucifixion than he does Isaiah's Servant. Recall from above that Mark's allusions to Isaiah's Servant motif is more subtle, echoing it more thematically than linguistically. Mark's evocations of the lament at Jesus' crucifixion are significantly more thematically and linguistically explicit, especially Jesus' cry of dereliction from the cross, a quote of Psalm 21:1. Whereas prior to Jesus' crucifixion, Mark more vaguely characterizes Jesus and his opponents as those of Isaiah's Servant, when the reader traverses the crucifixion in Mark 15:21–34, he or she knows unambiguously that, within Mark's narrative logic, Jesus is the psalmic lamenter par excellence (Mark 15:34) and his opponents are the paradigmatic opponents of the psalmic lamenter (Mark 15:24, 29, 36).

In summary, as Mark's plot unfolds in chapters 1–14, he presents Jesus and his opponents as, among other things, Isaiah's Servant and his

---

93. Jack Kingsbury notes that Mark's conflict motif "leads straight to the cross," and "the significance of the cross within the story of Mark is that the cross is the place where this story reaches its culmination" ("Significance of the Cross within Mark's Story," 374 and 379, respectively).

94. For a recent, succinct entry into foregrounding, see Cotrozzi, *Expect the Unexpected*, 1–9. Cf. Martín-Asensio, *Transitivity-Based Foregrounding in the Acts of the Apostles*; Dry, "Foregrounding: An Assessment," 435–50; Heimerdinger, *Topic, Focus and Foreground in Ancient Hebrew Narratives*, esp. 221–60; Douthwaite, *Towards a Linguistic Theory of Foregrounding*, esp. 17–50.

95. Martin Kähler's well-worn statement suggests this point well: The gospels are "passion narratives with an extended introduction" (*So-Called Historical Jesus*, 80n11). Stein rightly calls this a slight exaggeration, but does agree that it "correctly recognizes the central role that the death of Jesus plays in the [Gospel]" (*Mark*, 33). These assertions are especially accurate in light of Mark's own emphasis of Jesus' crucifixion throughout his gospel (cf. Mark 8:31; 9:31; 10:33–34) and his repeated use of σταυρόω (15:20, 24, 25, 27, 32) and σταυρός (Mark 15:21, 30, 32) in Mark 15:20b–32, when the crucifixion in Mark arrives (Marcus, *Mark 8–16*, 1049–50) . Cf. Kingsbury, "Significance of the Cross within Mark's Story," 370.

adversaries. When his focus shifts to the passion, Mark merges a psalmic lamenter motif with his Servant motif. In his brief accounts of Jesus' crucifixion and death, Mark decisively foregrounds Jesus and his opponents as those of the protagonist and antagonists of the psalmic lamenter.

Similarities and Differences

While sharing similar characteristics (the focus of most scholars), Mark's Servant and lamenter motifs are distinct in significant ways. In the previous section, the focus was on how Mark sequentially unfolds his narrative in relation to the Servant and lamenter motifs, noting the merging of one into the other. In this section, the focus is on Mark's portrait of the motifs as a whole. Basically, I argue that, amid overlapping traits, these two motifs contribute independently to Mark's narrative. Stated differently, each motif provides for Mark literary and theological themes that the other one does not. Specifically, the following two questions are addressed: What does Mark narratively accomplish by appropriating each motif and what are the similarities and distinctions between the two? Answering these questions introduces a more accurate picture of how Mark appropriates these two motifs than has previously been presented by conflating them.[96]

Mark appropriates Isaiah's Servant motif in order to accomplish several things (see discussion above). First, he uses it Christologically to identify Jesus as Isaiah's Servant (Mark 1:11). Second, he uses it to explain and to predict (within narrative time) Jesus' rejection, suffering, and vicarious death for others (Mark 10:45; 14:24). Third, he uses it to

---

96. Marcus ironically notes a distinction between Mark's use of Isaiah's Servant and what he calls the "sufferer in the Psalms" (i.e., the psalmic lamenter): "This figure [Isaiah's Servant] is important . . . in part because of two elements that go beyond the picture of the Righteous Sufferer in the Psalms: the Isaianic Servant not only suffers but also dies, and his suffering and death are not only necessary but also redemptive" ("Old Testament and the Death of Jesus," 218). Compare this with a similar statement by Marcus: "There is one important feature that the Isaian Servant Songs add to the picture of the Righteous Sufferer in the Psalms. . . . the psalms present a sequential movement: *first* suffering at the hands of one's enemies, *then* victory over them through the power of God. Although this sequence is not totally absent from Isa. 52:13—53:12 (see, e.g., 52:13; 53:10–12), it is mixed in with the idea that *already in his suffering* the Servant accomplishes a salvific purpose and thus wins an eschatological victory" (*Way of the Lord*, 194, italics original, citing Kee, "Function of Scriptural Quotations," 182–83). These statements are ironic, since Marcus suggests that Mark intends no distinction between the two figures ("Old Testament and the Death of Jesus," 214). This subsection explores in more detail what Marcus only notes in passing.

explain and to identify Jesus' opponents as those of the Servants' opponents (Mark 10:34; 14:65; 15:19) and to foreshadow and to describe Jesus' transition into their custody for crucifixion ("betrayal / handing over").

Mark also appropriates the psalmic lamenter motif in order to accomplish several things. First he uses it to identify Jesus as the Davidic lamenter.[97] Second, he uses it to identify Jesus' opponents as the paradigmatic lamenters' opponents.[98] Third, he uses it to paint Jesus in emotional hues. Until Gethsemane, the first place in Mark's gospel where he narrates Jesus' emotions, Mark simply describes Jesus' life, travels, ministry, etc. In Gethsemane, the Markan reader experiences for the first time a Jesus who is "overwhelmed with sorrow to the point of death" (Mark 14:34; evoking Ps 41/42). Another glimpse of an emotionally distraught messiah is found with Jesus' cry of dereliction in Mark 15:34 (evoking Ps 21:1). The lament provides Mark a natural OT source to explain Jesus' grief.

Finally, Mark uses the lament psalms to give a praying voice to Jesus, whose only two Markan prayers are laments (Mark 14:36; 15:34). One of these prayers is a near-verbatim quote of Psalm 21:1: "My God, my God why have you forsaken me" (Mark 15:34). In an insightful 1993 essay, Richard Hays argues that the early church pervasively used a hermeneutical device that portrays Jesus as a petitioner of the Psalms (almost exclusively the lament) in order to provide a matrix for their Christology.[99] Mark taps into this hermeneutical device; when the Markan Jesus prays, he prays within the tradition of the psalmic lament.

The reason that many scholars collapse these two figures indistinguishably together is because of the unmistakable similarities, which one finds both within their respective OT contexts and within Mark's narrative. First, both figures suffer terribly. Isaiah's Servant is mocked, beaten, spit upon, and shamelessly killed. The psalmic lamenter is wantonly degraded by enemies gambling for his clothes and by passerby derisively shaking their heads. Second, both figures face opposition from opponents who inflict physical and psychological pain on their subjects.

Although these figures share unmistakable similarities, they also possess notable differences, which are found both within their respective OT contexts and within Mark's narrative. First, Isaiah's Servant is not a

---

97. Ahearne-Kroll, *Psalms of Lament in Mark's Passion*. See discussion in chapter 1.

98. See previous section for discussion.

99. Hays, "Christ Prays the Psalms: Israel's Psalter as Matrix of Early Christology," 101–8.

petitioner, whereas the central role of the lamenter is that of a petitioner who petitions God to change his given plight. In Mark, when the two prayers of Jesus are recorded, he prays as a lamenter. Recall from above that Jesus' depiction as a psalmic petitioner is an established hermeneutical move that carries theological freight. In order to depict Jesus as an OT petitioner, Mark must go beyond his explication of Isaiah's Servant. He finds the most fitting OT motif to portray Jesus as a petitioner—a petitioner who prays to God in order to bring about change for his suffering—in the lament psalms. In isolation, Isaiah's Servant does not deliver the narrative goods that Mark needs in his portrayal of Jesus.

Second, in relation to his earthly opponents, Isaiah's Servant humbly submits to and embraces suffering; in relation to God, the lamenter struggles in prayer to remove it. The Servant is silent before his adversaries, while the lamenter is anything but silent before God. Mark taps into the distinct emphases of each motif in order to depict a messiah who simultaneously struggles with, yet calmly and quietly accepts, his suffering. Neither of these figures in isolation provides for Mark the OT background needed to depict this interesting literary interplay.

Third, God is consistently present for Isaiah's Servant[100] while he is pervasively absent for the lamenter.[101] Likewise, in Mark, Jesus, as the Servant, experiences God's presence (Mark 1:11; cf. 9:7) while, as the lamenter, he experiences his absence (Mark 14:36; 15:34). For reasons unknown to the modern interpreter, Mark desires to depict God's apparent absence at crucial moments in Jesus' life (Gethsemane and crucifixion). Isaiah's Servant does not provide for Mark this depiction, but the psalmic lamenter does.

Finally, Isaiah's Servant perceives that his death is endowed with purpose, that is, he suffers and dies vicariously for others while the lamenter does not fully understand his suffering. In the tradition of Isaiah's Servant, Mark's Jesus is acutely aware of the purpose of his suffering and death (Mark 9:31; 10:45). Conversely, in the tradition of the psalmic lamenter, Mark's Jesus questions God about being forsaken (Mark 15:34). Again, two similar but distinct OT figures provides Mark the scriptural

---

100. Note in Isaiah's Servant Songs, God either speaks (Isa 42:1–4; 49:3, 5–7) or is notably present (Isa 50:4; 52:12–13).

101. Note that the lamenter's expected "turn-to-trust" indicates the lamenter's disposition toward God in light of his absence and not that God has made his presence known.

concepts to present Jesus in a multifaceted way that highlights various aspects of his life and ministry.

Mark, then, is fully aware of the core similarities and distinctions between Isaiah's Servant and the psalmic lamenter; he reveals a messiah who embodies both the Servant and the lamenter, recognizing the similar and distinct contributions of each. Both function in Mark in ways that the other does not. Recognizing this enhances the modern reader's appreciation and understanding of Mark's more nuanced use of his Scriptures and brings more clarity to the literary and theological flow of his narrative. Additionally, it reinforces and advances Ahearne-Kroll's argument that collapsing Isaiah's Servant and the psalmic lamenter motifs indiscriminately together does injustice to Mark's complex narrative appropriation of each.[102]

Summary

Ahearne-Kroll, contrary to his predecessors, recognizes Mark's distinct understanding of the psalmic lament and refuses to collapse it indistinguishably into Mark's use of Isaiah's Servant motif. Whereas Ahearne-Kroll focuses his sole attention on Mark's appropriation of the psalmic lament, this section advances his work by exploring how Mark recognizes, understands, and appropriates both motifs in similar and distinct ways. Scholars have long recognized that Mark does this with other OT motifs (e.g., Jesus as a royal king and as Isaiah's Servant) but have, since Ruppert's 1972 *Jesus als der leidende Gerechte?*, indiscriminately merged his Servant and lamenter motifs, assuming that both are identical in the Markan narrative.

This section demonstrates that Mark establishes the Servant motif early in the gospel, merges it with his psalmic lamenter motif in the passion, and places it in the shadow of the lament motif at Jesus' crucifixion. In particular, Mark appropriates the Servant motif to, among other things, characterize Jesus and his opponents as those of the Servant, adding another layer to his trend to characterize them as paradigmatic OT heroes and villains. Thus, what Thielman notes in relation to Mark's Son of Man motif is pertinent to Mark's Servant and lamenter motifs: For Mark, the Son of Man pattern in Daniel 7 cannot tell the whole story; the Isaianic

---

102. Ahearne-Kroll, *Psalms of Lament in Mark's Passion*, 171–73.

Servant image is needed.[103] Likewise, the Servant pattern in Isaiah does not tell Mark's whole story; the psalmic lamenter image is needed.

CONCLUSION: NARRATIVE AND RHETORICAL IMPLICATIONS

Mark's characterization of Jesus' opponents as paradigmatic OT villains—namely, as those of King David, those of the lamenting David, and those of Isaiah's Servant—has narrative and rhetorical implications. Narratively, these portrayals enhance the character traits of Jesus' opponents. A character trait within a narrative is any attribute, either explicitly or implicitly stated, that a narrator uses to distinguish in a relatively enduring way one character from another.[104] For example, Judas is a "betrayer" (Mark 3:19; 14:10, 11, 18, 21, 41, 42, 44.), the crowd, a more rounded character group that does not become Jesus' outright opponent until the gospel's end, are sinners (Mark 14:41–43) and are easily manipulated (Mark 15:11), and John the Baptist possesses humility (Mark 1:7).

Jesus' opponents in Mark have many character traits: The religious authorities are mistaken about Jesus (Mark 3:22), "without authority" (Mark 1:22), "fearful" of people (Mark 11:18; 12:12; 14:1–2), manipulative (Mark 15:9–13), erroneous interpreters of Scripture (Mark 12:24), mistaken about the correct standards for making decisions (Mark 11:32; 12:12), and hypocritical (Mark 7:6; 12:38–40).[105] In light of my arguments in this chapter, another character trait is added to Jesus' opponents—namely, they also bear the sinister traits of their OT predecessors, the enemies of the Davidic psalmist (both King David and the lamenting David) and of Isaiah's Servant. Tapping into this mental image, Mark is able to paint a more vivid, concrete picture of Jesus' opponents in the minds of readers who were steeped in these OT traditions.

Mark's portrayal of Jesus' opponents as paradigmatic OT villains also provides a way forward in the narrative-critical debate concerning Mark's characterization of Jesus' opposition. Recall that the debate revolves around which characters to include in a unified group of opposition against Jesus. Beginning at the triumphal entry, the reader gradually realizes that Mark employs a hermeneutic of the OT in his characterization of

---

103. Thielman, *Theology of the New Testament*, 71.
104. Powell, *What Is Narrative Criticism?*, 54.
105. Ibid., 60–62; cf. Rhoads et al., *Mark as Story*, 117–23.

Jesus' opponents that eventually engulfs all of those who oppose Jesus. This hermeneutic is the unifying force that holds together Mark's concept of Jesus' opposition, allowing simultaneous consistency (the Jewish leaders' monolithic front against Jesus) and modification (e.g., the adding of the crowds, soldiers, and others to Jesus' opposition in the passion). In other words, although Mark forms major and minor characters (both individually and collectively) in opposition to Jesus, he does so under the guiding rubric of the OT. In composing his cast of characters who oppose Jesus, the edges that frame Mark's delineations of particular character groups (e.g., the Jewish leaders) blur because his overarching concern is with who aligns with the OT villains in opposition to Jesus the OT hero.

Rhetorically, these characterizations enhance Mark's evaluative point of view of Jesus' opponents. "Evaluative point of view," according to Powell, "may be defined as the standards of judgment by which readers are led to evaluate the events, characters, and settings that comprise the story." Mark's standard of judgment is what God thinks, and what God thinks is true and right (cf. Mark 8:33c).[106] A primary way that Mark and, presumably, his readers determine what God thinks is via the Hebrew Scriptures (cf. Mark 1:1–3, an OT quote that frames the entirety of Mark's message).[107] Those who "think the things of God" and not the "things of people," to borrow phrases from Petersen's groundbreaking work on points of view in Mark's gospel,[108] are those who act in accord with the Hebrew Scriptures as revealed in Jesus. Most of those in Mark's audience were painfully aware of the vicious and deplorable opposition the psalmic lamenter and Isaiah's Servant faced at the hands of their opponents. These OT villains always reflect those who, to apply Petersen's phrase to an OT phenomena, failed "to think the things of God." Mark's readers, then, understand Jesus' opponents as bad because the narrator, Jesus, *and* the Scriptures say they are. Mark appropriates these motifs, then, to provide an evaluative standard against which to places Jesus' opponents in order to substantiate his negative portrayal of them.

By merging Jesus' opponents with these OT villains, Mark strategically and increasingly enhances his already negative evaluative viewpoint

---

106. Powell, *What Is Narrative Criticism?*, 24. Cf. Rhoads, "Losing Life for Others in the Face of Death," 358–69. Boris Uspensky originally laid the groundwork for subsequent scholars to study point of view (*Poetics of Composition*).

107. Powell, *What Is Narrative Criticism?*, 24. Powell notes that God's point of view in the gospels is also revealed through angels, prophets, miracles, and dreams.

108. Petersen, "'Point of View' in Mark's Narrative."

of them as the narrative progresses.[109] As Jesus' opponents progress from those who oppose a king in Mark 11–12 to those who oppose a lamenter in Mark 15, the intensity of the reader's negative point of view significantly increases, since presumably, although it is disgraceful to oppose *King* David, it is intuitively worse to oppose a *lamenting* David—perhaps tantamount to the modern adage that one should never "kick a man when he is down." In essence, Mark adjudicates a quintessentially negative evaluative viewpoint by characterizing Jesus' opponents as OT villains at gospel's end.

---

109. This also coincides with Boomershine's rhetorical critical argument that Mark, via several narrative techniques (e.g.,character introductions, narrative commentary, character comments), seeks to regulate the emotional distance that he wants his readers to have with particular characters ("Mark, the Storyteller," 284–314).

3

Matthew's Appropriation of the Psalmic Lament

INTRODUCTION

MOST MODERN SCHOLARS ARGUE that Mark writes his gospel first and that Matthew utilizes Mark, and perhaps other sources, when writing the First Gospel. Matthew's utilization of Mark is more complex than an occasional parallel phrase or thought; rather, Mark provides Matthew with his primary structure and content, especially in the passion account. In light of this historical reconstruction of NT gospel chronology and Matthean dependence on Mark and in light of Mark's appropriation of the psalmic lament discussed in the previous chapter, it is apropos to examine how Matthew appropriates the same tradition. Such an examination advances Ahearne-Kroll's work, a need that he recognizes but notes is beyond the scope of his research.[1]

This is precisely where this chapter picks up the conversation, specifically to advance Ahearne-Kroll's work and the ancillary conclusions established in chapter 2 by exploring how Matthew appropriates the psalmic lament. The focus here is the same as the one in chapter 2—namely, to explore how Matthew uses the lament to characterize Jesus and Jesus' opponents interchangeably with, and as the climax to, his

1. Ahearne-Kroll, *Psalms of Lament in Mark's Passion*, 22.

characterization of Jesus and Jesus' opponents with other OT entities.² The arrangement of this chapter, however, differs slightly from the previous one (non-lament psalms; lament psalms; Isaiah's Servant), where it was necessary to follow the structure of Ahearne-Kroll's monograph in order to demonstrate more clearly a step-by-step advancement of his work. The following arrangement reflects more the flow of Matthew's narrative and includes a motif exclusive to Matthew (rejected prophet; Isaiah's Servant; non-lament psalms; lament psalms).

More precisely, the objectives and contributions of this chapter are fourfold. The first objective is to test Ahearne-Kroll's arguments on Matthew's gospel. Recall that Ahearne-Kroll demonstrates that Mark characterizes Jesus as the Davidic psalmic lamenter par excellence without indistinguishably collapsing it into his Isaianic Servant motif, thus giving a voice to the psalmic lamenter in the Second Gospel. This chapter demonstrates that Matthew, in relation to Mark, enhances the distinctions between his Isaianic Servant and psalmic lamenter motifs and expands and emphasizes the narrative content about Jesus as the Davidic lamenter par excellence, thus giving a voice to the psalmic lamenter in the First Gospel.³

Second, I test the advancements made to Ahearne-Kroll's work in chapter 2 on Matthew's gospel.⁴ Recall that chapter 2 establishes that Mark's characterization of Jesus as the lamenter par excellence is a part of a larger motif of characterizing Jesus as the paradigmatic OT hero (Isaiah's Servant, the Davidic king via non-lament psalms, and the psalmic lamenter) *and* Jesus' opponents as the paradigmatic OT villains (those of Isaiah's Servant, the Davidic king via non-lament psalms, and the psalmic lamenter). Also recall that chapter 2 establishes that the Markan hermeneutic that best explains his unification of Jesus' passion opponents is the category "paradigmatic OT villains." This chapter demonstrates that Matthew expands and emphasizes Mark's characterization of Jesus' op-

---

2. In doing this, I also advance Donald Senior's work. In a subsidiary point to a larger argument about Matthew's formula quotations, he briefly mentions, but does not pursue the fact, that Matthew uses the OT to characterize Jesus' opponents ("Lure of the Formula Quotations," 114–15).

3. Noting this "voice" of the psalmic lamenter in Matthew both supplements and challenges Eklund, who recognizes the influence of the lament on Matthew's depiction of Jesus but suggests that Matthew mutes that voice relative to Mark ("Lord, Teach Us How to Greive," 60–61). I, conversely, argue that Matthew amplifies Mark's voice of the lamenter.

4. These first two objectives examine Matthew via the redactional critical method discussed in chapter 1.

ponents as the paradigmatic OT villains, appropriating more extensively than Mark does this hermeneutical category.

The third objective is to test the overall thesis of chapter 2 (Mark's Jesus = paradigmatic OT hero; Jesus' opponents = OT paradigmatic villains) on a Matthean motif that is independent of Mark—Matthew's so-called rejected-prophet motif. I suggest that Matthew appropriates this motif to characterize Jesus as the paradigmatic OT hero and Jesus' opponents as the OT paradigmatic villains. Matthew's appropriation of this motif independent of Mark further confirms Matthew's expansion and emphasis of it.[5]

My final objective, by way of a conclusion, is to synthesize the foregoing explorations of Matthew's characterization of Jesus and Jesus' opponents, to examine Matthew's post-crucifixion characterization of Jesus' opponents via scenes found only in the First Gospel, to explore some rhetorical implications, and to summarize the contributions made in this chapter to Matthean scholarship.

Succinctly, I argue that Matthew expands and emphasizes Mark's characterization of Jesus as the Davidic king via non-lament psalms, as the psalmic lamenter par excellence, and as Isaiah's Servant, emphasizing, more emphatically than Mark does, Jesus as the paradigmatic OT hero. Simultaneously, Matthew expands and emphasizes Mark's characterization of Jesus' opponents as those of the Davidic king via non-lament psalms, those of the psalmic lamenter, and those of Isaiah's Servant, emphasizing, more emphatically than Mark does, Jesus' opponents as those of paradigmatic OT villains.[6] To augment and susbstantiate these arguments, I establish that Matthew, independently of Mark, develops his rejected-prophet motif similarly to his psalmic and Servant motifs—namely, to characterize Jesus and Jesus' opponents as the OT hero and villains, respectively. Matthew expands and emphasizes Mark's narrative in these regards to elicit, perhaps among other things, certain rhetorical effects.

---

5. By isolating Matthew's tandem use of these motifs (rejected prophet, Isaianic Servant, Davidic king via non-lament psalms, and Davidic lamenter), I do not intend to suggest that Matthew *only* had these motifs in mind; he wrote much more complexly than that. Instead, Matthean scholars have long recognized that he depicts Jesus within a complex tapestry of OT figures (for an extensive bibliography and a summary discussion, see Turner, *Matthew*, 32–37). Examining Matthean themes independently, however, is heuristically necessary but only within an exploratory framework that recognizes their interrelationships within the narrative as a whole.

6. R. T. France notes that Matthew is similarly more emphatic with his Galilee and Jerusalem motifs ("Matthew and Jerusalem," 108–27).

To make these arguments, I examine how Matthew in relation to Mark interchangeably appropriates the following OT texts and motifs in his characterization of Jesus and Jesus' opponents, coalescing and climaxing them with the psalmic lament at the crucifixion: (1) rejected prophet, (2) Isaiah's Servant, (3) non-lament Psalms 8, 109, and 117, and (4) the lament psalms.[7] After examining these texts and motifs, I synthesize and summarize them in a conclusion that explores their narrative and rhetorical impact on Matthew's story and reader.

OT REJECTED-PROPHET MOTIF IN CHARACTERIZING JESUS AND HIS OPPONENTS

From the beginning to the end of his gospel, Matthew characterizes Jesus closely with OT prophets, a fact well established by prior researchers (see below). Unexamined by these researchers is Matthew's characterization of Jesus' opponents as those of OT prophets. Exploring these two Matthean themes is necessary for my purposes here because it establishes a Matthean motif of characterization that is simultaneously independent from,[8] yet similar to, Mark's motif of characterizing Jesus as the OT paradigmatic hero and Jesus' opponents as the paradigmatic OT villains. Furthermore, establishing this motif validates and sets the stage to explore in the subsequent three sections how Matthew characterizes Jesus and Jesus' opponents as those of Isaiah's Servant and King David through non-lament psalms, climaxing his gospel with the lamenting David.

"Prophet" (and Cognates) within an OT Matrix

Before examining how Matthew characterizes Jesus as the rejected OT prophet par excellence and Jesus' opponents as those who reject this prophet, I must first establish that Matthew's concept of "prophet" derives from an OT matrix. This is important to establish because it shows that

---

7. Since Matthew climaxes his gospel with the lament psalms, and since the focus of this chapter is on how Matthew appropriates this motif, substantially more (roughly twice as much) attention is given to it in relation to each of the three other investigations. The exploration of the first three motifs, although offering their own unique contributions to Matthean research (especially in understanding how Matthew characterizes Jesus' opponents), serves, in essence, as a lengthy introduction to Matthew's appropriation of the psalmic lament.

8. Mark portrays Jesus explicitly as a prophet only twice (Mark 6:15; 8:28).

Matthew's characterization of Jesus and Jesus' opponents in tandem with prophets and their opponents parallels how Matthew characterizes Jesus and Jesus' opponents in tandem with Isaianic Servant and Davidic motifs examined below—namely, within an OT matrix.

Michael Knowles sums up well Matthew's interest in "prophets" and its cognates (προφήτης, προφητεύω, προφητεία, and ψευδοπροφήτης): Matthew employs these terms "44 times out of a total of 87 in the Synoptic Gospels (or 51% when Matthew constitutes only 37.4% of the Synoptic material) and 206 in the NT as a whole (or 21% for 13.3% of total NT material)."[9] It is clear that Matthew was profoundly affected by the concept of "prophets." It is also clear that he uses these terms within an OT matrix. Aside from generally anchoring his gospel in the OT, Matthew names specific OT prophets seven times (Matt 2:17; 3:3; 4:14; 8:17; 12:17; 24:15; 27:9), quotes unnamed OT prophets five times (Matt 1:22; 2:5, 15; 13:35; 21:4) and refers collectively to the OT prophets six times (e.g., "law and prophets"): Matthew 5:17; 7:12; 11:13; 16:14; 22:40; 26:56. These eighteen references, spanning the entirety of Matthew's gospel, inform his use of "prophet" (and cognates) when he does not specify a direct correlation with the OT (Matt 2:23; 5:12; 10:41; 11:9; 13:17; 13:57; 14:5; 21:11; 21:26, 46; 23:29–37). In other words, Matthew's concept of "prophet" derives from, and is defined by, the OT. When Matthew calls Jesus a prophet, then, he does so within an OT matrix.[10]

9. Knowles, *Jeremiah in Matthew's Gospel*, 149n1. Although Knowles's statistics reveal Matthew's interest in the concept of "prophet," they do conceal Luke's equal interest in the concept. Knowles fails to note that Mark only mentions the term prophet and its cognates nine times. Thus, the majority of the other occurrences in the Synoptics appear in Luke's gospel (thirty-two times). Furthermore, when statistics from Acts are included in the research (thirty-four times), Luke's interest in the concept is more pronounced. This oversight is explored at length in chapter 4.

10. This is not to say that Matthew limits Jesus to an OT prophet, for Matthew teaches, with specific reference to a prophet, that Jesus is greater than Jonah (Matt 12:41) and teaches, more broadly from a Christological perspective, that Jesus is God's Son (Matt 3:17). Matthew's Jesus may be more than an OT prophet, but he is not less than one. Additionally, when Matthew refers to his successors as prophets (Matt 23:34), he does so within an OT matrix (Matt 23:35). Jack Kingsbury, however, argues that Matthew's use of the term "prophet" in relation to Jesus is insignificant because those who claim Jesus as a prophet (e.g., the crowd) lack an adequate understanding of Jesus' identity and because Matthew specifically states that Jesus is "more than a prophet" (Matt 11:7–9) (*Matthew*, 88–92). Winkle rightly contends, however, that four of the five statements about Jesus in Mathew that begin with οὗτός ἐστιν ("this is"; as do the crowd's statement about Jesus as a prophet in Matt 21:11), identify Jesus accurately relative to Matthew's narrative logic ("Jeremiah Model for Jesus in the Temple,"

Of Heroes and Villains

Jesus as the OT Rejected Prophet Par Excellence

Matthew's characterization of Jesus as certain OT prophets is well argued by many.[11] Knowles, for example, argues that Matthew depicts Jesus as the prophet Jeremiah; Allison suggests that Matthew's Jesus is the "New Moses"; Huizenga argues that he is the "New Isaac"; and Ham believes he is Zechariah's "Shepherd-King."[12] The point of this section is not to explore the degree of specificity to which Matthew characterizes Jesus with particular OT prophets, which is less relevant for my purposes here; rather, the point is to show that Matthew characterizes Jesus more broadly as the OT prophet par excellence.[13]

Matthew's Jesus explicitly refers to himself as a prophet at least twice. In Matthew 13:57, Jesus references himself as a "prophet without honor" in relation to his hometown. In Matthew 12:38–42, Jesus likens himself to Jonah, whom Jesus identifies as a prophet in Matthew 12:39. Matthew's Jesus also implicitly refers to himself as a prophet twice. In Matthew 17:12–13, Jesus compares his suffering to John the Baptist, considered in Matthew's narrative to be a prophet (Matt 3:1–12; 14:5; 21:26; cf. Mal 4:5), via an allusion to the prophet Elijah.[14] In Matthew 26:31, Jesus references himself as the prophetic shepherd figure of Zechariah 13:7.

Other Matthean characters explicitly refer to Jesus as a prophet at least three times. In Matthew 16:14, Jesus' disciples recount that certain "people" refer to Jesus as "John the Baptist . . . Elijah . . . Jeremiah, or one of the prophets." In Matthew 21:11, the crowds call Jesus a "prophet from Nazareth in Galilee." In Matthew 21:46, the chief priests and Pharisees are afraid to arrest Jesus because the people believe him to be "a

---

158–59). Additionally, simply because Jesus is more than a prophet does not mean that he is not a prophet. For example, Matthew's identification with Jesus as other OT entities (e.g., Israel) does not mean that he is limited by that identity.

11. Cf. Schnider, *Jesus der Prophet*, 158–63; Leske, "Isaiah and Matthew," 152–69; Cousland, *Crowds in the Gospel of Matthew*, 208–13; Ham, *Coming King and the Rejected Shepherd*; and Nolland, "King as Shepherd," 133–46.

12. Knowles, *Jeremiah in Matthew's Gospel*; Allison, *New Moses*; Huizenga, *New Isaac*; Ham, *Coming King and the Rejected Shepherd*.

13. It is unnecessary to argue this point at length since others have aptly done so (Winkle, "Jeremiah Model for Jesus in the Temple," 158–63; 171–72). The following discussion, although drawing on the contributions of others, is primarily indebted to Knowles' monograph *Jeremiah in Matthew's Gospel*.

14. If Knowles is correct that Matthew's "Eli" transliteration in the cry of dereliction is a reference to Elijah, then Matthew makes a second connection between Jesus and Elijah in 27:46 (Knowles, *Jeremiah in Matthew's Gospel*, 158–59).

prophet." Implicitly, those in the Sanhedrin, who mock Jesus, refer to him as a prophet; they exclaim, "Prophesy to us, Christ. Who hit you" (Matt 27:68), insinuating that Jesus is a false prophet. Their accusation against Jesus as a false prophet indirectly indicates that Jesus claimed to be, and that others saw him as, a prophet.[15]

Matthew as narrator implicitly refers to Jesus as a prophet at least four times.[16] Concerning Matthew 16:21 and 23:37, Knowles notes, "It would appear that . . . at least part of the reason why Jesus 'must go to Jerusalem [δεῖ αὐτὸν εἰς Ἱεροσόλυμα ἀπελθεῖν]' (Matt 16:21; diff. Mark 8:31) is that Jerusalem is where all the prophets perish (Mt. 23:37 // Lk. 13:34; cf. Lk. 13:33)."[17] In Matthew 21:26–27, the questioning of Jesus' authority by the elders, Matthew sheds light on Jesus' authority via John the Baptist's authority. Knowles points out:

> If the authorities were unwilling to acknowledge the prophetic authority of John, so they will refuse to acknowledge the (implicitly prophetic) authority of Jesus. For the implication of Jesus' reply, "Neither will I tell you by what authority I do these things" (Mt. 21.7 // Mk. 11.33), is that their authority is one and the same.[18]

If their authority is one and the same, then Matthew implicitly depicts Jesus as a prophet. In Matthew 23:13–32, Jesus' "woes," as Turner rightly notes, "must be viewed against the background of the biblical prophets, who frequently cried woe against Israel's sins."[19] In 27:9–10, Matthew subtly depicts Jesus as Jeremiah and/or Zechariah.[20] D. A. Carson notes this subtle depiction in Matthew's redaction of Zechariah 11:13 in 27:9: "The one on whom a price is set is no longer a prophet ("me," Zech 11:13)

---

15. ibid., 157.

16. A fifth is included if Matthew intends an allusion to the prophet like Moses in Matt 17:5 ("listen to him"; cf. Deut 18:15) (cf. Winkle, "Jeremiah Model for Jesus in the Temple," 161–63).

17. Knowles, *Jeremiah in Matthew's Gospel*, 91.

18. Ibid., 155; cf. Allison, *New Moses*, 137–38.

19. Turner, *Matthew*, 550.

20. Modern interpreters find this fulfillment citation problematic, since Matthew attaches Jeremiah's name to a similar passage in Zech 11:12–13. For my purposes, it is unnecessary to address this issue since, in either case, Matthew characterizes Jesus as an OT prophet. For a survey of possible solutions to the problem, see Knowles, *Jeremiah in Matthew's Gospel*, 53–77.

but Jesus ("him," Matt 27:9)."[21] In other words, Matthew's replacement of Zechariah with Jesus identifies Jesus as a prophet.

Matthew further implies that Jesus is a prophet via numerous "traits that marked [him] and his ministry as specifically prophetic."[22] Such traits, Knowles notes, include the following: Jesus' endowment with the divine Spirit (Matt 3:16) as the source of his miraculous power and authority (Matt 7:29), his ecstatic experiences at his baptism (Matt 3:16–17), his temptation (Matt 4: 1–11), and his transfiguration (Matt 17:1–13), his insight into the inner thoughts and motivations of others (Matt 9:4; 12:25; 22:18), his prophetic predictions about his own death (Matt 16:21; 17:22–23; 20:18–19) and about Jerusalem (Matt 23:38; 24:2), and his "prophetic" symbolic actions, such as cleansing the temple (Matt 21:12–13) and cursing the fig tree (21:19). Similarly, Knowles continues, the content of Jesus' teaching (e.g., its rhetorical forms, polemic against cultic formalism, ethical emphasis, and call to repentance [Matt 4:17; 11:20 24]), his personal piety, intimacy with God, and divine calling to shape the national destiny of Israel are similar to the traits of the prophets.[23]

Matthew, therefore, characterizes Jesus as a prophet. He is not just any prophet, but his life and ministry are situated within the continuum, and as the culmination, of the OT prophets.[24] Jesus, then, is the OT prophet par excellence. The significance of this conclusion for my argument is that although Matthew establishes this characterization of Jesus as the OT prophet par excellence independent of Mark, it parallels Mark's more pervasive motif of characterizing Jesus as Isaiah's Servant, the Davidic king of the non-lament psalms, and the Davidic lamenter. This is more pronounced when one considers how Matthew characterizes Jesus' opponents in relation to this OT prophet motif. Before exploring this specific issue, however, I must make a brief digression on Matthew's general characterization of Jesus' opponents in order to note several well-known complications in delineating this character group, to suggest a way beyond these complications, and to frame all subsequent discussions of Jesus' opponents in this chapter.

---

21. Carson, *Matthew*, 565.

22. Knowles, *Jeremiah in Matthew's Gospel*, 149. To the degree that any one or more of these depict Matthew's Jesus as an OT prophet is to the same degree that it substantiates the argument of this section.

23. Ibid.

24. Cousland, *Crowds in the Gospel of Matthew*, 225.

Matthew's Characterization of Jesus' Opponents: A Way Forward

As with the Gospel of Mark (see discussion in chapter 2), scholars agree that Matthew's Jesus faces opposition from numerous characters. They are divided, however, on how to delineate them. Kingsbury and others argue that the Jewish leaders, comprised of the Pharisees, Sadducees, the chief priests, the elders, the scribes, and, in one instance, the Herodians, form a unified character group, since Matthew presents them as a monolithic front against Jesus.[25] Others disagree, suggesting that the term "Jewish leaders" imprecisely explains Matthew's characterization of Jesus' opponents because he is clearly aware of the differences between these groups.[26] Still others debate the varying degrees of emphasis that Matthew places on certain groups such as the Pharisees within this larger group of Jewish leaders[27] or whether to conflate "the crowd" with the leaders to comprise the larger character group "Israel."[28]

A way forward in this discussion is to understand that Matthew appropriates but significantly advances Mark's OT hermeneutic to characterize Jesus' opponents as the paradigmatic OT villains (recall discussion in chapter 2). This OT hermeneutic is the unifying force that holds together his concept of Jesus' opposition, allowing simultaneous consistency (the Jewish leaders' monolithic front against Jesus) and modification

---

25. Kingsbury, "Developing Conflict between Jesus and the Jewish Leaders in Matthew's Gospel," 58–59; cf. Anderson, *Matthew's Narrative Web*, 98 (cf. ibid., "Gender and Reading," 3–27); Tilborg, *Jewish Leaders in Matthew*, 1; Saunders, "'No One Dared Ask Him Anything More'"; Powell, "Religious Leaders in Matthew: A Literary-Critical Approach," 35–37; and Carter, *Matthew*, 228–31. Kingsbury finds the term "leaders" (ὁδηγοί) appropriate for denoting these characters, since Matthew uses it in describing them (Matt 15:14; 23:16, 24). For a helpful and succinct list of all references and scenes in which the Jewish leaders appear in Matthew, see Anderson, *Matthew's Narrative Web*, 99–101.

26. Barnet, *Not the Righteous but Sinners*, 3 (cf. France, "Matthew and Jerusalem," 117–19).

27. Gundry, for example, singles out the Pharisees as the main opponents of Jesus (*Matthew*, 306). Concerning the passion, Ulrich Luz specifies the high priests and elders as Jesus' most significant opposition (*Theology of the Gospel of Matthew*, 133–34).

28. Davies and Allison, *Matthew*, 1:302; Bauer, "Major Characters of Matthew's Story," 357–67; Luz, *Theology of the Gospel of Matthew*, 133–34. These scholars conflate the crowd with the leaders especially in light of Matt 27:24–25: "When Pilate saw that he was gaining nothing, but rather that a riot was beginning, he took water and washed his hands before the crowd [ὄχλου], saying, 'I am innocent of this man's blood; see to it yourselves.' And all the people [ὁ λαός] answered, 'His blood be on us and on our children!'"

(e.g., the adding of the crowds, soldiers, and others to Jesus' opposition in the passion, see below). In other words, although Matthew forms major and minor characters (both individually and collectively), he does so under the guiding rubric of the OT. In composing his cast of characters, the edges that frame Matthew's delineations of particular character groups (e.g., the Jewish leaders) blur because his overarching concern is with who aligns with the OT villains in opposition to Jesus the OT hero.

Establishing this way forward begins with exploring how Matthew characterizes Jesus' opponents in relation to the opponents of the OT prophets and continues in the explorations of Matthew's characterization of Jesus' opponents in the subsequent three sections.[29]

Jesus' Opponents as the Paradigmatic OT Prophets' Opponents

Matthew contrasts his characterization of Jesus as the OT prophet par excellence by explicitly characterizing Jesus' opponents as those of OT prophets at five junctures. In Matthew 21:46, the chief priests and Pharisees look for a way to arrest Jesus, but they fear the crowd, who believes Jesus to be a prophet; Jesus is depicted as a prophet (albeit to the ignorance of the religious leaders) and Jesus' opponents as those seeking to arrest and kill him. In Matthew 23:29–32, Jesus poignantly states that the scribes and Pharisees are "descendants of those who murdered the prophets."

In Matthew 23:37, Jesus ascribes blame to "Jerusalem" for killing the prophets. Jerusalem is identified in the larger context of Matthew 23:1–39 as the religious leadership who eventually kills Jesus.[30] In Matthew 26:68, the religious leaders of the Sanhedrin ironically call Jesus a prophet while

---

29. Aside from providing a way forward in understanding Matthew's characterization of Jesus' opponents, this chapter also advances an aspect of Anderson's work, who notes that Matthew uses numerous methods to emphasize the growing opposition to Jesus: repetition of epithets, actions (some depicted, some described), descriptions, doublets, and Jesus offering an authoritative legal interpretation and the leaders challenging it in later narratives (*Matthew's Narrative Web*, 102–32). This chapter advances Anderson's arguments by noting another Matthean repetition that emphasizes the growing opposition to Jesus—namely, his use of the OT to characterize Jesus' opponents as paradigmatic OT villains.

30. Hagner, *Matthew 14–28*, 680. Luz's conclusion that Matt 23:36 ("all this will come upon this generation") refers collectively to the crowd and Israel instead of the Jewish leaders (*Theology of the Gospel of Matthew*, 123–24) does not affect my argument here since at gospel's end the crowd and all of Israel become Jesus' opponents (Matt 27:25).

unwittingly acting in line with those "who murder the prophets" (Matt 23:31; cf. 23:37). In Matthew 27:9-10, Jesus is characterized as Jeremiah and/or Zechariah (see discussion above) and the chief priests, elders, and Judas are characterized as the opponents of these respective prophets— namely, as those who are involved in betrayal that results in the purchase of a field.

Matthew also implicitly characterizes Jesus' opponents as those of the OT prophets. In Matthew 5:11-12, those that persecute the disciples are likened to those who "persecuted the prophets who were before [them]." Matthew later identifies those who persecute the prophets as the religious leaders (Matt 23:29-32). In Matthew 16:21 (cf. Matt 20:18), there is a "divine necessity" for Jesus to go to Jerusalem (δεῖ αὐτὸν εἰς Ἱεροσόλυμα ἀπελθεῖν).[31] As noted above, Knowles is correct when he observes, "It would appear that in Matthew's gospel at least part of the reason why Jesus 'must go to Jerusalem' (16:21; diff. Mk 8:31) is that Jerusalem is where all the prophets perish (Mt. 23:37 // Lk. 13:34; cf. Lk. 13:33)."[32] To the degree that Knowles' observation is correct is to the same degree that those in Jerusalem who kill Jesus fulfill the divine necessity for the OT prophet par excellence to die. In Matthew 17:12-13, as Jesus is characterized as a prophet like Elijah, who in turn is compared with the prophet John the Baptist (see discussion above), the scribes are characterized as those who cause the suffering of these prophets.

Summary

Pervasively throughout his gospel, Matthew characterizes Jesus as the OT prophet par excellence and Jesus' opponents as the paradigmatic opponents of the OT prophet. Establishing this motif is important for what follows because it provides a Matthean motif that, although independent of Mark, functions similarly to the three motifs examined below: Isaiah's Servant, Davidic king of non-lament psalms, and Davidic lamenter. Additionally, establishing Matthew's characterization of Jesus' opponents as the paradigmatic villains of the OT prophet is the first step in providing a way forward concerning the narrative-critical debate about Matthew's characterization of Jesus' opponents.

---

31. On Matthew's verb δεῖ as a divine necessity, see Hagner, *Matthew 14-28*, 479.
32. Knowles, *Jeremiah in Matthew's Gospel*, 91.

Matthew's characterization of Jesus and Jesus' opponents with the OT prophet and prophets' opponents, respectively, coincides with three further Matthean motifs. I now turn attention to the way that Matthew characterizes Jesus and Jesus' opponents in relation to his Isaianic Servant motif followed by a discussion of his use of non-lament psalms. Finally, as demonstrated in the last section of this chapter, Matthew's motifs of characterizing Jesus and Jesus' opponents as these paradigmatic heroes and villains coalesce and climax at gospel's end with his appropriation of the psalmic lament.

ISAIAH'S SERVANT MOTIF IN CHARACTERIZING JESUS AND HIS OPPONENTS

As Matthew appropriates his OT prophet motif to characterize Jesus and Jesus' opponents, he simultaneously and similarly appropriates Isaiah's Servant motif. Herein, Matthew's characterization of Jesus and Jesus' opponents parallels Mark's narrative, where, as it was established in chapter 2, Mark characterizes Jesus and Jesus' opponents as the Isaianic Servant and the Servant's opponents, respectively. In this section, I focus on exploring Matthew's appropriation of the Servant motif in characterizing Jesus and Jesus' opponents. Specifically, I try to demonstrate that Matthew expands and emphasizes Mark's account by more emphatically characterizing Jesus as Isaiah's Servant and Jesus' opponents as the opponents of Isaiah's Servant.

This objective is more limited than the objectives in chapter 2, where I included in the discussion both an examination of Mark's broader appropriation of the Servant motif and an examination of how Mark merges the two motifs together. It would be redundant to undertake these same examinations in relation to Matthew for two reasons: (1) Mark and Matthew broadly appropriate Isaiah's Servant motif similarly (e.g., towards eschatological and explanatory ends)[33] and (2) both Mark and Matthew

33. Matthew's eschatological interests, for example, surface in Jesus' fulfillment of Isa 42:1-4 as one who will "lead justice to victory" (Matt 12:20c) and in whom "the nations will put their hope" (Matt 12:21). His explanatory interests surface in Matt 8:17, where Jesus' healing is explained in light of the Servant (Isa 54:3), and in Matt 20:28, where Jesus' death as a ransom is explained in light of the Servant's death (Isa 53:10-12; cf. Hagner, *Matthew 1-13*, 335-36; ibid., *Matthew 14-28*, 582-83). This is not to suggest that both authors appropriate the Servant motif identically. The distinctions are examined in the section below that explores Matthew's appropriation of the psalmic lament.

merge the two motifs together, crescendoing their respective gospels with the psalmic lament motif.

Three steps are needed in establishing how Matthew characterizes Jesus and Jesus' opponents in tandem with his Isaianic Servant motif. First, I delineate the Servant motif in Matthew, which lays the groundwork to explore the following two steps: Matthew's characterization of Jesus as Isaiah's Servant and Matthew's characterization of Jesus' opponents as the opponents of Isaiah's Servant.

Delineating Matthew's Isaianic Servant Allusions

There is little debate that Matthew alludes to Isaiah's Servant, primarily because Matthew directly quotes the motif briefly in 8:17 and extensively in 12:18–21.[34] Most interpreters agree that these two so-called fulfillment quotations refer to Isaiah's Servant and thus require no further comment.[35] Beyond these two quotes, there is a general consensus that Matthew further alludes to the Servant motif, but there is less agreement concerning the precise narrative junctures of these allusions. Thus, it is necessary to delineate briefly these allusions in order to frame the discussion that follows.

It is unnecessary to investigate each possible Matthean allusion to the Servant motif since Doug Moo presents a workable sampling of them: Matthew 3:17 (Isa 42:1; cf. Mark 1:11), 17:5[36] (Isa 42:1; cf. Mark 9:7), 20:28 (Isa 53:10–12; cf. Mark 10:45), 26:28 (Isa 53:12; cf. Mark 14:24), 63 (Isa 53:7; cf. Mark 14:61), 67–68 (Isa 50:6; cf. Mark 14:65), 27:12 (Isa 53:7; omitted in Mark); 14 (Isa 53:7; cf. Mark 15:5), and 30 (Isa 50:6; cf. Mark 15:19).[37]

Detecting intertextual allusions often exists on a continuum of certainty. One expects, then, that Moo rejects or overlooks some allusions that other scholars detect in the Matthean text. Examples include

---

34. Matthew's "quoting" of Isaiah is actually quite fluid (Davies and Allison, *Matthew*, 2:322–29, and Luz, *Matthew 8–20*, 191–92).

35. For a recent rejoinder, however, see Huizenga, *New Isaac*, 189–208 (cf. Huizenga, "Incarnation of the Servant," 25–58; and Novakovic, "Matthew's Atomistic Use of Scripture," 147–62).

36. Moo does not discuss Matt 17:5 ("This is my beloved Son, with whom I am well pleased") although it parallels Matt 3:17 and thus is included in the following investigation (cf. Hagner, *Matthew 14–28*, 494).

37. Moo, *Old Testament in the Gospel Passion Narratives*, 79–172.

Of Heroes and Villains

Matthew 4:17 (Isa 42:1), 11:5 (Isa 42:18), 20:19, 26:24 (Isa 52:13—53:12), 27:26 (Isa 50:6), 27:38 (Isa 53:12), and 57–58 (Isa 53:9).[38] Although these possible allusions and echoes are excluded from the examination below, they support the argument of this section—namely, that Matthew appropriates Isaiah's Servant motif to, among other things, characterize Jesus and Jesus' opponents as the Servant and the Servant's opponents, respectively.

Jesus as Isaiah's Servant

Although scholars debate the degree to which Matthew characterizes Jesus as Isaiah's Servant, there is a general consensus, unlike with Mark's gospel (see chapter 2), that Matthew portrays Jesus as the Servant.[39] This consensus primarily revolves around Matthew's lengthy OT quote of Isaiah 42:1–4, wherein Matthew applies the phrase "Behold, my servant" (ἰδοὺ ὁ παῖς μου[40]) to Jesus. It is, thus, unnecessary to argue specifically for a Matthean characterization of Jesus as Isaiah's Servant. For the purposes of this chapter, however, it is necessary to compare Matthew's characterization of Jesus with Mark's gospel in order to demonstrate that Matthew, by expanding Mark's account, depicts Jesus more emphatically as Isaiah's Servant.[41]

Matthew follows Mark closely in seven Isaianic allusions, each of which characterizes Jesus as the Servant: (1) God identifies Jesus as the Servant at the outset of Jesus' ministry (Matt 3:17 [Isa 42:1]; cf. Mark 1:11)[42] and (2) reaffirms the same identification at the Transfiguration (Matt 17:5 [Isa 42:1]; cf. Mark 9:7). (3) As the Servant, Jesus gives his life "as a ransom for others" (Matt 20:28 [Isa 53:10–12]; cf. Mark 10:45) and (4) "pours out his blood for the forgiveness of sins" (Matt 26:28 [Isa

---

38. Cf. Blomberg, "Matthew," 20, 38, 90, 97, 98.

39. See Gerhardsson, "Gottes Sohn als Diener Gottes," 73–106. Contrast with Hooker, "Did the Use of Isaiah 53 to Interpret His Mission Begin with Jesus," and Huizenga, *New Isaac*, 189–208 (cf. ibid., "Incarnation of the Servant," 25–58).

40. "Παῖς can mean 'child,'" Nolland rightly notes, "But since παῖς μου never means 'my child' in the LXX, but always 'my servant,' [then] that is most likely [the case] here" (Nolland, *Gospel Acccording to Matthew*, 492; cf. Acts 3:13, 26; 4:27, 30).

41. A fact well established by others (see Thielman, *Theology of the New Testament*, 96–97).

42. Matt 3:17 is a mixed citation that also echoes Ps 2:7 ("my Son") and Gen 22:2 ("beloved") (Beare, *Matthew*, 101–2).

53:12]; cf. Mark 14:24). (5) After his arrest, Jesus, in line with the Servant, remains silent before the high priest (Matt 26:63 [Isa 53:7]; cf. Mark 14:61). Matthew continues Isaiah's silence motif as (6) Jesus gives "no answer" to the chief priests and elders" (Matt 27:12 [Isa 53:7]; omitted in Mark) and (7) makes "no reply" to Pilate's question about Jesus' guilt (Matt 27:14 [Isa 53:7]; cf. Mark 15:5).

For the purposes of this chapter, it is noteworthy that in these seven allusions Matthew twice emphasizes Mark's characterization of Jesus as the Servant. First, in Matthew 27:12, Matthew adds a third allusion to Mark's two references of Jesus' "silence motif" (Mark 14:61; 15:5): "When [Jesus] was accused by the chief priests and the elders, he gave no answer" (cf. Isa 53:7). Additionally, as Hagner notes, in Matthew 27:14, Matthew further emphasizes Jesus' silence by replacing "οὐδὲν, 'nothing' (Mark 15:5), with πρὸς οὐδὲ ἓν ῥῆμα, 'to not even one charge,' and by the addition of λίαν, 'greatly,' to θαμάζειν, 'was amazed.'"[43]

These emphases are minor in comparison to Matthew's addition of two direct quotations of Isaiah's Servant (Matt 8:17 [Isa 53:4] and 12:15-21 [Isa 42:1-4]). These quotations indicate Matthew's clear interest in emphasizing certain attributes of Jesus as Isaiah's Servant. In Matthew 8:14-17, Matthew suggests that Jesus' healing ministry fulfills what Isaiah predicted through the Servant (Matt 8:17; cf. Isa 53:12), specifically highlighting that Jesus bears people's "infirmities" and their "diseases." Matthew continues his focus on Jesus as the Servant in 12:15-21, emphasizing that God chose Jesus to be the Servant (Matt 12:18a; cf. Isa 42:1a), whom he endows by the Spirit (Matt 12:18b; cf. Isa 42:1b) to carry out certain ministerial activities (Matt 12:18-21; cf. Isa 42:1c-4).

Matthew, then, expands and emphasizes Mark's characterization of Jesus as the Servant, adding numerous character traits to Jesus that extends beyond Mark's portrayal. Both Mark and Matthew portray Jesus as the Servant who dies silently before his accusers (Mark 14:61; 15:5; Matt 26:63; 27:12; 27:14) as a ransom for many (Mark 14:24; Matt 26:28). Matthew expands Mark's account by presenting Jesus also as the Isaianic Servant who heals (Matt 8:14-17), has God's Spirit (Matt 12:18b), does not quarrel (Matt 12:19), looks after the downtrodden (Matt 12:20), and brings justice and hope to the Gentiles (Matt 12:21).

---

43. Hagner, *Matthew 14-28*, 817.

Jesus' Opponents as Those of Isaiah's Servant

Matthew, like Mark, explicitly characterizes Jesus' opponents twice as those of the Servant. In Matthew 26:67–68, those present at Jesus' trial before the Sanhedrin spit (ἐμπτύω) on Jesus' face and repeatedly hit and mock him, while in Matthew 27:30 the soldiers repeat the same deeds. In a similar way, the antagonists in Isaiah 50:6 spit (ἐμπτύω) on the Servant and repeatedly hit and mock him. Although Matthew follows Mark in these characterizations of Jesus' opponents, Matthew, Nolland rightly explains, emphasizes the sinister character of Jesus' opponents in the Sanhedrin more than Mark does: "To further underline the revolting and insulting nature of [this] activity, Mark's 'on him' becomes 'on his face.'"[44] Although spitting on another is humiliating, spitting in another's face, Luz notes, is "an expression of the deepest contempt" (cf. the two uses of ἐμπτύω in LXX Num 12:14 and Deut 25:9).[45] Finally, Matthew omits Mark's "and the guards received [Jesus] with blows" (καὶ οἱ ὑπηρέται ῥαπίσμασιν αὐτὸν ἔβαλλον [Mark 14:65]) to enhance the allusion to LXX Isaiah 50:6 (ῥαπίσματα) by retaining the focus centrally on those administering the "hitting" (οἱ δὲ ἐρράπισαν [Matt 26:68:]).[46]

Matthew's characterization of Jesus' opponents as those of the Servant also implicitly surface in the lengthy quote of Isaiah 42:1–4 in Matthew 12:18–21. Some interpreters argue that this quote is entirely unrelated to Matthew's immediate context, with Nolland suggesting that Matthew's introduction to the quote in 12:15–16 provides for him only an "excuse" to include it.[47] Others, such as Davies and Allison, argue correctly, however, that "the entirety of Mt 12:18–21 serves Matthean themes and interests very well."[48] These interpreters note how Matthew's quote

---

44. Nolland, *Matthew*, 1134. Senior notes that although Matthew subordinates the spitting of the soldiers by changing Mark's indicative (ἐνέπτυον) to a participle (ἐμπτύσαντες), he more specifically emphasizes the totality of the act of spitting by changing Mark's simple dative (αὐτῷ; Mark 15:19) to the prepositional phrase εἰς αὐτόν (cf. Matt 27:27, 29, 30) (*Passion Narrative According to Matthew*, 269).

45. Luz, *Matthew 21-28*, 448. For an explanation of why Matthew omits Mark's "and to cover his face" (Mark 14:65), see Davies and Allison, *Matthew*, 3:535 (cf. Luz, *Matthew 21-28*, 447–48).

46. Davies and Allison, *Matthew*, 3:536 (cf. Luz, *Matthew 21-28*, 448).

47. Nolland, *Matthew*, 492 (*pace* Lindars, *Apologetic*, 145n1; Luz, *Matthew 8-20*, 191; and Strecker, *Weg der Gerichtigkeit*, 82–85).

48. Davies and Allison, *Matthew*, 2:324 (*pace* Beaton, *Isaiah's Christ in Matthew's Gospel*, 151–72; Hagner, *Matthew 1-13*, 337–38; Leske, "Isaiah and Matthew," 154–55;

Matthew's Appropriation of the Psalmic Lament

of Isaiah 42 includes themes that one finds throughout the rest of his gospel. For example, "I will put my Spirit on him" (Matt 12:18b) recalls Jesus' baptism (Matt 3:16) where God's Spirit descends upon Christ, and it foreshadows the immediately subsequent passage where the primary theme is Jesus' work via the Spirit (Matt 12:22–37). Similarly, the concern for the Gentiles in Matthew's Isaianic quote (Matt 12:21) harmonizes well with Matthew's broader interest in them (cf. Matt 28:19).[49]

Pertinent for the discussion at hand, B. Rod Doyle highlights aspects in Matthew's quote of Isaiah 42 that connect it to Jesus' opponents. Specifically, Doyle argues that Matthew quotes Isaiah at this narrative juncture in order to, among other things, contrast Jesus with the Pharisees.[50] Although three of Doyle's arguments are dubious,[51] five are convincing. (1) "I will put my Spirit (πνεῦμά) on him" (Matt 12:18b) contrasts with the Pharisees in the next pericope, who charge Jesus as one who "casts out demons only by Beelzebul the ruler of the demons" (Matt 12:24). This contrast comes sharply into view with the first clause of Jesus' response to the Pharisees: "But if it is by the Spirit of God (ἐν πνεύματι θεοῦ) that I cast out demons" (Matt 12:28). (2) As the Servant, Jesus "will not quarrel (ἐρίσει)" (Matt 12:19a). This most immediately reflects Jesus' refusal to engage the Pharisees in Matthew 12:14–15. More broadly it contrasts with the Pharisees who constantly quarrel over points of interpretation about the Law (Matt 9:11; 12:2, 24, 38; 15:2, etc.). (3) Jesus' voice will not be heard "in the streets (ἐν ταῖς πλατείαις)" (Matt 12:19b). This contrasts with the pharisaical "hypocrites ... [who love] to pray ... on the streets (τῶν πλατειῶν) to be seen by people."[52]

(4) As the Servant, Jesus will not condemn the weak: "A bruised reed he will not break, and a smoldering wick he will not quench" (Matt

---

Menken, *Matthew's Bible*, 51–65; and Neyrey, "Thematic Use of Isaiah 42," 457–73).

49. For a list of other Matthean themes related to Isa 42:1–4 that surface elsewhere in the gospel, see Davies and Allison, *Matthew*, 2:323–24.

50. Doyle, "Concern of the Evangelist: Pharisees in Matthew 12," 17–34.

51. (1) "My Servant (παῖς)" (Matt 12:18a) contrasts with the "wise and learned" Pharisees (Matt 11:25) via a supposed connection with παῖς and νηπίοις; (2) "he will proclaim justice to the nations" (Matt 12:18c), since it is linked to the Spirit (Matt 12:18b), contrasts with the Pharisees who are unable to see Jesus as one presenting and fulfilling justice as the Spirit-filled Son and Servant of God; and (3) "cry out" (Matt 12:19), by carrying the connotation "to bring attention to one's self," contrasts with the Pharisees who seek the attention of others (Matt 6:5, 16; cf. 23:5–7, 25–28) (Ibid., 20–21).

52. Davies and Allison note the same three thematic links between these pericopae (*Matthew*, 2:324).

12:20). This is in contrast to the scribes and Pharisees who "tie up heavy burdens, hard to bear, and lay them on people's shoulders" (Matt 23:4). (5) As the Servant, Jesus will "bring (ἐκβάλῃ) justice to victory" (Matt 12:20c). All occurrences of ἐκβάλλω in Matthew chapter 12, aside from the Isaianic Servant quote, occur in the conflict between Jesus and the Pharisees in Matthew 12:24–37, a controversy initiated by the Pharisees who contend that Jesus "casts out (ἐκβάλλει)" demons by Beelzebub. Jesus sums up the controversy by stating, "The good person out of his good treasure brings forth (ἐκβάλλει) good, and the evil person out of his evil treasure brings forth (ἐκβάλλει) evil" (Matt 12:35). Jesus as a "good person" who "brings forth (ἐκβάλλει) good things," including "justice" (Matt 12:20c), contrasts with the Pharisees as "evil" people who "bring forth (ἐκβάλλει) evil" (Matt 12:35; cf. 9:4).

Matthew, then, quotes Isaiah 42:1–4 in 12:18–21 not only to characterize Jesus but also as a foil to characterize Jesus' opponents. Jesus' opponents are the antitheses to Jesus. Jesus is the Isaianic Servant who possesses God's Spirit, is not quarrelsome, whose voice goes unheard in the streets, who does not condemn the weak, and who brings forth justice. Jesus' opponents, on the other hand, lack God's spirit, quarrel incessantly, hypocritically cry out in the streets for attention, burden the weak, and impede justice.

Summary

Pervasively throughout his gospel, Matthew follows Mark in characterizing Jesus and Jesus' opponents as Isaiah's Servant and as the Servant's opponents, respectively. Matthew, however, expands and emphasizes this Markan motif. This Matthean characterization of Jesus' opponents as the Servant's opponents is the second step in providing a way forward concerning the narrative-critical debate about how best to categorize Matthew's characterization of Jesus' opponents.

Matthew's characterization of Jesus and Jesus' opponents in tandem with the OT prophets and Isaiah's Servant coincides with two further Matthean motifs. I now turn attention to how Matthew characterizes Jesus and Jesus' opponents in relation to his appropriation of certain non-lament psalms. Finally, as demonstrated in the last section of this chapter, Matthew's motifs of characterizing Jesus and Jesus' opponents as these paradigmatic heroes and villains coalesce and climax at gospel's end with his appropriation of the psalmic lament.

NON-LAMENT PSALMS 8, 109, AND 117 IN CHARACTERIZING JESUS AND HIS OPPONENTS

As Matthew appropriates the OT prophet and Isaianic Servant motifs to characterize Jesus and Jesus' opponents—adding his OT prophet motif independent of, and expanding and emphasizing his Servant motif in relation to, Mark—Matthew simultaneously and similarly appropriates Psalms 8, 109, and 117. Examining Matthew's appropriation of these psalms in relation to his characterization of Jesus and Jesus' opponents directs attention in part back to Ahearne-Kroll's contributions, and my advancements of his work, discussed in the previous chapter.

As discussed in chapter 2, Ahearne-Kroll argues that Mark characterizes Jesus in chapters 10–12 as the royal Davidic messiah via the title "Son of David" (Mark 10:47–48; 12:35–40), a quote of Psalm 117 at the "triumphal entry" (Mark 11:9–10), a second quote of Psalm 117 in the story of the wicked tenant farmers (Mark 12:10–11), and a quote of Psalm 109 while Jesus teaches in the temple courts (Mark 14:62). Mark 10–12 parallels Matthew 21–23, quoting the same OT texts and characterizing Jesus with them. This section explores this theme in Matthew and demonstrates that he expands and emphasizes Mark's characterization of Jesus as the OT hero King David.

In chapter 2, I advanced Ahearne-Kroll's work by demonstrating that Mark characterizes Jesus' opponents as those of King David's in Mark 10–12 via references to Psalms 109 and 117. Matthew quotes these same OT texts and characterizes Jesus' opponents with them. This section explores these quotes in Matthew and demonstrates that he expands and emphasizes Mark's characterization of Jesus' opponents with the villains associated with King David.

So, in this section, I first test Ahearne-Kroll's thesis on Matthew's gospel—namely, that Mark characterizes Jesus as the royal Davidic messiah.[53] Second, I test the conclusions from chapter 2 on Matthew's

---

53. Ahearne-Kroll, *Psalms of Lament in Mark's Passion*, 57, 166. Recall that one of Ahearne-Kroll's primary arguments is that Mark downplays the militaristic overtones that accompanied Second Temple Davidic messianic expectations, presenting a redefinition of messiahship with respect to David. It is unnecessary to test this thesis on Matthew's gospel since Matthew follows Mark in depicting a serving and suffering

gospel—namely, that Mark characterizes Jesus' opponents as those of King David's.[54]

Jesus as the OT Davidic Messiah-King: Testing Ahearne-Kroll's Thesis on Matthew

Ahearne-Kroll demonstrates that Mark characterizes Jesus as, among other things, the royal Davidic messiah. I argue in this section that Matthew also characterizes Jesus as the OT Davidic messiah-king by appropriating Psalms 117, 8, and 109.[55] I also argue that Matthew expands and

---

messiah within the same Second Temple worldview that expected a militaristic messiah. Matthew, then, continues Mark's redefinition of messiahship with respect to David. Adding support to this is Matthew's more holistic portrayal of a Davidic messiah who, instead of militaristically initiating his kingship, presents himself as the "therapeutic son of David" (Duling, "Therapeutic Son of David," 392–409; cf. Luz, *Theology of the Gospel of Matthew*, 70–75; ibid, *Matthew 8-20*, 47–49; and Novakovic, *Messiah, The Healer of the Sick*). By "therapeutic," Duling means "healing." Matthew's Jesus, then, is not the expected militaristic messiah of the Second Temple era, but is a healing messiah that loves and helps the downtrodden.

54. Methodologically, this section follows Ahearne-Kroll and the advancements that I make to his work in chapter 2 by focusing on Psalms 109 and 117. Added to this investigation, however, is an examination of Matthew's appropriation of Psalm 8, since he quotes it in the same context as Psalm 117 (cf. Matt 21:1–17; see discussion below). In light of the general scholarly consensus that Matthew characterizes Jesus as the royal Davidic messiah, it is unnecessary, and beyond the scope of this chapter, to explore the following eleven possible allusions suggested by Blomberg's commentary on Matthew in Beale's and Carson's *Commentary on the New Testament Use of the Old Testament* and the NA[27]: (1) Matt 2:11 (Ps 71:10–11, 15): Kings from distant lands buy gifts and tribute to the ruler of Israel; (2) Matt 3:11 (Ps 117:26): "he who is coming after me"; (3) Matt 3:17 (Ps 2:7): "You are my son"; (4) Matt 4:6 (Ps 90:11–12): Satan quotes Psalm 90 at Jesus' temptation; (5) Matt 5:8 (Ps 23:3–5): "pure in heart"; (6) Matt 5:9 (Ps 33:15): "peacemakers"; (7) Matt 7:14 (Ps 15:11): the right path that leads to life; (8) Matt 8:11 (Ps 106:3): "from the east and the west"; (9) Matt 13:35 (Ps 77:2): "I will open my mouth in parables"; (10) Matt 16:18a (Ps 117:22): "rock"; and (11) Matt 17:5b (Ps 2:7): "This is my beloved Son" (excluded from these eleven possible allusions are ten psalmic references that Blomberg notes merely as background information to the particular passage under discussion with no intention to suggest a direct Matthean allusion: Matt 14:1–36; 16:1–4, 26, 27b; 18:6, 10–14; 19:22; 20:28; 23:19, 37). Noteworthy is that six of these eleven references (Matt 2:11; 3:11, 17; 13:35; 16:18a; 17:5b), to the degree that they represent allusions to their respective OT psalmic texts, confirm Matthew's tendency to characterize Jesus as the Davidic psalmist; each one either portrays Jesus reliving an aspect of David's life as depicted in the Psalms or records God addressing Jesus in the same way that he addresses the Davidic psalmist.

55. This is a well-established point in Matthean studies; for an extended discussion

emphasizes this notion by more pervasively weaving this characterization of Jesus through the entirety of his narrative, whereas Mark does not overtly introduce it until just prior to the triumphal entry (Mark 10:46–52); by expanding and emphasizing Mark's references to Psalm 117 in relation to his characterization of Jesus as David; and by presenting Jesus' temple cleansing, in contrast to Mark, as the work of David's son via the appellative "Son of David" and an added quote from Psalm 8:3.

Matthew follows Mark by appropriating Psalms 117 and 109 to characterize Jesus as the psalmic Davidic king.[56] In Matthew 21:9 (cf. Mark 11:9), the crowd quotes Psalm 117:26 ("Blessed is he who comes in the name of the Lord") in reference to Jesus as he enters Jerusalem. This quote follows a Matthean fulfillment citation of Zechariah 9:9 that clarifies Matthew's interest in presenting Jesus as king: "Say to the Daughter of Zion, 'Behold your king is coming to you.'" The crowd introduces their quote of Psalm 117:26 with the appellative "Son of David" (Matt 21:9a). Within Matthew's narrative logic, then, Jesus enters Jerusalem as the long awaited Davidic king of Psalm 117. In Matthew 21:42 (cf. Mark 12:10), Jesus identifies himself as the Davidic "stone" of Psalm 117:22. In Matthew 26:64 (cf. Mark 12:36), Jesus quotes Psalm 109:1 ("The Lord said to my Lord: 'Sit at my right hand'") to clarify his relationship with David as both son and Lord[57] and reconfirms this relationship in Matthew 26:64 with another allusion to Psalm 109:1 in a reply to the high priest's question about Jesus' messianic identity.

Matthew, however, expands and emphasizes Mark's characterization of Jesus as the royal Davidic messiah in at least three ways.[58] First, Matthew weaves this characterization of Jesus through his narrative more pervasively than Mark does. This is indicated by the sheer number of times that Matthew uses the title "Son of David" (nine times: Matt 1:1, 20; 9:27; 12:23; 15:22; 20:30–31; 21:9, 15) in relation to Mark (three times: Mark 10:47–48; 12:35) and by the number of times that

---

on, and a history of research of, Jesus as the Son of David in Matthew, see Novakovic, *Messiah, The Healer of the Sick*, 2–5 (cf. Strauss, *Davidic Messiah in Luke-Acts*, 15–31). The onus of this section is not to pave new ground in establishing Jesus' characterization as David but simply to supply a necessary step in the larger argument of this chapter. For an extended discussion on Matthew's presentation of Jesus as "King," see Ham, *Coming King and the Rejected Shepherd*, 108–14.

56. Keener, *Matthew*, 494–95.

57. Turner, *Matthew*, 540, and Hagner, *Matthew 14–28*, 650–51.

58. Christoph Burger argued a similar point in 1970 within a larger *traditionsgeschichtliche* concern (*Jesus als Davidssohn*, 72–91).

Matthew associates kingship to Jesus and/or David (nine times: Matt 1:6; 2:2; 21:5; 25:34, 40; 27:11, 29, 37, 42) in relation to Mark (six times: Mark 15:2, 9, 12, 18, 26, 32).

Note how Matthew prepares the reader for the blind man's (identified as "Bartimaeus" in Mark) appellative "Son of David" in Matthew 20:30–31 by explicitly stating from the gospel's first verse that Jesus is David's son (Matt 1:1) and by subsequently reiterating it four more times (Matt 1:20; 9:27; 12:23; 15:22). Mark, on the other hand, abruptly introduces this appellative just prior to the passion via Blind Bartimaeus (Mark 10:46–52). Recall from chapter 2 that this abrupt Markan introduction has sparked considerable debate about whether or not Mark characterizes Jesus with David; Matthew, however, dispels all doubt that Jesus is the Son of David by developing and expanding Mark's characterization of Jesus prior to the blind men's declarations.[59]

Second, Matthew emphasizes Mark's characterization of Jesus as the Davidic messiah-king by highlighting Jesus' Davidic sonship in his appropriation of Psalm 117:26 ("Hosanna to the Son of David! Blessed is he who comes in the name of the Lord!") in Matthew 21:9.[60] As Matthew's Jesus enters Jerusalem, he is coronated as king via a quote of Zechariah 9:9 ("behold, your king is coming to you" [Matt 21:5]) and via the crowds who quote Psalm 117:26.[61] Matthew emphasizes Jesus' Davidic sonship by dropping Mark's "Blessed is the coming kingdom of our father David" (Mark 11:10a) and adding "to the Son of David" (Matt 21:9b) to the crowd's exclamation "Hosanna" (Mark 11:9b):

---

59. See Duling, who notes that "it is well known in gospel studies that the Gospel of Matthew goes well beyond the Gospel of Mark in stressing Jesus as the 'Son of David'" ("Matthew's Plurisignificant 'Son of David,'" 99; cf. Kingsbury, "Title 'Son of David' in Matthew's Gospel," 591–602; Gibbs, "Purpose and Pattern in Matthew's Use of the Title 'Son of David,'" 446–62; and Suhl, "Der Davidssohn im Matthäus-Evangelium," 57–81). This is further confirmed below in the examination of Matthew's appropriation of the psalmic lament.

60. Thielman, *Theology of the New Testament*, 93–94.

61. Concerning Jesus' coronation as king, see Hagner, *Matthew 14–28*, 595–97. The crowd is a well-established Matthean character group (Cousland, *Crowds in the Gospel of Matthew*, 50–51). Little needs to be said here about this group since prior to the passion they remain relatively predictable (i.e., "flat"). In general, Matthew portrays the crowd as a group who, although "without faith" in Jesus, is predominantly "well disposed" toward him (Kingsbury, *Matthew as Story*, 23–24). More will be said about the crowds in the next section, where they make a decisive choice at gospel's end to converge with the Jewish leaders in rejecting Jesus. For an extensive discussion on Matthew's crowd, see Cousland, *Crowds in the Gospel of Matthew*.

> Mark 11:9b (quoting Ps 117:26): "Hosanna! Blessed is he who comes in the name of the Lord!"
>
> Matthew 21:9b (quoting Ps 117:26): "Hosanna *to the Son of David*! Blessed is he who comes in the name of the Lord" (italics added).

Matthew's use of the appellative "Son of David" in 21:9b echoes the same appellative that the blind men use in beckoning Jesus in Matthew 20:29–34[62] (and the same appellative used by two other blind men in Matt 9:27), stressing a connection between the two pericopae and emphasizing Jesus' characterization with David.[63]

Third, Matthew further emphasizes Jesus as David's Son in the immediately subsequent scene (Matt 21:12–17) by "focus[ing] on the cleansing of the temple as the work of the Son of David."[64] Matthew indicates that his focus at the temple is on David in 21:15 and 21:16 (both omitted by Mark). In Matthew 21:15, the children at the temple identify Jesus with David by exclaiming "Hosanna to the Son of David." This exclamation parallels the one shouted by the crowds to Jesus in Matthew 21:9 (cf. the blind men's same exclamations in Matt 20:30–31). The children's exclamation echoes not only the crowd's appellative "Son of David" but also implies an echo of the the crowd's accompanying quote of Psalm 117 in Matthew 21:9.[65] Matthew, then, extends Jesus' connection with David from the triumphal entry to the cleansing of the temple.

Matthew continues his emphasis on Jesus' temple cleansing as the work of David in 21:16 via the addition of another psalmic quote. In response to the Jewish leaders who react negatively to the children's appellative "Son of David" in Matthew 21:15, Jesus quotes Davidic Psalm 8:3 in Matthew 21:16: "Out of the mouth of infants and nursing babies you have prepared praise" (Matt 21:16c)—a psalm widely used messianically by early Christians (1 Cor 15:27; Eph 1:22; Phil 3:21; Heb 2:6–9; 1 Pet 3:22). Jesus, then, affirms the children's claim in Matthew 21:15 to his Davidic sonship by quoting this Davidic psalm in Matthew 21:16 in order to justify the praise that the children direct toward Jesus.[66]

---

62. Gundry, *Matthew*, 411.

63. Matthew continues a similar Davidic emphasis by requoting Ps 117:26 in 23:39: "For I tell you, you will not see me again, until you say, 'Blessed is he who comes in the name of the Lord.'"

64. Carson, *Matthew*, 441.

65. Gundry, *Matthew*, 413.

66. Keener, *Matthew*, 502.

This tripartite dialogue between the children, the Jewish leaders, and Jesus occurs within a narrative context that Matthew intentionally keeps connected with the triumphal entry scene. Whereas Mark distances Jesus' temple cleansing from his triumphal entry by placing it a day later (Mark 11:12), Matthew keeps the two scenes narratively and chronologically connected (Matt 21:12). The two scenes are so closely connected that scholars since the 1960s have increasingly regarded the two as a single pericope.[67] This close connection indicates, among other things, that one should read the children's exclamation in Matthew 21:15 ("Hosanna to the Son of David"; omitted in Mark) and Jesus' quote of Psalm 8:3 ("From the lips of children and infants you have ordained praise"; omitted in Mark) within the broader context of Matthew's emphasis on David in the triumphal entry.

Matthew, then, expands and emphasizes Mark's characterization of Jesus as the royal, psalmic, Davidic messiah. Matthew emphasizes Jesus' connection with David in the triumphal entry by adding the appellative "Son of David." He continues this emphasis in the temple scene by including another Davidic psalmic quote and by repeating the appellative "Son of David," an appellative that literarily connects Matthew's temple cleansing with his triumphal entry scene.

Jesus' Opponents as Those of the OT Davidic Messiah-King: Testing the Conclusions of Chapter 2 on Matthew

I demonstrated in chapter 2 that Mark characterizes Jesus' opponents as, among other things, those of King David's in Psalms 109 and 117. I demonstrate in this section that Matthew continues this characterization of Jesus' opponents and that, in the same way that Matthew expands and emphasizes Mark's characterization of Jesus with King David, Matthew also expands and emphasizes Mark's characterization of Jesus' opponents in relation to David's opponents. I argue this by examining how Matthew adds a quote of Psalm 8:3 in 21:16 to Mark's narrative in characterizing Jesus' opponents[68] and by examining how Matthew appropriates Mark's quotations of Psalm 117:22–23 in 21:42 and Psalm 109:1 in 22:44.

---

67. Luz, *Matthew 21–28*, 4.

68. Matthew also adds a second quote of Ps 117:26 in 23:39: "Blessed is he who comes in the name of the Lord" (cf. the crowds in Matt 21:9 who cite the same psalmic text at Jesus' triumphal entry). Jesus places this psalmic quote on the lips of his opponents—those who "kill the prophets" (Matt 23:37)—in the eschaton. It is impossible

Matthew follows Mark by appropriating Psalms 117 and 109 to characterize Jesus' opponents as those of the psalmic Davidic king. In Matthew 21:42, Jesus quotes Psalm 117:22 ("The stone that the builders rejected has become the capstone") in reference to Jesus' opponents. Prior to this quote, Jesus presents a parable about tenants who brutally kill a landowner's son (Matt 21:33–41). Jesus changes metaphors in Matthew 21:42 from the "tenants" who reject Jesus to the "builders" of Psalm 117:22 that reject Jesus. The builders about whom he speaks have a dual identity; they are simultaneously the opponents of the Davidic psalmist in 117:22 and also the opponents of Jesus.

In Matthew 22:44, Matthew again follows Mark by characterizing Jesus' opponents as those of Psalm 109. In clarifying his identity in relation to David, Jesus states that the Davidic king will "put [his] enemies under [his] feet" (Ps 109:1). It is beyond my scope here to address the longstanding discussions concerning the complicated interpretations of this passage.[69] Rather, my focus is on the simple fact that in quoting Psalm 109, Jesus references his opponents as those of David. This is significant, since the primary purpose of the passage centers on Jesus' identity as David's son. In other words, Matthew could have simply omitted Jesus' statement about "enemies" without altering the primary thrust of Jesus' argument.

Matthew expands and emphasizes Mark's characterization of Jesus' opponents as those of the Davidic king in at least three ways. First, Matthew adds a quote of Psalm 8:3 by Jesus in 21:16. As Jesus enters the temple after the triumphal entry, Matthew, following Mark, recounts Jesus' bold cleansing of the temple (Matt 21:12–14; cf. Mark 11:15–17). Matthew, however, adds a segment that includes Jesus' quote of Psalm 8:3. The chief priests and the scribes, after seeing "the wonderful things that [Jesus] did" and after hearing the children acclaim Jesus as "Son of

---

to know whether these opponents speak this psalm in repentant gladness (cf. Matt 21:9) or remorse in the face of judgment (cf. *1 Enoch* 62:5–6, 9–10; see also Hagner, *Matthew 14–28*, 681). In other words, in light of the dubiety of Matthew's characterization of Jesus' opponents via this quote of Ps 117:26, it is excluded from the discussion below. My argument in this section, however, is not affected by either conclusion. If Matthew intends to characterize them negatively, then my argument is supported. If he intends to characterize them positively, then it does not occur in narrative time but in the eschaton; thus, in the meantime, Jesus' opponents remain the paradigmatic OT villains who hideously mock and brutally kill Jesus.

69. For entries into the discussion, see Holladay, *Psalms through Three Thousand Years*, 117–19; Watts, "Psalms in Mark's Gospel," 36–41; Evans, "Praise and Prophecy in the Psalter and in the New Testament," 568; Subramanian, *Synoptic Gospels and the Psalms as Prophecy*, 560–65; and Gourgues, *À la droite de Dieu*.

David" (Matt 21:15–16a), "indignantly" question Jesus about the children's assertions. Jesus responds to them by quoting Psalm 8:3: "From the lips of children and infants you have ordained praise" (Matt 21:16b). Most important for the purposes of my argument at hand is the second part of Psalm 8:3 that Jesus does not quote but distinctly fits this context: "because of your enemies, to silence the foe and the avenger." Thus, in the psalm, God ordains the praise of children in order to silence the psalmist's enemies. In the same way, the praise from the children in Matthew 21:16, aside from explicitly and openly criticizing the religious leaders, implicitly characterizes Jesus' opponents as those of Psalm 8.

Second, Matthew emphasizes the culpability of Jesus' opponents by adding to Mark a caustic conclusion to his quote of Psalm 117:22–23 in Matthew 21:42: "Therefore I tell you that the kingdom of God will be taken away from you [the Jewish leaders; cf. Matt 21:45] and given to a people producing its fruit" (Matt 21:43).[70] Additionally, in the same pericope, Matthew portrays Jesus' opponents more negatively than Mark via the addition of the explanatory clause κακοὺς κακῶς ("evil wretches") in explaining the guilt of the parable's tenants (Matt 21:41).[71]

Third, Matthew emphasizes Mark's characterization of Jesus' opponents as those of the Davidic king by directing Jesus' quote of Psalm 109:1 to Jesus' Pharisaical opponents and by relocating Mark's conclusive statement, "No one dared to ask [Jesus] any more questions" (Mark 12:34). In Mark, Jesus directs his quote of Psalm 109:1 to the crowd gathered in the temple courts (Mark 12:37: "The great throng [ὄχλος] heard him gladly"). Matthew's version retains the temple setting (Matt 21:23) but changes the recipients of the quote to the Pharisees (Matt 22:41: "While the Pharisees were gathered together, Jesus asked them a question").

Additionally, Mark concludes his extended conflict narrative between Jesus and the religious leaders (Mark 11:27—12:34) prior to Jesus' quote of Psalm 109:1 with the following summary statement: "No one dared ask him anymore questions" (Mark 12:34). Matthew presents the same extended conflict narrative between Jesus and the religious leaders (Matt 21:23—22:46) and includes the same summary statement.[72] Matthew, however, moves this summary statement to the end of Jesus' quote of

---

70. France, "Matthew and Jerusalem," 118.

71. Hagner, *Matthew 14–28*, 618; cf. Davies and Allison, *Matthew*, 3:184; Nolland, *Matthew*, 875–76.

72. Matthew inserts the "Parable of the Wedding Banquet" in 22:1–14, representing a further indictment against the religious leaders.

Psalm 109:1, thus including the psalmic quote with his conflict narrative. When Matthew's Jesus, therefore, states that he is the Davidic messiah, whose "enemies" will be placed beneath "[his] feet" (Matt 22:44b, quoting Ps 109:1), he is not speaking *about* his opponents to a large crowd as in Mark. Rather, Matthew's Jesus is speaking *to* his opponents. This Matthean change of Jesus' conversation partner emphasizes the connection between Jesus' quote of Psalm 109:1 and Jesus' opponents.

Summary

The previous two sections establish that Matthew expands and emphasizes Mark's characterization of Jesus and Jesus' opponents as Isaiah's Servant and the Servant's opponents and that Matthew independently mirrors this method of characterization in his appropriation of his rejected-prophet motif. After the triumphal entry, Matthew again follows Mark in appropriating Psalms 109 and 117 (adding a quote from Psalm 8) in the same way, characterizing Jesus and Jesus' opponents as the Davidic king and as the opponents of the Davidic king, respectively. Continuing the trend that started with his Servant and prophet motifs, Matthew expands and emphasizes Mark's characterization of Jesus and Jesus' opponents in relation to these psalms. Matthew's characterization of Jesus' opponents as those of King David's is the third step in providing a way forward concerning the narrative-critical debate about how best to categorize Matthew's characterization of Jesus' opponents—namely, as the paradigmatic OT villains.

Matthew's characterization of Jesus and Jesus' opponents in tandem with the OT prophets, Isaiah's Servant, and the Davidic king coalesces and climaxes with his appropriation of the psalmic lament.

THE PSALMIC LAMENT IN CHARACTERIZING JESUS AND HIS OPPONENTS

As Matthew appropriates the OT prophet and Isaianic Servant motifs and Psalms 8, 109, and 117 to characterize Jesus and Jesus' opponents—adding his OT prophet motif independent of, and expanding and emphasizing his Servant and psalmic motifs in relation to, Mark—Matthew simultaneously appropriates the lament psalms similarly. Examining Matthew's appropriation of the lament psalms in relation to his characterization of

Jesus and Jesus' opponents, as in the previous section, directs attention in part back to Ahearne-Kroll's contributions, and the advancements of his work discussed in the previous chapter.

As discussed in chapter 2, Ahearne-Kroll argues that Mark characterizes Jesus in the passion as, among other things, the psalmic Davidic lamenter. Matthew's passion parallels Mark's passion, evoking these same psalmic texts and referencing the same themes of the Davidic lament. This section explores these texts and themes in Matthew and demonstrates that he expands and emphasizes Mark's characterization of Jesus as the OT Davidic lamenter.

In chapter 2, I advanced Ahearne-Kroll's work in relation to Mark's appropriation of the psalmic lament in two basic ways: (1) by establishing the differences and similarities between Mark's Isaianic Servant and Davidic lamenter motifs and, thus, demonstrating that Mark does not conflate the two motifs indistinguishably together, and (2) by demonstrating that Mark characterizes Jesus' opponents as those of the OT lamenting David. In this section, I establish that Matthew, like Mark, does not collapse his Servant and Davidic lamenter motifs indistinguishably into one, and that Matthew expands and emphasizes Mark's characterization of Jesus' opponents as the villains associated with the lamenting David.

Succinctly, I argue that Matthew follows Mark by distinguishing certain aspects of his Isaianic Servant motif from his lamenting David motif. Additionally, Matthew follows Mark by characterizing Jesus as the Davidic lamenter while simultaneously characterizing Jesus' opponents as those of the lamenting David, climaxing his gospel and coalescing his characterization of Jesus' opponents with this motif. Matthew, however, develops and expands his characterization of Jesus as the lamenter par excellence and simultaneously expands and emphasizes his characterization of Jesus' opponents as those of the psalmic lamenter.

To demonstrate this, first I establish the similarities and differences between Matthew's Servant and lamenter motifs, since scholars tend to conflate them (see chapter 2). Establishing these similarities and distinctions validates an independent investigation into Matthew's lamenter motif. Second, I delineate Matthew's evocations of the psalmic lament. With these evocations established, third, I test Ahearne-Kroll's thesis concerning Jesus as the psalmic lamenter on Matthew's gospel. Similarly, fourth, I test the advancements made to Ahearne-Kroll's thesis in chapter 2 concerning Mark's characterization of Jesus' opponents in relation to the psalmic lament on Matthew's gospel. Finally, I examine some supplementary data that substantiates the argument of this section.

Similarities and Differences

Before exploring how Matthew characterizes Jesus and Jesus' opponents in relation to the psalmic lament, it is first necessary to demonstrate that Matthew does not collapse his Servant and lamenter motifs indistinguishably together. Establishing this is necessary in order to validate independent enquiries into each. This investigation overlaps with the investigation of the differences and similarities between the two motifs in Mark's gospel (chapter 2); thus, the following discussion is truncated and, where appropriate (especially in the first half of this subsection), attention is directed to chapter 2, where the following conclusions overlap with that argument. An independent investigation of this issue in Matthew is needed, because Matthew significantly expands Mark's presentation of Jesus as Isaiah's Servant. I argue that, amid overlapping traits, these two motifs contribute independently to Matthew's narrative.

Matthew follows Mark in appropriating Isaiah's Servant motif to accomplish several things (see discussion in chapter 2). First, he uses it Christologically to identify Jesus as the Servant (Matt 3:17 [Isa 42:5]; 12:18–21 [Isa 42:1–4]; cf. Mark 1:11). Second, he uses it to explain and to predict (within narrative time) Jesus' rejection, suffering, and vicarious death for others (Matt 20:28 [Isa 53:10–12]; 26:28 [Isa 53:12]; cf. Mark 10:45; 14:24). Third, he uses it to explain and to identify Jesus' opponents as those of the Servants' opponents (Matt 26:67 [Isa 50:6]; 27:30 [Isa 50:6]; cf. Mark 10:34; 14:65; 15:19).

Matthew expands Mark's use of the Servant motif via two direct Isaianic quotes (Matt 8:17 [Isa 53:4]; 12:18–21 [Isa 42:1–4]) in order to accomplish additional things (see discussion above): The Matthean Jesus is also the Isaianic Servant who heals (Matt 8:14–17), has God's Spirit (Matt 12:18b), does not quarrel (Matt 12:19), looks after the downtrodden (Matt 12:20), and brings justice and hope to the Gentiles (Matt 12:18; 21).

Matthew follows Mark in also appropriating the psalmic lamenter motif in order to accomplish several things (cf. discussion in chapter 2 and below). First he uses it to identify Jesus as the Davidic lamenter. Second, he uses it to identify Jesus' opponents as the paradigmatic lamenters' opponents. Third, he uses it to paint Jesus in emotional hues, especially in Gethsemane. Finally, he uses the lament psalms to give a praying voice to Jesus.

As in Markan research, the reason that many scholars collapse these two figures indistinguishably together is because of their unmistakable similarities, which one finds both within their respective OT contexts and within Matthew's narrative (see discussion in chapter 2). First, both figures suffer terribly. Isaiah's Servant is mocked, beaten, spit upon, and shamelessly killed. The psalmic lamenter is wantonly degraded by enemies gambling for his clothes and by passerby derisively shaking their heads. Second, both figures face opposition from opponents who inflict physical and psychological pain on their subjects.

Although these figures share unmistakable similarities, they also possess notable differences, which are found both within their respective OT contexts and within Matthew's narrative (see discussion in chapter 2): (1) Isaiah's Servant is not a petitioner, whereas the central role of the lamenter is that of a petitioner who asks God to change his given plight, (2) in relation to his earthly opponents, Isaiah's Servant humbly submits to and embraces suffering (Matt 12:19); in relation to God, the lamenter struggles in prayer to remove it, (3) God is consistently present for Isaiah's Servant, while he is pervasively absent for the lamenter, and (4) Isaiah's Servant perceives that his death is endowed with purpose, that is, he suffers and dies vicariously for others, while the lamenter does not fully understand his suffering.

When Matthew expands Mark's Isaianic Servant motif by adding two direct quotations (Matt 8:17; 12:18–21), Matthew highlights attributes of the motif that are distinct from attributes found in the psalmic lament. In other words, Matthew chooses Isaianic material to add to his gospel for narrative purposes that psalmic lament material could not provide. First, Matthew's added features from Isaiah's Servant are missional: Jesus, as the Servant, heals (Matt 8:14–17; cf. Isa 53:4), ministers to the downtrodden (Matt 12:20; cf. Isa 42:3), and brings justice and hope to the Gentiles (Matt 12:21; cf. Isa 42:4c). The lament psalms do not portray a missional sufferer; rather, they portray a sufferer who desires to avoid suffering (cf. Ps 21:1–2; 41:5–7) and one who questions it (cf. Ps 21:1; 68:15). This portrayal coincides with Matthew's characterization of Jesus as the psalmic lamenter, who in Gethsemane desires to avoid suffering (Matt 26:39: "let this cup pass from me") and at the crucifixion questions it (Matt 27:46: "why have you forsaken me"). Suffering, for the lamenter, is something to stop and not something that serves a missional end.

Second, Matthew's Isaianic Servant is endowed with the Spirit (Matt 12:18b; cf. Isa 42:1b) to accomplish the foregoing missions. Within Matthew's narrative logic, the Spirit is closely connected with God's presence (cf. Matt 3:16; 12:18; 28:19). Thus, Jesus' endowment with the Spirit is tantamount to empowerment by God. The lament psalms do not portray the sufferer as a Spirit-endowed person who basks in God's presence while suffering missionally but as one who desperately seeks God within his suffering because the sufferer perceives God's absence (cf. Ps 21:1b–2; Ps 68:1–3). This portrayal coincides with Matthew's characterization of Jesus as the psalmic lamenter who feels forsaken by God (Matt 27:46).

Matthew, then, is aware of similarities and distinctions between Isaiah's Servant and the psalmic lamenter. Matthew's Jesus takes on attributes of both the Servant and the lamenter, appropriating the similar and distinct contributions of each. In other words, both Matthean motifs function in ways that the other one does not. Therefore, collapsing Isaiah's Servant and the psalmic lamenter motifs indiscriminately together does injustice to Matthew's complex narrative appropriation of each. Furthermore, recognizing this distinction justifies the independent investigation of Matthew's psalmic lament motif in his narrative.

Delineating Matthew's Lament Evocations

Recall from the methodology discussed in chapter 1 that the focus in examining the gospels' lament allusions is placed on simple evocations of the psalmic lament, those intertextual echoes that refer to one, and only one, text. According to Craig Blomberg's commentary on Matthew in Beale's and Carson's *Commentary on the New Testament use of the Old Testament*, the NA^{27}, and Moo's *Old Testament in the Gospel Passion Narratives*, there are twenty possible psalmic lament allusions in Matthew. Five more are added when one includes the Markan allusions relegated to "Supplementary Data" in chapter 2 that Matthew appropriates but Blomberg, Moo, and the NA^{27} overlook. Out of these twenty-five allusions, at least nine are simple evocations: Matthew 7:23 (Ps 6:9); 26:38 (Ps 41/42); 27:34 (Ps 68:22); 27:35 (Ps 21:20), 39–40 (Ps 21:9; two times), 42–43 (Ps 21:9), 46 (Ps 21:1), and 48 (Ps 68:22). Before delineating these nine evocations, the other sixteen that are omitted from the examination proper need to be addressed.

Of Heroes and Villains

Data Omitted

As I stated previously, as with many intertextual inquiries, certainty often exists on a continuum, and detecting them is sometimes as much an art as it is a science. My intention in this section's investigation into the psalmic lament is to determine simple evocations more conservatively than liberally in order to more firmly establish my conclusions. Matthew may have intended any one of the following sixteen texts as an allusion or simple evocation to these referents. Since every one of these sixteen texts support the thesis of this chapter, absolute precision in delineating them is less important. Most are easily excluded because they share lexical parallels with more than one OT passage, no lexical parallels with any specific OT passage, and/or no broader thematic parallels with the proposed referents. A few, however, are simply too difficult to conclude with certainty. The following examines these sixteen texts and provides the reasons they are excluded from the examination proper. I return brief attention to these sixteen texts at the end of this section in order to demonstrate how they support the present argument that Matthew appropriates the psalmic lament to characterize Jesus and Jesus' opponents.

(1) Matthew 8:12 ("weeping and gnashing of teeth" [ὁ κλαυθμὸς καὶ ὁ βρυγμὸς τῶν ὀδόντων]; cf. Matt 13:42, 50; 22:13; 24:52; 25:30) shares lexical parallels with lament Psalm 34:16 (ἔβρυξαν ἐπ' ἐμὲ τοὺς ὀδόντας αὐτῶν). Likewise, however, it shares similar lexical parallels with Job 16:9 (ἔβρυξαν ἐπ' ἐμὲ τοὺς ὀδόντας), Psalm 36:12 (βρύξει ἐπ' αὐτὸν τοὺς ὀδόντας αὐτοῦ), Psalm 111:10 (τοὺς ὀδόντας αὐτοῦ βρύξει), and Lamentations 2:16 (ἔβρυξαν ὀδόντας).[73] With no thematic parallels offered as clues to precise referents, it is apparent that Matthew had in mind broader OT themes rather than one specific citation, thus his "weeping and gnashing of teeth" references do not qualify as simple evocations.

(2) Matthew 8:23–27 (Jesus' calming of the storm) shares possible thematic parallels with lament MT Psalms 3:5 and 4:8 (the ability to sleep untroubled in God's protective power) and lament MT Psalms 35:23; 44:23–24; and 59:4 (God sleeping during moments of disaster and in need of awakening). These same parallels, however, are also found in Leviticus 26:6; Job 11:18–19; Proverbs 3:23–24; and Isaiah 51:9.[74] With no lexical parallels to anchor Matthew's thematic similarities with specific OT texts, Matthew 8:23–27 does not qualify as a simple evocation.

---

73. Blomberg, "Matthew," 30.
74. Ibid., 33.

(3) Matthew 13:41 (καὶ τοὺς ποιοῦντας τὴν ἀνομίαν) shares lexical parallels with lament Psalm 140:9 (καὶ ἀπὸ σκανδάλων τῶν ἐργαζομένων τὴν ἀνομίαν).[75] The same parallels, however, are also found in non-lament Psalm 36:1 (καὶ τοὺς ποιοῦντας τὴν ἀνομίαν)[76] and Zeph 1:3 (והמכשלות את־הרשעים ... אסף אדם).[77] With no broader Matthean thematic parallels offered as clues to precise referents, Matthew 13:41 does not qualify as a simple evocation.

(4) Matthew 23:21 (καὶ ἐν τῷ κατοικοῦντι αὐτόν) shares similar wording with lament Psalm 25:8 (καὶ τόπον σκηνώματος δόξης σου). A stronger lexical parallel, however, is found in non-lament Psalm 134:21 (ὁ κατοικῶν Ιερουσαλημ).[78] In light of the thin lexical connections between Matthew 23:21 and these respective texts and with no broader Matthean thematic parallels offered as clues to precise referents, Matthew 23:21 does not qualify as a simple evocation.

(5) Matthew 23:27 ("for you are like whitewashed tombs [τάφοις]") and (6) Matthew 23:29 ("for you build the tombs [τάφους] of the prophets") share one lexical parallel (τάφους) with lament Psalm 5:10 ("their throat is an open grave [τάφος]").[79] This possible evocation is difficult to determine. It is omitted from the examination proper because it shares only one lexical similarity and the thematic similarity—namely, the concept of comparing wicked people to open graves (Matt 23:27)—is forced. This thematic similarity is forced because Matthew compares the scribes (as a whole) to "whitewashed tombs" and the psalmist compares their "throats" to "open tombs."

(6) Matthew's possible simple evocation of Psalm 30:14 in 26:3–4 is the most challenging to determine. Matthew 26:3–4 (τότε συνήχθησαν οἱ ἀρχιερεῖς ... καὶ συνεβουλεύσαντο) shares two lexical parallels (βουλεύω and συνάγω) and similar thematic trends (a slandered man oppressed on all sides by opponents who plot to kill him) with Psalm 30:14 (ἐν τῷ ἐπισυναχθῆναι αὐτοὺς ἅμα ἐπ' ἐμὲ τοῦ λαβεῖν τὴν ψυχήν μου ἐβουλεύσαντο), which leads many to conclude that Matthew intends a psalmic allusion.[80] Furthermore, Luke's quote of Psalm 30:6 in 23:46 (cf.

---

75. Ibid., 48.

76. Ibid.

77. See Davies and Allison, *Matthew*, 2:430; Nolland, *Matthew*, 560; Schweizer, *Matthew*, 310; Hagner, *Matthew 1–13*, 394; and Carson, *Matthew*, 326.

78. Blomberg, "Matthew," 84.

79. Ibid., 85.

80. Moo, *Old Testament in the Gospel Passion Narratives*, 235; Davies and Allison,

Acts 7:59) indicates that at least one writer contemporary with Matthew was shaped by Psalm 30.

Most convincing, however, is Matthew's redactions of Mark 14:1:

> Mark 14:1: καὶ <u>ἐζήτουν</u> οἱ ἀρχιερεῖς καὶ οἱ γραμματεῖς πῶς αὐτὸν ἐν δόλῳ κρατήσαντες ἀποκτείνωσιν
>
> Matthew 26:3–4: ³ Τότε <u>συνήχθησαν</u> οἱ ἀρχιερεῖς . . . ⁴ καὶ <u>συνεβουλεύσαντο</u> ἵνα τὸν Ἰησοῦν δόλῳ κρατήσωσιν καὶ ἀποκτείνωσιν
>
> Psalm 30:14: ἐν τῷ <u>ἐπισυναχθῆναι</u> αὐτοὺς ἅμα ἐπ' ἐμὲ τοῦ λαβεῖν τὴν ψυχήν μου <u>ἐβοθλεύσαντο</u>

Note that Matthew changes Mark's ἐζήτουν to συνεβουλεύσαντο, which parallels the psalmist's ἐβοθλεύσαντο. This parallel is strengthened in light of the fact that συνεβουλεύσαντο is a Matthean *hapax legomena*. In other words, it is unlikely coincidental that Matthew would depart from Mark and parallel Psalm 30:14 with a *hapax legomena*. Furthermore, it is unlikely coincidental that Matthew's added description of the chief priests and elders (Matt 26:3; συνήχθησαν) would incidentally coincide with the psalmist's ἐπισυναχθῆναι.[81]

Although these thematic similarities and redactions almost certainly confirm a Matthean allusion to Psalm 30:14, it is excluded as a simple evocation due to Matthew's *hapax legomena* δόλῳ that possibly alludes to Psalms 9:28; 34:20; and 51:11; Proverbs 12:20; and/or Jeremiah 5:27.[82] It is impossible to ensure, therefore, that Matthew only had in mind Psalm 30; thus, Matthew 26:3–4 is excluded as a simple evocation.

(7) Matthew 26:21 (καὶ ἐσθιόντων αὐτῶν) shares a lexical parallel (ὁ ἐσθίων ἄρτους μου) and similar thematic trends (a Davidic figure betrayed by a meal companion and close friend into the hands of enemies) with Psalm 40:10.[83] It is Matthew's redaction of Mark, however, that causes speculation concerning an intentional Matthean evocation. Matthew refines Mark's awkward use of the definite article (ὁ ἐσθίων; Mark 14:18)[84] by changing it to a genitive absolute (ἐσθιόντων αὐτῶν). Mark's awkward use of the definite article coupled with the retention of ἐσθίων is a decisive

---

Matthew, 3:439; Carson, *Matthew*, 524.

81. Matthew omitted the psalmist's ἐπι probably to avoid the redundancy with σύν (Nolland, *Matthew*, 1047–48n19).

82. See Hagner, *Matthew 14–28*, 754.

83. Blomberg, "Matthew," 90.

84. Concerning the awkwardness of this phrase, see Marcus, *Mark 8–16*, 950.

Matthew's Appropriation of the Psalmic Lament

clue to his simple evocation of Psalm 40:10 (see chapter 2).[85] Matthew's redaction of Mark away from the psalmist's ὁ ἐσθίων, then, decreases the likelihood of a Matthean evocation of the psalm.[86]

(8) Matthew 26:39 ("not as I will, but as you will [θέλω]") shares the similar idea of submitting to God's will (θέλω) in lament Psalms 39:9[87] ("I desire to do your will [θέλημα], O my God") and 142:10[88] ("Teach me to do your will [θέλημα]") and the psalmist's willing spirit in MT lament Psalm 51:12 ("uphold me with a willing spirit"). The thin linguistic link (Matthew's use of the verb instead of the noun and the widespread use of θέλω/θέλημα [152 times in the LXX alone]) and the possibility of two psalmic references excludes Matthew 26:39 as a simple evocation.

(9) Matthew 26:41 ("The spirit [πνεῦμα] indeed is willing [πρόθυμον]") shares a lexical similarity with MT Psalm 51:14 ("uphold me with a willing spirit [ורוח נדיבה]"). Jesus, who is praying in Gethsemane and who returns to find his disciples sleeping, warns them that "the spirit is willing (πνεῦμα πρόθυμον; cf. MT Ps 51:14: ורוח נדיבה), but the body is weak." This possible evocation is difficult to determine. It is omitted from the examination proper based on a thin linguistic link.

(10) Matthew 26:59–60 ("[they] were seeking false testimony [ψευδομαρτυρίαν] against Jesus . . . many false witnesses [ψευδομαρτυρίαν] came forward") shares lexical and thematic (a Davidic figure surrounded and accused by false witnesses) similarities with Psalm 26:12 ("false witnesses [μάρτυρες ἄδικοι] have risen against me, and they breathe out violence [καὶ ἐψεύσατο ἡ ἀδικία]").[89] This passage, which is difficult to determine, is excluded as a simple evocation because Matthew uses the same term ψευδομαρτυρία in 15:19 and its verb form (ψευδομαρτυρήσεις) in 19:18 without any reference to an OT passage. In these two passages, especially Matthew 15:19, Matthew's Jesus uses ψευδομαρτυρία to explain a parable spoken against the Pharisees. Instead of intending to evoke Psalm 26:12, Matthew's use of the same term in Matthew 26:59–60 may simply parallel Matthew 15:19. In essence, determining Matthew's referent in 26:59–60 is too difficult to ensure a simple evocation.

---

85. Ibid., 950.

86. Nolland, *Matthew*, 1065.

87. There is debate concerning the classification of Psalm 39 (see Craigie, *Psalm 1–50*, 313–14).

88. Blomberg, "Matthew," 93.

89. Ibid. (cf. Davies and Allison, *Matthew*, 3:523).

(11) Matthew 26:63 records Jesus' silence before the high priest, which, Blomberg suggests, "may echo David's [silence] in [Ps 38:10]."[90] This text, however, does not qualify as a simple evocation because it more likely parallels Isaiah 53:7 (see discussion above), there are no broader thematic similarities between Matthew 26:63 and Psalm 38 (e.g., no psalmic opposition that causes the psalmist's silence), and the linguistic similarity rests solely on two dissimilar terms (Matthew's ἐσιώπα and the psalmist's ἐκωφώθην).

(12) Matthew 27:2 records some of the religious leaders "handing over" (παρέδωκαν) Jesus to Pilate, which shares a lexical overlap with Psalms 26:12 (παραδῷς) and 73:19 (παραδῷς) and Isaiah 53:6 (παρέδωκεν). Matthew 27:2 is not a simple evocation because it possibly alludes to more than one OT text.

(13) Matthew 27:23 ("what evil [κακὸν] has he done") shares one lexical parallel with Psalms 37:21 ("Those who repay my good with evil [κακὰ] slander me") and 108:5 ("They repay me evil [κακὰ] for good"). This possible allusion is excluded from the examination proper as a simple evocation because of a thin linguistic connection based on a widely used term (κακός occurs 293 tims in the LXX alone) and on its possible allusion to more than one psalm.

(14) Matthew 27:29 ("they mocked [ἐνέπαιξαν] [Jesus]") shares a lexical similarity with Psalm 21:8 ("all who see me mock [ἐξεμυκτήρισάν] me"; cf. MT Ps 22:8: ילעגו)[91] and shares a broad mocking motif. Although Matthew depends heavily upon Psalm 21 in the subsequent crucifixion scene, the thin linguistic similarity that shares only one dissimilar term excludes Matthew 27:29 as a simple evocation.

(15) Matthew 27:44 (the robbers crucified with Jesus "reviled him [ὠνείδιζον αὐτόν]) shares a lexical parallel with Psalms 41:11 ("my adversaries taunt [ὠνείδισάν] me") and 68:10 ("those who reproach [ὀνειδιζόντων] you have fallen on me"). This reference is omitted from the examination proper because it possibly alludes to more than one psalm.

(16) In Matthew 27:50, Jesus takes his final breath at his death "with a loud cry (φωνὴν)", which shares a lexical parallel with Psalm 30:23 ("you heard the voice [φωνῆς] of my pleas for mercy"). Although Matthew 27:50 shares thematic parallels with Psalm 30 (a suffering man who cries out for help), the linguistic connection depends too much on a

---

90. Blomberg, "Matthew," 93.
91. Cf. NA[27].

popular word that occurs fifty-nine times in the LXX Psalms. It is difficult to ensure, therefore, that Matthew links Jesus' φωνήν specifically with the psalmist's φωνῆς.

Evocation of Psalm 6:9 in Matthew 7:23

Scholars widely agree that Matthew 7:23 evokes Psalm 6:9.[92] The linguistic links between the passages are obvious:

Matthew 7:23: ἀποχωρεῖτε ἀπ' ἐμοῦ οἱ ἐργαζόμενοι τὴν ἀνομίαν

Psalm 6:9: ἀπόστητε ἀπ' ἐμοῦ πάντες οἱ ἐργαζόμενοι τὴν ἀνομίαν

Matthew's entire phrase in 7:23 is almost identical to Psalm 6:9, with two variations notwithstanding: He replaces the psalmist's imperative of ἀφίστημι with the imperative of ἀποχωρέω and adds πάντες.[93] Matthew linguistically follows Psalm 6:9 more closely than he follows the similar phraseology in Job 21:14; 22:17; Psalm 138:19 (ἀπόστητε ἀπ' ἐμοῦ πάντες ἐργάται ἀδικίας [cf. Justin, *1 Apology* 16:11 and *Dialogue* 76:5; *2 Clement* 5:4]), retaining verbatim οἱ ἐργαζόμενοι τὴν ἀνομίαν.[94] Matthew, then, intended his readers to recognize 7:23 as a simple evocation of Psalm 6:9.

Evocation of Psalms 41:6, 12, and 42:5 in Matthew 26:38

In chapter 2, I suggested via Ahearne-Kroll's arguments that Mark 14:34 (περίλυπός ἐστιν ἡ ψυχή μου) is a simple evocation of Psalms 41:6, 12, and 42:5 (τί περίλυπος εἶ ψυχή) based on the lexical, syntactical, and thematic relationship between the texts and based on external data found in 1QH 16:32. Matthew 26:38 copies Mark's evocation of Psalm 41/42 verbatim (περίλυπός ἐστιν ἡ ψυχή μου) within the same syntactical and thematic context (Gethsemane).

It seems, then, that Matthew, like Mark, evokes Psalm 41/42. It is possible, however, that Matthew was unaware of Mark's evocation and unknowingly copied the phrase. I addressed this issue in chapter 1, where I argued that Matthew, indeed, detects Mark's evocation of Psalm 41/42

---

92. Nolland, *Matthew*, 341; Davies and Allison, *Matthew*, 1:718; Luz, *Matthew 1–7*, 380; and Hagner, *Matthew 1–13*, 188.

93. Matthew's rationale for these minor alterations are irrelevant for the following examination. For a discussion, see Davies and Allison, *Matthew*, 1:718.

94. Cf. Davies and Allison, *Matthew*, 1:718.

based on Matthew's use of λυπέω ("I grieve") and περίλυπος ("excessive grief") in relation to Mark's use of the same terms. There is no need to repeat that argument here.

Evocation of Psalm 68:22 in Matthew 27:34

Most commentators argue correctly that Matthew 27:34 represents a simple evocation of Psalm 68:22.[95] Linguistically, Matthew evokes the psalmist at two crucial junctures:

> Matthew 27:34: ἔδωκαν αὐτῷ πιεῖν οἶνον μετὰ χολῆς μεμιγμένον
>
> Psalm 68:22: ἔδωκαν εἰς τὸ βρῶμά μου χολὴν

Thematically, the similar settings between Psalm 68 and Matthew's crucifixion scene are striking—namely, that in both accounts the protagonist undergoes abuse and mocking that include the sarcastic offering of sour wine to drink.

Furthermore, writers contemporary with Matthew evoke Psalm 68:22, revealing a broader Second Temple interest in the psalm. John more explicitly evokes Psalm 68:22 by thrice repeating ὄξος in 19:28-30 while 1QH 12:11 (ולצמאם ישקום חומץ) quotes nearly verbatim MT Psalm 69:21b (ולצמאם ישקוני חמץ). Luke also alludes to Psalm 68:22 in a similar context (Luke 23:36; cf. chapter 4). Additionally, the popular use of Psalm 68 in general by other NT writers to describe Jesus and his ministry increases the possibility that Matthew evoked Psalm 68:22 (Mark 3:21 [Ps 68:9]; Rom 15:3 [Ps 68:10]; John 2:17 [Ps 68:10]; Rom 11:9 [Ps 68:23]; and Acts 1:20 [Ps 68:27]).

Most convincing, however, is Matthew's redactions of Mark 15:23:

> Mark 15:23: καὶ ἐδίδουν αὐτῷ ἐσμυρνισμένον οἶνον· ὃς δὲ οὐκ ἔλαβεν
>
> Matthew 27:34 ἔδωκαν αὐτῷ πιεῖν οἶνον μετὰ χολῆς μεμιγμένον
>
> Psalm 68:22: ἔδωκαν εἰς τὸ βρῶμά μου χολὴν

Note that Matthew changes Mark's imperfect ἐδίδουν to the aorist ἔδωκαν in order to parallel the psalmist's use of ἔδωκαν. Furthermore, Matthew adds χολῆς, a Matthean *hapax legomena*, to ensure an evocation of Psalm

---

95. Hagner, *Matthew 1-13*, 834-35; Schweizer, *Matthew*, 511; Nolland, *Matthew*, 1191; Carson, *Matthew*, 575; and Davies and Allison, *Matthew*, 3:612-13.

Matthew's Appropriation of the Psalmic Lament

68:22. These redactions indicate that Matthew explicitly molds Mark's text to echo Psalm 68:22 in his own narrative.

Evocation of Psalm 21 in Matthew 27:35, 39–40, 42–43, 46

As most scholars agree,[96] Matthew follows Mark in presenting a sustained explication of Psalm 21 at Jesus' crucifixion and death by referencing 21:1, 8–9, and 19. It is unnecessary to discuss these evocations at length, since the same arguments given by Ahearne-Kroll (mentioned in chapter 2 above) in relation to Mark also apply to Matthew. In essence, each Matthean passage reflects significant linguistic parallels with these respective psalmic referents:

> Psalm 21:19: διεμερίσαντο τὰ ἱμάτιά ... ἱματισμόν ... ἔβαλον κλῆρον
>
> Matthew 27:35: διεμερίσαντο τὰ ἱμάτιά ... βάλλοντες κλῆρον
>
> Psalm 21:8–9: ἐκίνησαν κεφαλήν ... σωσάτω αὐτόν
>
> Matthew 27:39–40: κινοῦντες τὰς κεφαλὰς αὐτῶν ... σῶσον σεαυτόν
>
> MT Psalm 22:1: אלי אלי למה עזבתני
>
> Matthew 27:46: ηλι ηλι λεμα σαβαχθανι

Furthermore, these texts thematically parallel the Psalm 21 psalmist, who undergoes suffering at the hands of his enemies, and Psalm 21 as a whole was popular during the Second Temple era (see chapter 2).

Matthew, however, evokes Psalm 21 once more than Mark does (Matt 27:42–43; Ps 21:9), clarifying Mark's less-certain allusion to the same psalm (Mark 15:30–31; see "Supplementary Data" in chapter 2):

> Matthew 27:42–43: ἄλλους <u>ἔσωσεν</u> ἑαυτὸν οὐ δύναται <u>σῶσαι</u> ... πέποιθεν ἐπὶ τὸν θεόν <u>ῥυσάσθω</u> ... <u>θέλει</u> αὐτόν εἶπεν
>
> Psalm 21:9: ἤλπισεν ἐπι κύριον <u>ῥυσάσθω</u> αὐτόν <u>σωσάτω</u> αὐτόν ὅτι <u>θέλει</u> αὐτόν
>
> Mark 15:30–31: <u>σῶσον</u> σεαυτὸν ἄλλους <u>ἔσωσεν</u> ἑαυτὸν οὐ δύναται <u>σῶσαι</u>

---

96. Blomberg, "Matthew," 98; Hagner, *Matthew 14–28*, 835–44; Davies and Allison, *Matthew*, 3:614–25; Nolland, *Matthew*, 1192–1207; and Carson, *Matthew*, 576–79.

Note that while Mark 15:30–31 only parallels Psalm 21:9 via variations of σῴζω, Matthew retains these parallels and adds ῥυσάσθω and θέλει, ensuring an evocation.

Evocation of Psalm 68:22 in Matthew 27:48

Although there are only two lexical similarities between Psalm 68:22 ("they gave me sour wine [ὄξος] to drink [ἐπότισάν]") and Matthew 27:48 ([a bystander] filled [the sponge] with sour wine [ὄξους] . . . and gave it to [Jesus] to drink [ἐπότιζεν]"), Ahearne-Kroll's arguments mentioned in chapter 2 for a Markan evocation of Psalm 68 can equally be applied to Matthew:[97] (1) the two texts share similar settings, (2) other Second Temple writers evoke Psalm 68:22 (John 19:28–30; 1QH 12:11; Luke 23:36), and (3) the use of Psalm 68 in general was popular among other NT writers to describe Jesus and his ministry (Mark 3:21 [Ps 68:9]; Rom 15:3 [Ps 68:10]; John 2:17 [Ps 68:10]; Rom 11:9 [Ps 68:23]; and Acts 1:20 [Ps 68:27]). Increasing the likelihood that Matthew evokes Psalm 68:22 in Matthew 27:48 is his evocation of the same psalmic text in Matthew 27:34 (see discussion above). Matthew's clear evocation of Psalm 68:22 just prior to Jesus' crucifixion suggests that Matthew detects Mark's evocation of the same psalm just subsequent to Jesus' crucifixion.

Summary

I regard the following passages as non-simple evocations—intertextual allusions that refer to two or more texts—and are excluded from the examination below: Matthew 8:12; 8:23–27; 13:41; 23:21, 27, 29, 41; 26:3–4, 21, 39, 41, 59–60, 63; 27:2, 23, 29, 44, 50. These possible allusions, however, are explored as supplementary evidence below and support the argument of this chapter. The following eight passages are regarded as simple evocations—intertextual allusions that refer to one and only one text: Matthew 7:23; 26:38; 27:34, 35, 39, 43, 46, 48. These eight passages are the focus of the following exploration of Matthew's characterization of Jesus and Jesus' opponents with the psalmic lamenter and the lamenter's opponents, respectively.

---

97. Ahearne-Kroll, *Psalms of Lament in Mark's Passion*, 74–77. Cf. Hashimoto, "Function of the Old Testament Quotations," 295.

Jesus as the Psalmic Lamenter Par Excellence: Testing Ahearne-Kroll's Thesis on Matthew

Ahearne-Kroll demonstrates that Mark characterizes Jesus as, among other things, the psalmic lamenter par excellence. In this section, I demonstrate that Matthew follows Mark in this characterization of Jesus. I further demonstrate that Matthew expands and emphasizes Mark's characterization of Jesus as the psalmic lamenter by adding another psalmic lament quotation in the Sermon on the Mount and in his redactions of Mark's Gethsemane and crucifixion accounts.

Matthew follows Mark in presenting Jesus as a lamenter in Gethsemane (Matt 26:36–46). In Matthew's Gethsemane account, Jesus, a distraught petitioner (Matt 26:38; cf. Mark 14:34) who is surrounded by opposition (Matt 26:45; cf. Mark 14:41), prays to God in order to bring about change for his plight (Matt 26:39, 42, 44; cf. Mark 14:35, 39). Aside from these traits that parallel those of OT lamenters (recall the definition of the lament established in chapter 1), Jesus also evokes psalmic lament 41/42 via his threefold prayer refrain (Matt 26:39, 42, 44; cf. Mark 14:35, 39 [Ps 41:6, 12; 42:5]).

Matthew also follows Mark by characterizing Jesus as a psalmic lamenter at the crucifixion. Jesus is surrounded by opponents (Matt 27:11–44; cf. Mark 15:1–32) that Matthew and Mark extensively parallel with those of Psalm 21 (see below). Additionally, Jesus prays to God in the words of the Psalm 21 lamenter: "My God, my God, why have you forsaken me?" (Matt 27:46; cf. Mark 15:34).

Matthew, however, expands and emphasizes Mark's motif of characterizing Jesus as the psalmic lamenter in at least three ways. First, prior to the passion, Matthew adds an evocation of Psalm 6:9 in 7:23. Near the end of his Sermon on the Mount, Jesus explains the eschatological outcome of false prophets who "bear bad fruit" because they stem from "bad tree[s]" (Matt 7:15–22). In rendering his final judgment, Jesus evokes Psalm 6:9 in Matthew 7:23: "Depart from me, you workers of lawlessness." In this first Matthean evocation of the psalmic lament, Matthew characterizes Jesus as the Davidic lamenter but not as the lamenter who petitions God to change his plight. Such a petition is unnecessary within the eschatological context of Jesus' evocation[98]; for, in "that day" (Matt 7:22) Jesus no longer represents the ridiculed lamenter but he represents

---

98. The future tense ἐροῦσιν and ὁμολογήσω in Matt 7:21 and 7:22, respectively, clearly indicate Matthew's eschatological setting.

the vindicated lamenter (Matt 7:23).⁹⁹ This characterization of Jesus as a vindicated lamenter parallels the precise context of Psalm 6:9:

> Away from me all you who do evil, for the Lord has heard my weeping. The Lord has heard my cry for mercy; the Lord accepts my prayer. All my enemies will be ashamed and dismayed; they will turn back in sudden disgrace.

Matthew, then, presents Jesus as the psalmic lamenter in 7:23, but, since the setting of the pericope is the eschaton, Jesus is the vindicated lamenter and not the earthly lamenter that one finds in Gethsemane and at the crucifixion.

Second, Matthew expands Mark's Gethsemane account precisely in tandem with the threefold prayer refrain of Psalm 41/42 (41:6, 12; 42:5). The following comparison clarifies this expansion:
Mark:

- Jesus evokes Psalm 41/42 in Mark 14:34 ("My soul is very sorrowful, even to death").

- Recounts Jesus' prayer in Mark 14:36 ("remove this cup from me").

- States that Jesus prayed "the same thing" in Mark 14:39 (without actually rewriting the prayer).

- Insinuates a third prayer in Mark 14:41 by noting Jesus' return a "third time."

Matthew:

- Retains Mark's evocation of Psalm 41/42 in Matthew 26:38 ("My soul is very sorrowful, even to death").

- Retains the Markan Jesus' first prayer in Matthew 26:39 ("let this cup pass from me").

- Expands Mark by recording Jesus' second prayer in Matthew 26:42 ("My Father, if this cannot pass unless I drink it").¹⁰⁰

- Expands Mark by clarifying what Mark leaves obscure—namely, that Jesus' third trip away from the disciples included a third prayer

---

99. Cf. Carson, *Matthew*, 193. Recall from chapter 1 that laments almost always contain a "turn-to-praise" that often predicts vindication from enemies.

100. It is additionally possible that Matthew intensifies Jesus' second prayer (Matt 26:39) relative to his first one (Matt 26:42) by adding οὐ to δύναται and the demonstrative τοῦτο to ποτήριον (Senior, *Passion of Jesus in the Gospel of Matthew*, 112).

that parallels the first two (Matt 26:44: "[Jesus] went away and prayed for the third time, saying the same words again").[101]

Matthew also emphasizes Jesus' grief in Gethsemane more than Mark does.[102] This is indicated by Matthew's replacement of Mark's ἐκθαμβεῖσθαι ("distressed"; Mark 14:33) with λυπεῖσθαι ("grieve"; Matt 26:37).[103] The definitions of these terms presented in BDAG indicate the lexical distinctions between the two: ἐκθαμβέω carries the connotations of distress as it relates to being overwhelmed, amazed, and/or alarmed, while λυπέω carries the connotations of distress as it relates to sadness, sorrow, and grief.[104] These distinctions are confirmed in Mark's three other uses of ἐκθαμβέω: The crowd is "amazed" (ἐξεθαμβήθησαν; Mark 9:15) when they see Jesus; Mary Magdalene and Mary, the mother of James, are "alarmed" (ἐξεθαμβήθησαν; Mark 16:5) when they see celestial beings inside of Jesus' empty tomb; and, in response to these two women, one of the celestial beings encourages them not to be "alarmed" (ἐκθαμβεῖσθε; Mark 16:5). Mark, then, never uses the term ἐκθαμβέω to imply grief or sadness. This is confirmed further by noting Mark's two uses of λυπέω to describe the grief/sadness of the "rich young man" over his wealth (Mark 10:22) and the grief/sadness of the disciples over Jesus' betrayal (Mark 14:19). Mark, then, uses these two terms distinctly to highlight different aspects of particular characters.

When Matthew, then, replaces Mark's ἐκθαμβέω with λυπέω in Matthew 26:37, he subtly emphasizes Jesus' grief in Gethsemane. This observation is strengthened in light of Matthew's replacement of Mark's καί with τότε, binding Jesus' allusion to Psalm 41/42 in Matthew 26:38 with Matthew's statement about Jesus' sorrow in Matthew 26:37:[105]

---

101. Beare, providing no evidence, suggests that Jesus' third prayer is one for God's will to be done and not one of petition for deliverance (*Matthew*, 515). It is more likely that Jesus prays the "same thing" (Matt 26:44c) that he prays in Matt 26:39 and 42 in its entirety.

102. Brown, *Death of the Messiah*, 1:28–29, suggests just the opposite but does not provide supporting evidence.

103. Beare, citing only the NEB for support, suggests that Matthew's replacement of ἐκθαμβέω with λυπέω makes Mark's depiction of Jesus' grief milder (*Matthew*, 514). Ἐκθαμβέω conveys stronger emotion, but this is not tantamount to stronger grief (cf. Senior, *Passion Narrative According to Matthew*, 103–4).

104. BDAG, 303 and 604, respectively.

105. Senior, *Passion Narrative According to Matthew*, 104.

> Matthew 26:37–38: "[Jesus] began to be sorrowful and troubled. Then [τότε] he said to them..."
>
> Mark 14:33–34: "[Jesus] began to be greatly distressed and troubled. And [καί] he said to them..."

This coincides well with Matthew's replacement of Mark's use of the indicative παραλαμβάνει with the nominative participle παραλαβών in Matthew (cf. Mark's use of the indicative παραλαμβάνει [Mark 14:33]) that, as Gundry recognizes, "allows the emphasis to fall on Jesus' sorrow and distress":[106]

> Mark 14:33: "And he took [παραλαμβάνει] with him Peter and James and John, and began to be greatly distressed and troubled."
>
> Matthew 26:37: "And taking [παραλαβών] with him Peter and the two sons of Zebedee, he began to be sorrowful and troubled."

This further coincides with Matthew's general tendency to highlight the grief of certain characters. Note, for example, Matthew's addition of σφόδρα ("deeply") to Mark's λυπεῖσθαι ("grieved") in describing the disciples' grief over Jesus' betrayal (Matt 26:22; cf. Mark 14:19), and note also Matthew's description of the servants "deeply grieving" (ἐλυπήθησαν σφόδρα) in the parable of the Unmerciful Servant (account omitted by Mark) (cf. Matt 14:9; 17:23; 19:22; 26:22). Finally, Matthew's emphasis on Jesus' sorrow in Gethsemane is emphasized in light of the fact that Matthew tends to eliminate and tone down the Markan Jesus' expressions of emotion (Matt 15:30 [cf. Mark 7:34]; 16:2 [cf. Mark 8:12]; 13:58 [cf. Mark 6:6]; 19:15 [cf. Mark 10:16]; 19:22 [cf. Mark 10:21]).[107]

Third, Matthew expands and emphasizes Mark's characterization of Jesus as the psalmic lamenter par excellence in the crucifixion. Recall from chapter 1 that in his crucifixion account, Matthew retains Mark's evocations of Psalms 21:1 (Mark 15:34; Matt 27:46), 19 (Mark 15:24; Matt 27:35), 8 (Mark 15:29; Matt 27:39), and 68:22 (Mark 15:36; Matt 27:48). Matthew expands these by adding evocations of Psalm 21:9 in Matthew 27:43 and Psalm 68:22 in Matthew 27:34, revealing Matthew's interest in setting Jesus' crucifixion more squarely within the psalmic lament tradition and his increased interest in presenting Jesus as the psalmic lamenter par excellence.

---

106. Gundry, *Matthew*, 532.
107. Cf. Beare, *Matthew*, 512.

Jesus' Opponents as Those of the Psalmic Lamenter's: Testing the Conclusions of Chapter 2 on Matthew

Chapter 2 demonstrated that Mark characterizes Jesus' opponents as, among other things, those of the psalmic lamenter. Likewise, in this section, I demonstrate that Matthew characterizes Jesus' opponents similarly. Additionally, I argue that Matthew expands and emphasizes this notion via an evocation of Psalm 6:9 in 7:23 and by adding two evocations at Jesus' crucifixion.

Matthew follows Mark in characterizing Jesus' opponents as those of the psalmic lamenter's opponents in his Gethsemane account. As demonstrated in the previous section, Matthew's spotlight in Gethsemane is squarely on Jesus as the lamenter who imbibes the attributes of the psalmist of Psalm 41/42. Matthew, however, also portrays Jesus' opponents in tandem with the psalmic lamenter's opponents. As Jesus' lament draws to an end, Matthew transitions the reader in 26:45–49 to Jesus' arrest, a crucial turn of narrative events in relation to Matthew's portrayal of Jesus' opponents.[108] Matthew makes clear the significance of this turn of events at four critical moments prior to 26:45–49 (expanding Mark's three accounts in this regard), where four times Jesus and/or Matthew predicts Jesus' death (Matt 16:21; 17:22–23; 20:17–19; 26:2). At three of these junctures, they disclose the identity of those who will kill Jesus (Matt 16:21; 17:22; 20:17: chief priests, scribes, and "men") and, at the final three junctures, Jesus stresses his "betrayal" (παραδίδωμι) into the hands of the opponents (Matt 17:22–23; 20:17–19; 26:2).

These predictions are finally fulfilled at the transition between Jesus' lament in Gethsemane and his arrest in Matthew 26:45–49. In Matthew 26:45, Jesus is "betrayed [παραδίδοται] into the hands of sinners [τῶν ἁμαρτωλῶν]." These sinners are identified in Matthew 26:47–49 as the crowds, the chief priests, and the elders of the people. When Matthew 26:45–49 is read within its immediate Gethsemane context and within Matthew's use of the lament psalms in the broader context of his passion, it becomes clear that Matthew intends his reader to understand these opponents in tandem with the psalmic lamenters' opponents. Brief attention is now turned to demonstrating this.[109]

---

108. Note that Matthew keeps Jesus' arrest closely connected with his Gethsemane scene: Καὶ ἔτι αὐτοῦ λαλοῦντος ("And while he was still speaking"; Matt 26:47).

109. This argument closely resembles the one about Mark's Gethsemane scene in chapter 2 above.

Of Heroes and Villains

Matthew's reader, who understands that he presents Jesus as a psalmic lamenter in Gethsemane and who was familiar with the pervasive role that opponents play in the psalmic laments,[110] would naturally see a parallel between Jesus, who is praying in Gethsemane as a lamenter, and his opponents who appear at the end of his lament (Matt 26:45). In other words, if Jesus, a lamenter (Matt 26:38–44), experiences opposition and betrayal by sinners (ἁμαρτωλῶν; Matt 26:45) in a passage where he evokes a psalmic lament (Matt 26:38), a genre in which protagonists constantly face hostile opponents, it is quite reasonable to conclude that Matthew intentionally portrays the crowds, the chief priests, and the elders of the people (Matt 26:47–49) in tandem with those of the psalmic lamenter.

Strengthening this argument is the fact that the plural form ἁμαρτωλῶν appears in the LXX almost exclusively in the Psalms (twenty-two times; the only other occurrences are in Num 17:3; 32:14; Amos 9:8; Isa 14:5). This increases the likelihood that Matthew's readers, who are already thinking of Jesus as the psalmic lamenter, would have thought of the "sinners" in Matthew 26:45 within a psalmic matrix. Also strengthening this argument is Matthew's emphasis on Jesus' arrest (and accompanying death) as fulfillment of Scriptures (Matt 26:54, 56; cf. Mark 14:49). This argument is still further strengthened when one examines how Matthew continues to evoke the lament at Jesus' crucifixion.

Matthew also follows Mark in characterizing Jesus' opponents as those of the lamenter's opponents via evocations from Psalms 21 and 68 in Matthew 27:32–48. In Matthew 27:35, the soldiers cast lots for Jesus' clothes in the same way that the lamenter's opponents do in Psalm 21:19. In Matthew 27:39, the passerby derisively shake their heads at Jesus just as the lamenter's opponents do in Psalm 21:8–9. After crying out to God as the lamenter par excellence in Matt 27:46 via a quote of Psalm 21:1, an unnamed man, echoing the soldiers' offer of wine in Matthew 27:34, offers Jesus wine vinegar to drink (Matt 27:48) in a way similar to the lamenter's opponents in Psalm 68:22 who mockingly offer the lamenter the same drink.

Matthew, however, expands and emphasizes Mark's characterization of Jesus' opponents as those of the psalmic lamenter in at least three ways. First, Matthew adds to Mark a psalmic quote in 7:23 where Jesus identifies certain "false prophets" as the "workers of lawlessness" of Psalm 6:9. In Psalm 6:9, the vindicated lamenter declares his triumph over his

---

110. Dhanaraj, *Theological Significance of the Motif of Enemies*.

opponents. Similarly, in Matthew 7:23, the eschatologically vindicated Jesus declares his triumph over his opponents. Although Jesus leaves the specific identity of these "false prophets" unstated,[111] it clear that he views them in tandem with the opponents of Psalm 6.

Matthew, second, adds an evocation of Psalm 68:22 in 27:34 where soldiers offer Jesus "wine to drink, mixed with gall." In the same way that the lamenter's opponents "scorn," "disgrace," and "shame" the lamenter—offering him no "sympathy" and no "comfort" (Ps 68:21)—by giving him gall and vinegar to eat and drink (Ps 68:22), Jesus' opponents do the same thing by offering him an unpalatable drink.[112] Mark similarly mentions the offering of Jesus wine at the outset of Jesus' crucifixion, but recall from above that Matthew intentionally aligns the scene with Psalm 68 by changing Mark's imperfect ἐδίδουν to the aorist ἔδωκαν and by adding χολῆς (cf. Ps 68:22: ἔδωκαν ... χολὴν). Matthew, then, intentionally expands Mark's narrative in order to portray the soldiers more specifically as the opponents of the psalmic lamenter.

Third, Matthew adds an evocation of Psalm 21:9 in 27:43 where the chief priests, scribes, and elders (note Matthew's addition of the "elders") mockingly say to Jesus, "He trusts in God; let God deliver him now." In the same way, the lamenter's opponents, who the psalmist depicts as "bulls," "roaring lions," "dogs," and "wild oxen," sarcastically deride the lamenter of Psalm 21. Mark similarly mentions the mockery of these Jewish leaders, but recall from above that Matthew intentionally parallels this account with Psalm 21:9 by adding ῥυσάσθω and θέλει (cf. Ps 21:9: ῥυσάσθω ... θέλει).

---

111. Suggestions concerning their identity include Pharisees (Hill, "False, Prophets and Charismatics" 343–48; Lagrange, *L'Évangile selon Saint Matthieu*, 152), Essenes (Daniel, "'Faux prophètes,'" 45–79), Zealots (Cothenet, "Les prophètes chrétiens dans L'Évangile selon saint Matthieu" 281–308), antinomians (Turner, *Matthew*, 217–18), and those in general who appear on the surface to be something they are not (Hagner, *Matthew 1–13*, 183).

112. Based on *b. Sanh.* 43a, where wine mixed with gall is used as a sedative to ease a crucified victim's pain, and based on Prov 31:6, where wine is used to ease one's pain, the soldiers' act of giving Jesus "wine mixed with gall" to drink might be an act of compassion (*pace* Blomberg, *Matthew*, 416). It is more likely, however, in light of the soldiers, who in the immediate context barbarically beat Jesus (Matt 27:27–31), and in light of the context of Psalm 68, where the psalmist's opponents ridicule him incessantly, that Matthew intends the soldiers' act in 27:34 as one of mockery (*pace* Turner, *Matthew*, 660; Nolland, *Matthew*, 1190–91; Luz, *Matthew 21–28*, 530; Davies and Allison, *Matthew*, 3:612–13; Hagner, *Matthew 14–28*, 834–35; Carson, *Matthew*, 575; cf. discussion in chapter 2).

Matthew again expands Mark's narrative in order to portray the Jewish leaders more specifically as the opponents of the psalmic lamenter.

Supplementary Data

Recall from the previous discussion that there are many possible echoes of the lament psalms in Matthew that do not meet the criteria spelled out in chapter 1 as a simple evocation. Although these echoes are not examined in the discussion above, it is noteworthy to mention that they support the foregoing argument that Matthew characterizes Jesus and Jesus' opponents as the psalmic lamenter and the psalmic lamenter's opponents, respectively. In all but two (Matthew's "weeping and gnashing" motif[113] and Matt 23:21 [cf. MT Pss 26:8; 135:21]) of the following possible echoes, Matthew focuses on characterizing Jesus (three times) and especially his opponents (thirteen times) in tandem with the psalmic lament. Furthermore, these possible echoes further confirm Matthew's trend to expand and emphasize Mark's motif of characterizing Jesus and Jesus' opponents as the lamenter and the opponents of the lamenter, respectively. In other words, to the degree that any one or more of these references echo the psalmic lament is to the same degree that it substantiates the preceding argument.

Recall from the discussion above that, methodologically, these possible echoes are chosen from the NA²⁷, Craig Blomberg's commentary on Matthew in Beale's and Carson's *Commentary on the New Testament Use of the Old Testament*, and by examining how Matthew appropriates all the possible Markan echoes of the psalmic lament discussed in the "Supplementary Data" of chapter 2.

Supplementary Data Used to Characterize Jesus' Opponents

- Matthew 13:41 (omitted by Mark): Jesus, in explaining what the kingdom of heaven is like, states that in the eschaton the angels will weed out "everything that causes sin (σκάνδαλα) and all who do evil (τοὺς ποιοῦντας τὴν ἀνομίαν)" (cf. Ps 140:9b: καὶ ἀπὸ σκανδάλων τῶν ἐργαζομένων τὴν ἀνομίαν; see also Ps 139:6: σκάνδαλον).

---

113. Matt 8:12; 13:42, 50; 22:13; 24:51; 25:30. Other OT passages that contain this motif include Job 16:9; 37:12; 112:10; and Lam 2:16. One could, however, argue that these passages characterize Jesus' opponents at the judgment (cf. Matt 7:23).

Matthew's Appropriation of the Psalmic Lament

- Matthew 23:27, 29 (two times) (omitted by Mark): Jesus compares the scribes and Pharisees to open tombs (τοὺς τάφους) (cf. Ps 5:10: τάφος).

- Matthew 26:3–4a (par. Mark 14:1: Matthew adds ἐβουλεύσαντο to Mark): The chief priests and the elders of the people "gather together" (συνήχθησαν) in order to "plot" (συνεβουλεύσαντο) Jesus' arrest (Ps 30:14: ἐπισυναχθῆναι . . . ἐβουλεύσαντο).

- Matthew 26:4 (par. Mark 14:1) The chief priests and the elders of the people plot to kill Jesus by "stealth" (ἐν δόλῳ) (cf. Ps 9:28: δόλου).

- Matthew 26:21 (par. Mark 14:18): Jesus identifies Judas as his betrayer "while [Jesus and his disciples were] eating" (ἐσθιόντων αὐτῶν) (cf. Ps 40:10: ὁ ἐσθίων).

- Matthew 26:59 (par. Mark 14:55): "The chief priests and the whole Sanhedrin were seeking (ἐζήτουν) for evidence against Jesus so that they could put him to death (θανατώσωσιν αὐτόν)" (cf. Ps 36:32: ζητεῖ τοῦ θανατῶσαι αὐτόν).

- Matthew 26:59–60 (par. Mark 14:55–56; Matthew adds a second ψευδομαρτυρίαν): The chief priests and the Sanhedrin seek "false witnesses" (ψευδομαρτυρίαν [2x]) against Jesus in order to put him to death (cf. Ps 26:12: μάρτυρες . . . ἐψεύσατο).

- Matthew 26:63 (par. Mark 14:61b): The high priest demands that Jesus states whether or not he is "the Son (υἱός; cf. Ps 85:16: υἱὸν;) of God."

- Matthew 27:2 (par. Mark 15:1): The religious leaders bind Jesus and "hand him over (παρέδωκαν; cf. Pss 26:12 and 73:19: παραδῷς) to Pilate."

- Matthew 27:23 (par. Mark 15:14): Pilate asks the crowd, "What crime (κακόν; cf. Pss 37:21 and 108:5: κακά) has [Jesus] committed?"

- Matthew 27:29 (cf. Mark 15:18; Matthew adds ἐνέπαιξαν to Mark): The soldiers kneel before Jesus and mock (ἐνέπαιξαν) him (cf. Ps 21:8: ἐξεμυκτήρισάν; MT Ps 22:8: ילעגי).

- Matthew 27:44 (par Mark 15:32): The robbers crucified with Jesus "reviled him (ὠνείδιζον αὐτόν; cf. Pss 41:11 [ὠνείδισάν με] and 68:10 [ὀνειδιζόντων σε])." [/BL 1–12]

Of Heroes and Villains

Supplementary Data Used to Characterize Jesus

- Matthew 8:23–27 (par. Mark 4:35–41) Jesus sleeps during a storm and needs awakening similarly to God who sleeps during moments of need (MT Pss 3:5; 4:8; 35:23; 44:23–24; 59:4).

- Matthew 26:41 (par. Mark 14:38): Jesus speaks the words of the psalmist to warn his sleeping disciples in Gethsemane that "the spirit is willing (τὸ μὲν πνεῦμα πρόθυμον; cf. MT Ps 51:14: ורוח נדיבה ורוח), but the body is weak."

- Matthew 26:63 (par. Mark 14:61a): When the Sanhedrin questions Jesus, he "remained silent (ἐσιώπα; cf. MT Pss 38:14: :39:10; כאלם אלמתי) and gave no answer."

- Matthew 27:50 (par. Mark 15:37): At his death, Jesus takes his final breath "with a loud cry (φωνὴν; cf. Ps 30:23: φωνῆς)."

Matthew retains verbatim ten of Mark's possible evocations of the psalmic lament (Matt 8:23–27; 26:4, 21, 41; 59, 63; 27:2, 23, 44, 50), redacts three closer to the lament (Matt 26:3–4a, 59–60; 27:29[114]), and adds two lament evocations of his own (Matt 13:41; 23:29). Interestingly, out of the sixteen possible Markan evocations examined in the supplementary evidence of chapter 2, Matthew only omits one possible psalmic echo—Mark 15:13—by replacing Mark's ἔκραξαν with λέγουσιν, thus editing away from a possible allusion to Psalm 21:6 (ἐκέκραξαν).[115] This supplementary data, to the degree that they echo the psalmic lament, substantiates the foregoing argument that Matthew expands and emphasizes Mark's characterization of Jesus and Jesus' opponents as the psalmic lamenter and the psalmic lamenter's opponents, respectively.

Summary

In the first three sections of this chapter, I establish that Matthew expands and emphasizes Mark's characterization of Jesus and Jesus' opponents in

---

114. Mark 15:23 (the offering of Jesus wine at his crucifixion) is omitted here, since it is discussed above as a simple evocation. Recall that Matthew shapes this account into an evocation of Ps 68:22.

115. One might also include Matthew's redaction away from Ps 40:10 in 26:21, Jesus' identification of Judas at the Last Supper (Ps 40:10: ὁ ἐσθίων—Mark 14:18: ὁ ἐσθίων—Matt 26:21: ἐσθιόντων αὐτῶν). As noted above, however, some still see a Matthean echo of Ps 40:10 in 26:21.

tandem with his Isaianic Servant motif and his use of Psalms 8, 109, and 117, and that Matthew independently mirrors this method of characterization in his appropriation of his rejected-prophet motif. In this section, I demonstrate that Matthew appropriates the psalmic lament similarly by characterizing Jesus and Jesus' opponents as the psalmic lamenter par excellence and as the lamenter's opponents, respectively, expanding and emphasizing both in relation to Mark. This characterization represents the final step in providing a way forward concerning the narrative-critical debate about how best to categorize Matthew's characterization of Jesus' opponents—namely, as the paradigmatic OT villains (see chapter conclusion below for a synthesis of this argument).

Matthew's lament motif, in contrast to the previous three motifs examined above, serves at least two further and interrelated purposes. First, Matthew amalgamates and unifies his entire cast of villains as those of the psalmic lamenter. Note that in Gethsemane Matthew characterizes the crowd, chief priests, elders, and Judas as villains of the psalmic lamenter (Matt 26:47–48), while at the crucifixion he includes the soldiers (Matt 27:34, 35), the passerby (Matt 27:39), an unnamed man (Matt 27:48), and, once again, the Jewish leaders: the chief priests, scribes, and elders (Matt 27:42–43). Every character and character group (Jew and Gentile[116]), then, amalgamate into a climactic unified force of opposition against Jesus as the paradigmatic villains of the psalmic lamenter.

This amalgamation and unification of Matthew's cast of characters is enhanced by, second, Matthew's use of the psalmic lament to crescendo his characterization of Jesus as the psalmic lamenter par excellence and Jesus' opponents as the lamenter's opponents. Every

---

116. Pilate is not directly characterized as the opponent of the psalmic lamenter, but his soldiers are—as those who carry out Pilate's demands to flog and crucify Jesus (Matt 27:26–37, 62–66). In light of Pilate's self-declaration of innocence (Matt 27:24), some suggest that Matthew intends to exonerate Pilate and the Romans from guilt regarding Jesus' death (Beare, *Matthew*, 531; Bonnard, *L'Évangile selon Saint Matthieu*, 398; Plummer, *Matthew*, 391; Schweizer, *Matthew*, 508–9; Tilborg, *Jewish Leaders in Matthew*, 93–94). Davies and Allison, however, are correct: "The point is not Pilate's exoneration—as though Matthew extols cowardice. Pilate's 'see to it yourselves' no more excuses him than 'see to it yourselves' excuses the chief priests and elders (27:4)" (*Matthew*, 3:590; cf. Luz, *Matthew 21–28*, 500; Hagner, *Matthew 14–28*, 827; Carson, "Jewish Leaders in Matthew's Gospel," 173–74; Cargal, "His Blood Be Upon Us and Upon Our Children," 107–8, 111–12). Furthermore, Pilate's complicity with Jesus' death is clear in Matt 27:27, where the "governor's soldiers" carry out the crucifixion; presumably, if Pilate were truly guiltless, he would have stopped his soldiers from proceeding with the horrific acts that follow.

Matthean theme is an outstretched finger pointing ultimately to Jesus' passion and resurrection.[117] For example, Matthew's rejected prophet is climactically rejected at the crucifixion, his Servant serves by giving his life "as a ransom for many" at the crucifixion, and his Davidic king unexpectedly establishes his kingdom at the crucifixion. When Matthew's literary conflict between Jesus and the opponents finally reaches its destination at the crucifixion, he presents it through a hermeneutic of the psalmic lament as his narrative climax that serves as the denouement for the story's hero and cast of villains.

CONCLUSION: NARRATIVE AND RHETORICAL IMPLICATIONS

Since the 1980s, scholars have rightly highlighted and emphasized Matthew's literary features, offering insightful correctives to redaction criticism and bringing Matthean studies into an exciting new era. Without expunging redaction criticism but using it as a handmaiden to narrative criticism, this chapter explores how Matthew characterizes Jesus and Jesus' opponents. Examining these characterizations required individualized focus on four interrelated but distinct Matthean motifs. Such an individualized examination is necessary but narratively artificial. In this conclusion, before summarizing the contributions that this chapter makes to Matthean scholarship, I focus on these four motifs more holistically within the overall flow of Matthew's narrative in order to accomplish the following three things.

First, I synthesize via a summary Matthew's appropriation of these four motifs—prophet, Servant, Davidic king via non-lament, and lament—in characterizing Jesus and Jesus' opponents within the overall flow of his narrative.[118] This summary serves as a prelude, second, to ex-

---

117. Allison correctly states, "[Matthew's] passion and resurrection ... constitute the climax of [his] story" (*Studies in Matthew*, 217). Allison further argues that Martin Kähler's appellative about Mark ("a passion narrative with an extended introduction") (*So-Called Historical Jesus*, 80n11]) is equally true for Matthew's gospel in light of the breadth of material directly associated with Matthew's passion (Allison, *Studies in Matthew*, 233).

118. It is beyond the scope of this conclusion, but beckons further research, to synthesize the findings of this chapter with other narrative features of Matthew's gospel such as his Immanuel motif, which likely serves as a link between his Servant and Son of God motifs (Nolland, *Matthew*, 492), his established ecclesiology, and his role of characterization as it relates to his fulfillment motif (for an entry into these discussions

plore Matthew's characterization of the soldiers, Pilate, the Jewish leaders, and the crowd in three scenes subsequent to Jesus' crucifixion. Since only Matthew continues these post-crucifixion characterizations, it is necessary to explore them briefly in order to consummate the foregoing narrative summary. Third, in this conclusion I explore some rhetorical effects that Matthew's characterization of Jesus and Jesus' opponents as the paradigmatic OT hero and villains had on his readers.

Synthesis/Summary

In summarizing Matthew's characterization of Jesus and Jesus' opponents in appropriating the OT prophet, Servant, and psalmic non-lament and lament motifs, one must remember that Jesus is the central focus of the narrative. Every character, event, and subplot serves Matthew's larger purpose to explain, defend, and magnify Jesus' identity and mission. Matthew's Jesus represents a complex nexus through whom the culmination of salvation history flows and in whom Matthew's present and subsequent generations must "hope" (Matt 12:21). Matthew channels salvation history through Jesus by portraying him from every angle as one who fulfills, authoritatively interprets, imbibes, and recapitulates Israel's Scriptures in order to initiate a following that his disciples will garner from "all nations" (Matt 28:19).

In writing a narrative that centrally focuses on Jesus, Matthew relates a story replete with characters and conflict and that intentionally flows toward a climactic ending. The main characters, aside from Jesus, are the disciples, the Jewish and Gentile leaders, and the crowd. Matthew presents the conflict as a classic struggle between the hero, Jesus, and the villains, the Jewish leaders. Hanging in the balance are the crowd and the disciples, as the reader discovers how each will respond to the hero and villains. Matthew builds upon this basic plot in complexly creative ways. For example, Jesus simultaneously fulfills the OT, inaugurates a kingdom, trains a group of disciples, battles demons, heals the multitudes, dies on behalf of others, and conquers the grave.

One way, among many others, that Matthew builds upon this plot is by characterizing Jesus and Jesus' opponents as various paradigmatic OT heroes and villains. These characterizations, which are sometimes overt

---

with accompanying bibliographies, see Allison, *Studies in Matthew*, 234–35; cf. Turner, *Matthew*, 32–47, and Hagner, *Matthew 1–13*, liii–lvii, lix–lxiv).

and sometimes subtle, coincide with Matthew's crescendoing conflict motif. Prior to the triumphal entry (chapters 1–20), Matthew characterizes Jesus as, among other things, Isaiah's Servant and the paradigmatic OT prophet. Jesus is the Servant from God (Matt 3:17; 12:18; 17:5), who heals (Matt 8:17), fulfills Scripture (Matt 8:17; 12:17), does not quarrel (Matt 12:19), cares for the downcast (Matt 12:20), and dies as a ransom for others (Matt 20:28). Jesus is also a prophet (Matt 13:57; 16:14), who is greater than those of the OT (Matt 12:38–42) and, as his predecessors (Matt 23:30–31), is rejected by his opponents (Matt 17:12–13). Also prior to the triumphal entry, Matthew constructs a group of characters, the Jewish leaders, in opposition to Jesus, but Matthew does not yet link this opposition to particular OT villains (except indirectly as a foil in Matt 12:18–21 and in the eschaton in Matt 7:23[119]). This changes when Jesus enters Jerusalem.

From the triumphal entry to Gethsemane, Jesus dons an additional OT heroic image, the Davidic psalmic king,[120] while his opponents begin to emerge as paradigmatic OT villains. Jesus, while continuing as the paradigmatic OT prophet (Matt 21:26–27, 46) and Isaiah's Servant (Matt 26:28), becomes the Davidic messiah-king (Matt 21:1–17; 22:44). In each instance where Matthew characterizes Jesus as the Davidic psalmist, he also characterizes Jesus' opponents (the Jewish leaders) as the psalmists' villains (Matt 21:1–17; 22:44). At the same time, Jesus' opponents emerge as the paradigmatic opponents of the OT prophets via Jesus' scathing indictment in Matthew 23:29–32 ("Woe to you, scribes and Pharisees, hypocrites").

From Gethsemane to the crucifixion, Jesus, continuing as Isaiah's Servant (Matt 26:63; 27:12, 14, 30), dons yet another OT heroic character, the David psalmic lamenter (Matt 26:36–47; 27:46). At the same time, Jesus' opponents, while continuing as those of Isaiah's Servant (Matt 26:67–68; 27:30) and as those of the paradigmatic OT prophet (Matt 27:9), become the villains of the psalmic lamenter (Matt 26:47; 27:32–54). Two important things occur with Matthew's characterization of Jesus' opponents in tandem with those of the psalmic lamenter:

---

119. These characters of the eschaton are akin to Powell's characters who exist in Matthew's "story world" (the world perceived by the implied author that extends from creation to eternity) but do not function as characters in the story proper (Powell, "Religious Leaders in Matthew," 37–38).

120. Jesus' kingship begins at gospel's beginning (Matt 2:2), but his specific, royal link with the Psalms does not overtly begin until the triumphal entry (for a more subtle Matthean introduction of this royal theme, cf. Matt 3:17).

Matthew climaxes his gospel and amalgamates and unifies Jesus' opposition through a focused explication of two lament psalms. Lament Psalms 21 and 68 provide the OT material with which Matthew crescendos his characterization of Jesus and is the glue that unites the opposition against Jesus. Matthew coalesces Jesus' entire opposition, including those who join the opposing side late in the gospel (e.g., the crowd and the soldiers), by characterizing them as the villains of the lament psalms. The lament psalms, then, serve Matthew's narrative to climax and coalesce his characterization of Jesus and Jesus' opponents as those of the OT hero and villains.

Post-crucifixion Scenes

Interestingly, Matthew, unlike Mark, continues characterizing Jesus' opposition in three scenes subsequent to the crucifixion—namely, the soldiers, the Jewish leaders, Pilate, and the crowd (Matt 27:54, 62–66; 28:11–15).[121] These scenes reveal that while most of Matthew's characters continue to bear the label "villain," at least one can discard it.

In the first scene, the terrified soldiers, along with a centurion, exclaim in relation to Jesus' supernatural death (Matt 27:50–53), "Surely he was the Son of God" (Matt 27:54). It is difficult to know if Matthew intends this exclamation as a conversion or as an ignorant gesture, since these same soldiers[122] just moments earlier hideously mock and kill Jesus and, as discussed below, continue in overt opposition to Jesus in two subsequent scenes. In other words, at this narrative juncture, does Matthew change their status as villains? This question has interested Matthean scholars for over half a century, resulting in three general interpretive

---

121. As Cousland rightly argues, the crowds prior to the passion are the same crowds in the passion—Matthew does not posit a different crowd (*Crowds in the Gospel of Matthew*, 227–28; contra Minear, "Disciples and the Crowds in the Gospel of Matthew," 35; Blomberg, *Matthew*, 412; Saldarini, *Matthew's Christian-Jewish Community*, 38).

122. Matthew clarifies the identity of those attending the centurion via his use of τηρέω: Those "keeping guard" (τηροῦντες) with the centurion in Matt 27:54 are the *soldiers* who were "keeping guard" (ἐτήρουν) over Jesus in Matt 27:36. For a more detailed argument that the soldiers who crucify Jesus are the same soldiers who exclaim "Surely he was the Son of God," see Sim, "'Confession' of the Soldiers in Matthew 27:54," 404–6.

Of Heroes and Villains

conclusions: (1) the soldiers convert,[123] (2) the soldiers do not convert,[124] and (3) the modern interpreter simply cannot know.[125] If these soldiers convert, then their status as villains change, but if they do not convert then their status remains unchanged.

These soldiers do not convert; rather, the broader context clarifies that, although the soldier's confession itself in Matthew 27:54 is not specifically villainous or a specific act of mockery, Matthew continues to portray the soldiers collectively as villains opposed to Jesus. Sim notes the context prior to the soldiers' exclamation and rightly concludes that Matthew's trajectory of characterizing them as "bad" prior to Jesus' crucifixion increases the likelihood that their exclamation is not a confession of faith.[126] Sim and others, however, have not considered how Matthew continues to characterize the soldiers in two subsequent post-crucifixion scenes: Matthew 27:62–66 and 28:11–15. Attention, then, is turned to these two scenes before returning to address the soldiers' exclamation in Matthew 27:54.

In the second post-crucifixion scene that features Jesus' opponents, a concern arises about Jesus' tomb (Matt 27:62–66). Five characters previously denoted as villains appear in this scene: chief priests, Pharisees, Pilate, the crowd/people,[127] and soldiers.[128] The chief priests and the

---

123. Nils Alstrup Dahl argues that the appellative is a conversion that foreshadows the conversion of the Gentiles to Christ in Matt 28:19 ("go and make disciples of all nations") (Dahl, "Passion Narrative in Matthew," 49; cf. Senior, *Passion of Jesus in the Gospel of Matthew*, 324, and Hagner, *Matthew 14–28*, 852–53). Gundry agrees, adding that Matthew's echo of Matt 17:6 (the disciples' fear at Jesus' transfiguration) in Matt 27:54 via a repeated use of ἐφοβήθησαν σφόδρα indicates a conversion (Gundry, *Matthew*, 578; cf. Nolland, *Matthew*, 1217–21). Davies and Allison also agree, adding further that a similar conversion of onlookers by a martyr's faith occurs in 3 Macc 6:16–29 (*Matthew*, 3:635). Nolland suggests that it represents the culmination of what others throughout Matthew's gospel said of Jesus (*Matthew*, 1217–21). Finally, Turner understands it as foil to the invectives hurled at Jesus since 27:27 (*Matthew*, 671).

124. Kingsbury argues that the soldiers' use of the past tense ("surely he was [ἦν] the Son of God") suggests an end to Jesus' sonship and not an understanding of Matthew's permanence of it (*Matthew as Story*, 90). Blomberg contends that the appellative is a confession of Jesus as a good man but falls short of a Christian conversion (*Matthew*, 422, citing Plummer, *Luke*, 539). David C. Sim argues that it represents a cry of defeat ("Confession," 401–24).

125. Carson, *Matthew*, 582.

126. Sim, "Confession," 404–6.

127. Recall that the crowd (ὄχλος) and the Jewish people (λαός) unite in Matt 27:24–25.

128. Matthew initially calls this a "guard" (κουστωδίαν; a collective singular: note the plural οἱ δὲ πορευθέντες ἠσφαλίσαντο in 27:66) but clarifies in 28:12 that they are

Pharisees approach Pilate with a dilemma; they are concerned that the disciples might steal Jesus' body in order to feign a resurrection. Their concern is that the thievery might deceive "the people." To prevent this deception, Pilate sends soldiers to seal and guard the tomb. Matthew indicates that the reader is to regard these soldiers as the same ones at Jesus' crucifixion: All are sent from Pilate (Matt 27:27, 65) and all are linked via the term τηρέω (Matt 27:36, 54; 28:4). For my purposes here, note that the chief priests, the Pharisees, and Pilate continue to function as villains who are opposed to Jesus (calling him a "deceiver" [Matt 27:63]), who do not understand Jesus' pending resurrection, and who liken Jesus' disciples to thieves. The soldiers continue as handmaidens to Pilate, obeying his orders to guard the tomb against possible deception. Interestingly, Matthew depicts the crowd as possible subjects of reconciliation, for the chief priests and Pharisees are primarily concerned that the Jewish crowd might believe the "deception" of the resurrection (Matt 27:64).[129]

In the final post-crucifixion scene that features Jesus' opponents, a conspiracy to cover up the resurrection unfolds. Five characters previously denoted as villains appear in this scene: the soldiers, chief priests, elders, the governor (i.e., Pilate; cf. Matt 27:2: "Pilate the governor"), and the Jewish crowd. The soldiers report the resurrection to the chief priests, who meet with the elders to concoct a plan to bribe the soldiers with money to lie about what they saw. The chief priests and elders tell the soldiers to say that Jesus' disciples stole his body during the night. The soldiers take the bribe and spread the lie, which "circulated widely among the Jews" until the time of Matthew's writing (Matt 28:15c). Note that the chief priests and elders, in the face of indisputable evidence about Jesus' resurrection, continue to function as villains who oppose Jesus by concocting a lie. Also note that the soldiers, as some of the first eyewitnesses to the resurrection, accept a monetary bribe to squelch the public spread of the news. Finally, Matthew depicts Pilate, the governor, as one who will cause trouble for the soldiers if the news about Jesus' resurrection surfaces. Interestingly, Matthew again depicts the crowd (Ιουδαίοις) as possible subjects of reconciliation by implicitly suggesting that they have a propensity to believe the message about Jesus' resurrection (Matt 28:15).[130]

"soldiers" (τοῖς στρατιώταις).

129. This Matthean depiction of the crowd is astutely noted by Cousland, *Crowds in the Gospel of Matthew*, 238.

130. Again, astutely noted by Cousland, ibid.

Of Heroes and Villains

Returning momentarily to the soldiers' exclamation, "Surely he was the Son of God," these scenes provide answers to the long-debated issue about their intentions. It is unlikely that Matthew would depict the soldiers as OT villains who horridly beat, mock, and kill Jesus while conspiring with the religious leaders, and then depict them as converts to Christ immediately following the crucifixion, only to re-depict them a few verses later (and only within two days of narrative time: Matt 27:62; 28:1) as lying villains in cahoots with the religious leaders and Pilate. It is more likely that the centurion and the soldiers, in their fearful disposition,[131] ignorantly and ironically state, albeit truthfully within Matthew's narrative logic, that Jesus "was the Son of God." This scenario of Jesus' opponents claiming ironic but true statements about Jesus fits better within Matthew's narrative (e.g., the sign on Jesus' cross, "This is Jesus, the King of the Jews" and the soldiers' "prophesy to us Christ, who hit you") than a Christian conversion placed awkwardly within a context that previously and subsequently suggest otherwise.

These scenes, then, solidify Matthew's characterization of the Jewish leaders and Pilate as continued villains opposed to Jesus and his mission[132] and provide an unexpected twist concerning Matthew's characterization of the crowd. Although the crowd merges with the Jewish people and becomes the OT paradigmatic villain in killing the paradigmatic OT hero, Matthew portrays them subsequent to the crucifixion and resurrection as people who hang in the balance between obstinate rejection of Jesus' resurrection and reconciliation to him. This indicates that, within Matthew's narrative logic, at least some characters are able to recant their villainous opposition to Jesus.

Rhetorical Implications

The final scene provides a segue into a discussion of Matthew's intended rhetorical effect of these characterizations. The villains concoct a lie to conceal Jesus' resurrection, which Matthew states, "has been widely circulated among the Jews to this very day" (Matt 28:15; cf. Matt 28:20c). Matthew's characterization of Jesus' opponents, then, exceeds

---

131. Sim ("Confession," 408–12) corrects Senior's argument (*Passion Narrative According to Matthew*, 323–28), which is based on a supposed Matthean pattern in Matt 9:8; 17:6; 28:8; and 27:54, that the soldiers' "fear" is tantamount to their conversion to faith.

132. Cf. Powell, "Religious Leaders in Matthew," 168–71.

the boundaries of his narrative, intentionally converging with Matthew's contemporary readership.

The rhetorical effect of Matthew's characterization of Jesus and Jesus' opponents as the OT hero and villains is similar to the rhetorical effect that Mark intends for his readers (see chapter 2): It enhances Matthew's evaluative point of view of Jesus and Jesus' opponents. Recall that "evaluative point of view," according to Powell, "may be defined as the standards of judgment by which readers are led to evaluate the events, characters, and settings that comprise the story." Matthew's standard of judgment, like Mark's, is what God thinks, and what God thinks is true and right (Matt 16:33; cf. Mark 8:33c).

As with Mark, a primary way that Matthew and, presumably, his readers determine what God thinks is via the Hebrew Scriptures (cf. Matthew's fulfillment quotations).[133] Those who "think the things of God" and not the "things of people" are those who act in accord with the Hebrew Scriptures as revealed in Jesus. Matthew makes clear that anyone who acts in accordance with the villains of the OT fails "to think the things of God." Matthew's readers, then, understand Jesus' opponents as bad because the narrator, Jesus, *and* the Scriptures say they are. Matthew appropriates these motifs, then, to provide an evaluative standard against which to places Jesus' opponents in order to substantiate his negative portrayal of them.

Matthew, however, builds on Mark's gospel in ways that significantly enhance his evaluative point of view of Jesus and Jesus' opponents. This chapter demonstrates that Matthew expands and emphasizes Mark's characterization of Jesus as Isaiah's Servant, the Davidic king, and the Davidic lamenter. Simultaneously he expands and emphasizes Mark's characterization of Jesus' opponents as those of Isaiah's Servant, the Davidic king, and the Davidic lamenter. Substantiating this is Matthew's independent characterization of Jesus and Jesus' opponents as the paradigmatic OT prophet and the OT prophets' opponents. Matthew intends these expansions and emphases rhetorically to move Jesus and Jesus' opponents in opposite evaluative directions.[134] Stated more concretely, if one

---

133. Powell, *What Is Narrative Criticism?*, 24. Powell notes that God's point of view in the gospels is also revealed through angels, prophets, miracles, and dreams.

134. One can rightly argue that, since Matthew's readers probably did not know Mark's gospel, Matthew's expansions and emphases of Mark's characterizations could not have had a rhetorical affect on his readers. This, however, does not negate Matthew's intention to do so. It is unlikely that Matthew wrote his gospel with modern

Of Heroes and Villains

views Mark's depictions of Jesus and Jesus' opponents at certain opposite points on a "good-to-evil" continuum,[135] then Matthew significantly slides these two characters in opposite directions along the same continuum.[136]

Contributions

This chapter advances Matthean scholarship in at least the following five ways. First, it advances Ahearne-Kroll's work by applying his conclusions about Mark to the Gospel of Matthew—namely, that Matthew, like Mark, characterizes Jesus as the Davidic lamenter who shuns Second Temple militaristic expectations. Closely related to this, second, this chapter gives a clearer voice to Matthew's psalmic lamenter motif that has only little been recognized, a motif that contributes to Matthew's narrative independently of his appropriation of Isaiah's Servant.

Third, this chapter advances Powell's 1988 dissertation that establishes the character traits of Jesus' opponents in Matthew—they are evil, hypocritical, and spiritually blind[137]—by adding one more: Jesus

---

rigid narrative-critical categories in mind whereby his compositional intentions bypassed how he appropriated his primary source—the Gospel of Mark.

135. This concept of a good-to-evil continuum is taken from Black, who notes two poles in Matthew: righteousness and disobedience (Black, *Rhetoric of the Gospel*, 44). The continuum of "good-to-evil" is used instead of "righteous-to-disobedience" since the concept pervades Mark's and Matthew's narratives (good: Matt 3:10; 5:16, 45; 7:17–19; 12:33, 34; 19:16; 22:10; etc.; evil: Matt 5:11, 39, 45; 7:11; 9:4; 12:34, 35, 43; 13:41). Other concepts/continuums equally reflect this notion: godly-to-evil; godly-to-satanic; obedience-to-disobedience; righteousness-to-disobedience; and righteousness-to-unrighteousness. The point is that within their narrative worldview, Mark and Matthew see their characters as good or evil.

136. That Matthew's characters can slide on a continuum between these two poles is evident in his characterization of the crowd, who at gospels' beginning is positively predisposed toward Jesus (Matt 9:8), becomes his enemy in the passion (Matt 27:25), and returns to a neutral position after the resurrection (Matt 27:64). Similarly, Peter, who Jesus addresses as Satan (Matt 16:23) and who outright denies knowing Jesus (Matt 26:69–75), is also lauded for recognizing Jesus as the Messiah (Matt 16:16–17). The notion of Jesus sliding on this continuum is perhaps slightly inadequate if Matthew, as David B. Howell argues, considers Jesus to be the standard of good and evil (*Matthew's Inclusive Story*, 181–84). Jesus' "goodness," however, as Howell concedes, is directly correlated with his relationship to, and fulfillment of, Scripture (ibid., 185–86). Thus, in the sense that Matthew characterizes Jesus more centrally as one who fulfills and reenacts Scripture, Matthew, in relation to Mark, slides Jesus toward the "good" side of the continuum.

137. Powell, "Religious Leaders in Matthew," 184–200.

opponents are also the OT paradigmatic villains. Fourth, this chapter complements the works of many interpreters who have written at length about Matthew's characterization of Jesus as certain OT figures (e.g., OT rejected prophet par excellence and Isaiah's Servant) by exploring Matthew's characterization of Jesus' opponents as those of the same OT figures.

Fifth, Matthew's characterization of Jesus' opponents as paradigmatic OT villains provides a way forward in the debate to understand how Matthew characterizes Jesus' opposition. Beginning at the triumphal entry, the reader gradually realizes that Matthew employs a hermeneutic of the OT in his characterization of the Jewish leaders, a hermeneutic that eventually engulfs practically all of Jesus' opponents. This hermeneutic is the unifying force that holds together his concept of Jesus' opposition, allowing simultaneous consistency (the Jewish leaders' monolithic front against Jesus) and modification (e.g., the adding of the crowds, soldiers, and others to Jesus' opposition in the passion). In other words, although Matthew forms major and minor characters (both individually and collectively) in opposition to Jesus, he does so under the guiding rubric of the OT. In composing his cast of characters who oppose Jesus, the edges that frame Matthew's delineations of particular character groups (e.g., the Jewish leaders) blur because his overarching concern is with those who align with the OT villains in opposition to Jesus.

4

Luke's Appropriation of the Psalmic Lament?

INTRODUCTION

The previous two chapters explored a motif that begins with Mark, and that Matthew expands and emphasizes toward particular literary and rhetorical ends—namely, the characterizing of Jesus and Jesus' opponents as paradigmatic OT hero and villains, coalescing and climaxing these characterizations with their appropriation of the psalmic lament. Since Luke also establishes Jesus and Jesus' opponents as literary characters within an unfolding narrative (see discussion below) and, since most modern scholars argue that Luke uses Mark as a primary source,[1] it is apropos to examine how Luke more generally appropriates Mark's motif of characterizing Jesus and Jesus' opponents as OT hero and villains and

---

1. Research into Luke's use of sources, especially in his passion account, has an extremely long and complicated history, as a cursory glance at Jay M. Harrington's lengthy monograph reveals (*Lukan Passion Narrative*, 117–676). The arguments in this chapter are valid if Luke is read in isolation of purported sources. Noting possible Lukan redactions of Mark, however, confirms, albeit to a limited degree, Luke's intentions in appropriating these OT motifs. This approach is consistent with the method discussed in chapter 1—namely, that redaction criticism can serve as a handmaiden to narrative criticism.

Luke's Appropriation of the Psalmic Lament?

more specifically to what degree he appropriates the psalmic lament in this motif of characterization.[2]

Such an examination, augmenting the advancements made in chapter 3 to Ahearne-Kroll's monograph as it relates to Matthew's gospel, advances Ahearne-Kroll's work as it relates to Luke's gospel.[3] In undertaking this task, I ask two general questions: (1) Does Luke follow Mark in understanding and appropriating the psalmic lament to characterize Jesus? (2) To what degree does Luke follow Mark in characterizing Jesus and Jesus' opponents as paradigmatic OT hero and villains? Answering these two questions is the cumulative goal of the following two arguments.[4]

First, although Luke follows Mark in appropriating psalmic lament literature, he does very little to characterize Jesus as the Davidic lamenter. In other words, there is little indication that Luke's narrative, contrary to Mark and Matthew, reflects an understanding of the core elements of the psalmic lament in his characterization of Jesus.[5] Thus, whereas Ahearne-

---

2. Luke writes a two-volume work (Tannehill, *Narrative Unity of Luke-Acts*, 1:xiii–xiv), but he intends that each can be read both independently and corporately since, after all, Luke's gospel was apparently "published" prior to Acts and was intended to be "intelligible to the Christians for whom it was written" (C. Kavin Rowe's methodology in *Early Narrative Christology*, 25; cf. Carson and Moo, *Introduction to the New Testament*, 212). Although my focus in this chapter is on Luke's gospel, pertinent data from Acts is examined in order to supplement the primary investigation. This chapter, however, is not an investigation of Luke's second volume, an investigation that exceeds my purposes here. Gail O'Day offers an initial step in investigating the intersection of intertextual studies and narrative characterization in "Citation of Scripture as a Key to Characterization in Acts," 207–21.

3. Recall that this is precisely the need that Ahearne-Kroll envisions (Ahearne-Kroll, *Psalms of Lament in Mark's Passion*, 22).

4. By isolating these Lukan motifs, I do not intend to suggest that Luke *only* uses the OT for the purposes of characterization. Others have argued, for example, that Luke uses the OT apologetically (as "proof from prophecy") (Conzelmann, *Theology*, 157–59; Cadbury, *Making of Luke-Acts*, 303–5), in a promise-fulfillment schema (Rese, *Alttestamentliche Motive in der Christologie des Lukas*, 38–42, 209; and Bock, *Proclamation from Prophecy and Pattern*, 273), to explain how Gentiles become the heirs of salvation (Conzelmann, *Theology*, 157, 162–63), and ecclesiologically as a redefinition of God's people (Tyson, *Luke-Acts and the Jewish People*). For a summary of these arguments, consult Mallen, *Reading and Transformation of Isaiah in Luke-Acts*, 4–9. I also do not intend to suggest that the motifs discussed in this chapter completely explain Luke's complex portrait of Jesus. Concerning the complexity of Luke's portrait of Jesus, see Rowe, *Early Narrative Christology*; Strauss, *Davidic Messiah in Luke-Acts*; and Bovon, *Luke the Theologian*, 167–223.

5. Recall from chapter 1 that a lament is essentially a distressful complaint/question/appeal directed toward God (a prayer) in order to bring about change for a

Kroll, as discussed in chapter 2, gives a voice to the psalmic lamenter in Mark, and chapter 3 gives a voice to the psalmic lamenter in Matthew, this chapter demonstrates that with respect to Jesus there is but a vague whisper of the lamenter's voice to be heard in Luke.[6] Instead of presenting Jesus as a lamenter seeking to bring about change for his plight, Luke is more concerned, as Bock correctly argues, with characterizing Jesus as an innocent, righteous sufferer more in line with Isaiah's Servant.[7] Luke, then, does what many scholars erroneously and myopically ascribe to the passion accounts of Mark and Matthew (see chapters 2–3 above)—Luke focuses on Jesus as Isaiah's righteous sufferer.

Second, I argue that Luke's characterization of Jesus as the paradigmatic OT hero is prominent throughout his gospel—his characterization of Jesus as the Davidic lamenter notwithstanding. Luke's characterization of Jesus' opponents as paradigmatic OT villains is also present, but Luke omits an important aspect of this motif of characterizing Jesus' opponents that significantly impacts his narrative. Specifically, Luke downplays the significance of characterizing Jesus' opponents as those of the Davidic psalmist at the crucifixion by excluding the crowd as Jesus' opponents, by omitting two Markan evocations of the Psalms, and by highlighting various participants at the crucifixion who do not oppose Jesus.

I address these two arguments by exploring the following three Lukan motifs, the first two of which function, in essence, as an extended introduction to the exploration of the third motif. First, I establish that Luke appropriates an OT rejected-prophet motif (independent of Mark but parallel to Matthew) in characterizing Jesus as an OT prophet and Jesus' opponents as those of the OT prophets. Second, I establish that Luke follows Mark in appropriating Isaiah to, among other things, characterize Jesus as the Servant but downplays Mark's characterization of Jesus' opponents as those of the Servant, retaining only one possible allusion.

Third, I argue that Luke appropriates the psalmic literature to characterize Jesus and Jesus' opponents as King David and King David's opponents, respectively. Herein, Luke significantly depends upon, but

---

real or perceived problem. A NT writer's evocation of OT lament literature in concert with the appropriation of this definition of the lament increases the likelihood that the respective writer understands how the lament functions.

6. Eklund disagrees, arguing rather that Luke definitely portrays Jesus as a lamenter, especially in Gethsemane and on the cross ("Lord, Teach us How to Grieve," 26–62). I address her arguments below.

7. Bock, *Luke 9:51–24:53*, 1862.

simultaneously departs from, this Markan motif of characterization. Recall that Mark characterizes Jesus as the psalmic Davidic king at the triumphal entry, merges this motif with an appropriation of the psalmic lament in Gethsemane, and climaxes it via the lament at the crucifixion. Luke follows Mark in appropriating the Davidic psalms to characterize Jesus as the Davidic king, but he does not overtly follow Mark in characterizing Jesus as the Davidic lamenter who prayerfully struggles with God to change his plight. Luke, instead, emphasizes Jesus as Isaiah's innocent, righteous Suffering Servant.

Related to this, I demonstrate that Luke appropriates the Davidic psalms to characterize Jesus' opponents as those of the Davidic psalmist. Herein, Luke significantly depends upon, but simultaneously departs from, this Markan motif of characterization. Recall that Mark characterizes Jesus' opponents as those of the psalmic Davidic king at the triumphal entry, coalesces this characterization with the crowd and the soldiers as a unified force of opposition against Jesus via the psalmic lament in Gethsemane, and climaxes this unified force of opposition via the lament at the crucifixion. Luke follows Mark in appropriating the Davidic psalms to characterize Jesus' opponents (including the soldiers at the crucifixion) as those of David. Luke, however, does not follow Mark in using the lament as a motif of characterization in Gethsemane, and he does not use the lament to coalesce the crowd into a unified force of opposition with Jesus' opponents. Furthermore, Luke, at Jesus' crucifixion, appropriates but downplays Mark's characterization of Jesus' opponents as those of the Davidic psalmist.

After exploring these three Lukan motifs, I examine some supplementary data that adds support to the foregoing arguments, and, additionally, some narrative and rhetorical implications via a conclusion.

OT PROPHET MOTIF IN CHARACTERIZING JESUS AND HIS OPPONENTS

Noted at length as early as 1957,[8] the focus of a dissertation in 1975,[9] and discussed extensively by commentators and theologians over the last thirty-five years, scholars have long recognized that Luke characterizes

---

8. Gils, *Jésus prophète d'après les Évangiles synoptiques*.
9. Greene, "Portrayal of Jesus as Prophet in Luke-Acts."

Of Heroes and Villains

Jesus as the paradigmatic OT prophet par excellence[10] independently of Mark but parallel to Matthew.[11] Others have noted, albeit briefly, that Luke characterizes Jesus' opponents as those of the OT prophets.[12] My purpose here, aside from providing an introductory foundation to the third section, is to summarize via previous research Luke's characterization of Jesus as the paradigmatic OT prophet and to advance previous research by clarifying Luke's characterization of Jesus' opponents as the paradigmatic opponents of the OT prophets. Exploring these Lukan motifs of characterization demonstrate that Luke establishes a characterization of Jesus and Jesus' opponents as OT hero and villains independently of Mark. Furthermore, they validate and set the stage to explore in the subsequent two sections how Luke appropriates Isaiah's Servant and the Davidic psalms to characterize Jesus and Jesus' opponents.

---

10. Kingsbury rightly cautions against elevating Luke's Jesus as the prophet par excellence to the level of a christological title ("Jesus as the 'Prophetic Messiah' in Luke's Gospel," 41–42). Kingsbury, however, goes too far in suggesting that Luke refuses to interpret Jesus' identity in terms of a prophet, suggesting, instead, that Luke interprets Jesus' *ministry* prophetically (ibid., 41). In spite of sound arguments that Luke presents John the Baptist instead of Jesus as the "great prophet" (ibid., 37–38) and that Jesus identifies himself as the Messiah in juxtaposition to the crowd's identification of him as a resurrected prophet of long ago (Luke 9:18–20; ibid., 35–39), Kingsbury does not adequately explain why Jesus directly calls himself a prophet in Luke 13:33 (cf. ibid., 40) and why two trustworthy preachers (trustworthy within Luke's narrative logic), Peter and Stephen, identify Jesus as a prophet like Moses (Acts 3:22 and 7:37 [cf. the Emmaus disciples in 24:19–21]; cf. ibid., 40–41). Kingsbury's argument that the term "prophet" is not a Lukan christological title is heeded, but his argument that Luke's Jesus is not a prophet is challenged below.

11. Various scholars argue that Luke associates Jesus with specific OT prophets. For example, Marshall, *Luke*, 286, suggests that Luke portrays Jesus as Elijah (Luke 4:24; 7:39; 9:8, 19; 24:19). Feiler, *Jesus the Prophet*; Bovon, "La figure de Moïse dans L'oeuvre de Luc," 47–62; and Moessner suggest that Luke portrays Jesus as Moses (*Lord of the Banquet*). Here, I do not explore Luke's characterization of Jesus with specific OT prophets or Luke's understanding of other characters who function as prophets (cf. Luke 1:76; 2:36; Acts 11:27; 15:32; 21:10; see Johnson, "Christology of Luke-Acts," 54–56]); rather, I simply note his general interest in presenting Jesus as a prophet. In exploring this motif, I should mention that, although Luke's Jesus functions as a paradigmatic OT prophet, Jesus is not limited to it. Luke's Jesus is also, among other things, Messiah (Luke 2:11), Lord (Luke 2:11), King (Luke 19:38), and Son of God (Luke 1:32).

12. Tannehill, *Narrative Unity of Luke-Acts*, 1:97–98.

"Prophet" (and Cognates) within an OT Matrix

Before summarizing how Luke characterizes Jesus as the OT prophet par excellence, first I establish that Luke's concept of "prophet" (προφητεύω, πρφήτης, προφῆτις) derives from an OT matrix.[13] This is important to note because it shows that when Luke uses the term(s) in relation to Jesus and/or Jesus' opponents, he does so with the OT in mind. In his gospel, Luke refers to "prophet(s)" thirty-two times. A quick glimpse at these references reveals that Luke uses this term within an OT matrix. He names specific OT prophets three times (Luke 3:4; 4:17; 11:50–51) and refers collectively to the OT prophets eight times (e.g., "the Prophets and Psalms": Luke 1:70; 6:23; 16:16, 29, 31; 18:31; 24:25, 27). These eleven references, spanning the entirety of Luke's gospel, inform his use of "prophet" (and cognates) when he does not specify a direct correlation with the OT (Luke 1:67, 76; 2:36; 4:24, 27; 6:23; 7:16, 26 [two times], 39; 9:8, 19; 10:24; 11:47, 49; 13:28, 33, 34; 20:6; 22:64; 24:19).

This trend is more pronounced in Acts, where Luke names specific OT prophets ten times (Acts 2:16, 30; 3:22, 23; 7:37; 8:28, 30, 34; 13:20; 28:25) and refers collectively to the OT prophets fourteen times (Acts 3:18, 21, 24, 25; 7:42; 10:43; 13:15, 27, 40; 15:15; 24:14; 26:22, 27; 28:23). Luke's concept of "prophet," then, derives from, and is defined by, the OT. When he calls Jesus a prophet, he does so within an OT matrix.

Jesus as the OT Prophet Par Excellence

Luke's Jesus explicitly refers to himself as a prophet twice. In Luke 4:24, Jesus states that "no prophet is acceptable in his hometown." In Luke 13:33, Jesus sees it as a "divine necessity" (δεῖ) to die in Jerusalem (cf. Luke 9:22; 17:25; 27:4)[14] because, he says, "It cannot be that a prophet should perish away from Jerusalem."[15] Other characters also explicitly refer to Jesus as

---

13. This coincides with Franklin's point that Luke, in his understanding of Jesus, "was dominated by Old Testament categories" (*Christ the Lord*, 49). See Greene for an extensive investigation into the broader background of the term "prophet" ("Portrayal of Jesus as Prophet in Luke-Acts," 13–32).

14. Concerning δεῖ as a so-called "divine necessity," see Nolland, *Luke 9:1—18:34*, 2:741 and Bock, *Luke 9:51—24:53*, 1248.

15. Kingsbury downplays the significance of Jesus' self-identifications as a prophet, arguing that these identifications should be interpreted in light of Peter's confession that Jesus is the Messiah and not "one of the prophets of long ago [that] has come back to life" (Luke 9:18–20) (Kingsbury, "Jesus as the 'Prophetic Messiah' in Luke's Gospel," 38–40).

a prophet.¹⁶ In Luke 7:16, after raising a widow's son from the dead, the crowd says in reference to Jesus that "a great prophet has arisen among us." In Luke 7:39, a Pharisee questions Jesus' status as a prophet ("if this man were a prophet"), thus revealing that others attached this label to him. In Luke 9:8, "some were saying" that Jesus was "one of the prophets of old [who] had risen." In Luke 9:18–19, Jesus asks his disciples, "Who do the crowds say that I am?" The disciples include in their response that the crowds think that Jesus is "one of the prophets of old [who has] risen."¹⁷ In Luke 24:19, two disciples traveling to Emmaus identify Jesus as a "prophet mighty in word and deed" (cf. the description of Moses in Acts 7:22: "he was mighty in his words and deeds").

Luke's gospel is also replete with implicit traits ascribed to Jesus that parallel those of OT prophets.¹⁸ Since these traits have been discussed at length by others, only several are noted here.¹⁹ In Luke 6:24–26 and 11:42–51, Jesus speaks "woes" against oppressors and the religious leaders, respectively, as OT prophets often did (cf. Isa 5:11–30). In Luke 19:43, while weeping over Jerusalem, Jesus uses the phrase "the days will come" in predicting Jerusalem's fall. OT prophets frequently use this phrase to

---

Jesus' twofold point in Luke 9:18–20, however, is that, although he is not a *resurrected* prophet, he is the Messiah. Jesus is not rejecting the status of a prophet (especially in light of his claims in Luke 4:24 and 13:33), but he is rejecting the notion that he is Elijah or another prophet from OT antiquity.

16. Tannehill rightly notes that "those who speak of Jesus as a prophet in Luke may not understand him completely, but this title does not represent a distortion to be rejected" (*Narrative Unity of Luke-Acts*, 1:97).

17. Kingsbury rightly argues that Jesus focuses in Luke 9:18–20 on his identity as the Messiah and not on his identity as a prophet (Kingsbury, "Jesus as the 'Prophetic Messiah' in Luke's Gospel," 36–39). As mentioned above, however, Jesus is not expunging the identity of a prophet but the identity of a *resurrected* prophet. Mentioning Luke 9:18–20 here simply emphasizes that other Lukan characters recognize prophetic traits in Jesus.

18. An implication of Kingsbury's argument is that these implicit traits simply signify the "prophetic character" of Jesus' ministry and not his identity as a prophet (cf. "Jesus as the 'Prophetic Messiah' in Luke's Gospel," 41–42). If Luke's Jesus, however, speaks like a prophet and acts like a prophet, it seems reasonable to conclude that, within Luke's narrative logic, he is a prophet.

19. For full discussions, see Greene, "Portrayal of Jesus as Prophet in Luke-Acts"; Bock, *Luke 1:1—9:50*, 29–30; Thielman, *Theology of the New Testament*, 122–23; Bovon, *Luke the Theologian*, 201–3; Friedrich, "προφήτης," 6:846–47; Tannehill, *Narrative Unity of Luke-Acts*, 1:97; Feiler, "Jesus the Prophet," 116–95; Carroll, "Luke's Crucifixion Scene," 114; Karris, *Luke: Artist and Theologian*, 18–20, 93–94; Johnson, "Christology of Luke-Acts," 58–59; and Moessner, *Lord of the Banquet*, 47–56.

indicate future events of great significance (cf. 1 Sam 2:31; 2 Kings 20:17; Jer 7:32-34; 31:38; 33:14; 49:2; Isa 39:6; Zech 14:1).²⁰ In Luke 23:28-31, Jesus, quoting Hosea 10:8 ("they shall say to the mountains, 'Cover us, and to the hills, Fall on us'"), speaks as a prophet against Jerusalem.²¹

Adding support to Luke's characterization of Jesus as a paradigmatic OT prophet in the gospel is Luke's explicit portrayal of Jesus as an OT prophet in Acts.²² In Acts 3:22-23 ("For Moses said, 'The Lord our God will raise up for you a prophet like me'"), Peter identifies Jesus as the predicted Mosaic prophet of Deuteronomy 18:15-19 ("The LORD your God will raise up for you a prophet like me"), and, in Acts 7:37, Stephen repeats the same Deuteronomic prophecy. In Acts 2:22, Peter argues that Jesus was a man accredited by God to perform "mighty works and wonders and signs"—events that often accompanied OT prophets (cf. Deut 13:1; Isa 8:18; 20:3).²³ In Acts 4:27, the early believers recount that God "anointed" Jesus, which Gils rightly notes, is "a major trait of all prophetic portrayal."²⁴

Luke, therefore, characterizes Jesus as a prophet, a prophet whose life and ministry are situated within the continuum, and as the culmination, of the OT prophets. Jesus, then, is the OT prophet par excellence. This is more pronounced when one explores how Luke characterizes Jesus' opponents in relation to this OT prophet motif.

Jesus' Opponents as the Paradigmatic OT Prophets' Opponents

Luke contrasts his characterization of Jesus as the OT prophet par excellence by explicitly characterizing Jesus' opponents as those of OT prophets at least three times. In Luke 11:47-52 (absent in Mark; par. Matt 23:29-32), Jesus chastens the "lawyers" (νομικοῖς) with a "woe oracle" that accuses them of being descendents of those who killed the prophets. In Luke 13:33-35 (omitted in Mark; par. Matt 23:37-39), Jesus is depicted

20. Bock, *Luke 9:51—24:53*, 1561, citing Schweizer, *Luke*, 300.

21. Greene, "Portrayal of Jesus as Prophet in Luke-Acts," 119-20. Cf. Bock, *Luke 1:1—9:50*, 38.

22. I discuss only a few of these here. For full discussions, see Greene, "Portrayal of Jesus as Prophet in Luke-Acts"; Tannehill, *Narrative Unity of Luke-Acts*, 1:97; and Moessner, *Lord of the Banquet*, 50-56.

23. Greene, "Portrayal of Jesus as Prophet in Luke-Acts," 62-64 (cf. Bock, *Acts*, 120; Johnson, *Acts*, 50; Polhill, *Acts*, 111; and Pesch, *Die Apostelgeschichte*, 120).

24. Gils, *Jésus prophète d'après les Évangiles synoptiques*, 71 (cited in Bovon, *Luke the Theologian*, 203).

as a prophet and Jerusalem is depicted as his murderer. In Luke 22:63, the soldiers (οἱ ἄνδρες[25]) mockingly and ironically call Jesus a prophet while unwittingly acting in line with those "who murder the prophets" (cf. Luke 11:47–53; 13:33–35).

Luke also implicitly characterizes Jesus' opponents as those of the OT prophets. In Luke 4:14–30, Jesus directly identifies himself (Luke 4:24) as a prophet in Nazareth by quoting Isaiah 61:1–2.[26] Luke portrays the inhabitants of Nazareth as those who furiously reject Jesus and who seek to kill him (Luke 4:28–30). In Luke 6:23, 26, those that persecute the disciples are identified as the descendants of those who persecuted the prophets. Luke later identifies those who persecute the prophets as the scribes (Luke 11:49). In Luke 7:39, a Pharisee antagonistically questions Jesus' status as a prophet because of his interactions with a sinful woman; Jesus' identity as a prophet is ironically noted by the Pharisee's sarcastic comment, while the Pharisee is unwittingly portrayed as the prophet's opponent.

Adding support to Luke's characterization of Jesus' opponents as the paradigmatic opponents of the OT prophet in the gospel is Luke's portrayal of Jesus' opponents as those of OT prophets in Acts. In Acts 2:22, Luke portrays Jesus as a prophet who performed miracles, wonders, and signs, and the "men of Jerusalem . . . [and] wicked men" (Acts 2:22, 23) as those who crucified him. In Acts 3:11–24, Luke portrays Jesus as a prophet like Moses (Acts 2:22–23) and the "men of Israel" as those who kill him (Acts 3:13). In Acts 7:37–53, Luke again portrays Jesus as a prophet like Moses (Acts 7:37) and the Sanhedrin as those who kill the prophets (Acts 7:51–53).

Summary

Luke characterizes Jesus and Jesus' opponents as the paradigmatic OT prophet and as the opponents of the OT prophets, respectively. Establishing this motif is important because it shows that Luke establishes a motif of characterization independent of Mark that functions similarly to the two motifs examined below—namely, his Isaianic Servant and Davidic motifs. Now I turn attention to how Luke characterizes Jesus and Jesus'

---

25. Because of Luke's abrupt narrative shift in Luke 22:63 it is difficult to identify precisely these men who mock and beat Jesus. Bock is probably correct that, based on the larger literary context of Luke 22:47–65, these men are the "temple guards" (i.e., soldiers) of Luke 22:52 (*Luke 9:51—24:53*, 1789).

26. Evans, *Luke*, 269.

opponents in relation to his Isaianic Servant motif followed by a discussion of his use of the psalmic literature.

ISAIAH'S SERVANT MOTIF IN CHARACTERIZING JESUS AND HIS OPPONENTS

As Luke appropriates his OT prophet motif to characterize Jesus, he simultaneously appropriates Isaiah's Servant motif similarly—Luke's Jesus is, among other things, Isaiah's Servant. Herein, Luke's characterization of Jesus derives in part from, and expands upon, Mark's gospel. Recall from chapter 2 that Mark characterizes both Jesus and Jesus' opponents as the Servant and the Servant's opponents, respectively. Although following Mark in characterizing Jesus as the Servant, Luke downplays Mark's characterization of Jesus' opponents as those of Isaiah's Servant. Exploring these Lukan characterizations of Jesus and Jesus' opponents is the primary purpose for this section.

A secondary purpose is to establish that Isaiah's Servant is the primary hermeneutical grid for Luke's interpretation of his passion narrative. As argued in the previous two chapters, Isaiah's Servant, in contrast with prevailing scholarly assumptions, is not Mark's and Matthew's controlling OT hermeneutical grid in depicting their respective passion accounts; rather, it is the psalmic lamenter motif. Luke's gospel, however, reflects this prevailing scholarly assumption—Luke's depiction of Jesus as Isaiah's Servant takes a more central OT hermeneutical role in his passion account. Establishing this role here sets the stage for exploring Luke's appropriation of the Davidic psalms in my final section.

Delineating Luke's Isaianic Servant Allusions

Before discussing Luke's appropriation of Isaiah's Servant motif in characterizing Jesus and Jesus' opponents, I need to delineate Luke's allusions to it. As discussed in the previous two chapters, it is often difficult to delineate intertextual allusions, an interpretive enterprise that is often both an art and a science. Most interpreters, however, agree, especially in light of Luke's direct quote of Isaiah 53:12 in 22:37, that Luke incorporates Isaiah's Servant into his narrative.[27] Although sug-

---

27. Cf. Bock, *Luke 9:51—24:53*, 1747–49; Nolland, *Luke 18:35—24:53*, 3:1076–77; and Green, *Luke*, 775–76.

gested Lukan allusions to the Servant are numerous,[28] there is no need here to investigate all of them, since each one supports the argument of this chapter, and since Doug Moo presents a workable sampling of them: Luke 3:22 (Isa 42:1; cf. Mark 1:11), 18:32–34 (Isa 50:6; cf. Mark 10:33–34), 22:20 (Isa 53:12; cf. Mark 14:24), 37 (Isa 53:12; absent in Mark); 23:9 (Isa 53:7; cf. Mark 14:61).[29]

Jesus as Isaiah's Servant

Luke follows Mark closely four times in characterizing Jesus as Isaiah's Servant:[30] (1) God identifies Jesus as the Servant at the outset of Jesus' ministry: "You are my beloved Son; with you I am well pleased" (Luke 3:22 [Isa 42:1]; cf. Mark 1:11).[31] (2) In one of his passion predictions, Jesus states that, in fulfillment of the prophets, Jesus, like Isaiah's Servant, will be "handed over," "mocked," and "spit upon" (Luke 18:32–34 [Isa 50:6]; cf. Mark 10:33–34). (3) At the Last Supper, Jesus, as the Servant, says that

---

28. See, e.g., Leske, "Influence of Isaiah on Christology in the Gospels of Matthew and Luke," 241–69; Seccombe, "Luke and Isaiah," 252–59; and Mallen, *Reading and Transformation of Isaiah in Luke-Acts*, 134–58.

29. Moo, *Old Testament in the Gospel Passion Narratives*, 79–172. Omitted from Moo and the discussion below is Jesus' quote of Isa 61:1–2 in 4:18–19 ("The Spirit of the Lord is on me . . . to preach good news to the poor"; traditionally not considered to be an Isaianic Servant passage). Commentators often note the similarities between Isa 61:1–2 and Isaiah's Servant and that Luke may have interpreted Isa 61 similarly to the servant passages (cf. Marshall, *Luke*, 183; some also note the passage's affinity with Luke's prophet motif [cf. Bock, *Luke 1:1—9:50*, 405–6]). For a full discussion, see Bock, *Proclamation from Prophecy and Pattern*, 108–11. Although this text is omitted from the discussion below, it supports the argument of this section that to the degree that Luke has in mind Isaiah's servant passages in quoting Isa 61 is to the same degree that Luke characterizes Jesus as Isaiah's Servant in Luke 4:18–19.

30. Luke excludes two Markan allusions to Isaiah's Servant. In Luke 23:3 and Luke 22:66-67, Luke omits the Markan Jesus' "silence motif" that linguistically and thematically connects the passages to Isa 53:7. These omissions prove insignificant, since Luke includes similar silence motifs in relation to Herod in Luke 23:9 ("but [Jesus] made no answer") and another one in the Ethiopian Eunuch's lengthy quote of Isa 53:7-8 in Acts 8:32–33 ("like a lamb before its shearer is silent, so he opens not his mouth").

31. Luke's redaction of Mark 9:7 ("This is my Son, whom I love [ἀγαπητός]. Listen to him") at the Transfiguration in 9:35 ("This is my Son, my Chosen One [ἐκλελεγμένος]; listen to him")—changing ἀγαπητός to ἐκλελεγμένος—perhaps aligns the passage more so with Isa 42:1 (בחיר ["chosen"]), thus adding another Lukan characterization of Jesus with Isaiah's Servant and strengthening the connection between the two motifs in Luke 3:22 (cf. Bock, *Luke 1:1—9:50*, 874; Nolland, *Luke 9:21—18:34*, 2:501–2).

he will pour out his blood for his disciples (Luke 22:20 [Isa 53:10–12]; cf. Mark 14:24).[32] Finally, Jesus, like Isaiah's Servant, remains silent before his accusers (Luke 23:9 [Isa 53:7]; cf. Mark 14:61).

Luke's interest in characterizing Jesus as Isaiah's Servant in his second volume adds supplementary evidence to Luke's allusions to the motif in his first volume. In Acts 3:13, Peter specifically calls Jesus the "servant" (παῖδα) who was "handed over" (παρεδώδατε) to die.[33] In Acts 3:26, Peter again uses the title "servant" (παῖδα) in identifying Jesus.[34] In Acts 8:32–35, the Ethiopian Eunuch, while reading a lengthy quote of Isaiah 53:7–8 ("Like a sheep he was led to the slaughter"), asks Philip, "Who is [Isaiah] talking about?" Philip replies by identifying Jesus as the Isaianic figure of Isaiah 53.[35]

Luke adds to Mark a direct quote of the Isaianic Servant in Luke 22:37 that indicates a unique Lukan interest that is pertinent to the argument of my next section below.[36] While Mark focuses on the disciples' desertion of Jesus via a quote of Zechariah 13:7 ("I will strike the shepherd, and the sheep will be scattered" [Mark 14:27–31; cf. Matt 26:31–35]),[37] Luke frames his entire crucifixion account with Jesus' quote of Isaiah 53:12: in Luke 22:37:

> For I tell you that this Scripture must be fulfilled in me: "And he was numbered with the transgressors." For what is written about me has its fulfillment.

---

32. There is a longstanding text-critical issue concerning Luke 22:17-20. Although some MSS omit Luke 22:19b-20: "This is my body, which is given for you " (D and some Old Latin MSS), most include it (P[75], ℵ, A, B, C, L, T, W, Δ, Q, Ψ, etc). Bock is correct that the longer text is original because of its widespread attestation and because it is the more difficult reading (Bock, *Luke 9:51—24:53*, 1722). For full discussions with accompanying bibliographies, see Bock, *Luke 9:51—24:53*, 1721-22, Moo, *Old Testament in the Gospel Passion Narratives*, 127-30, and Nolland, *Luke 18:35—24:53*, 3:1040.

33. Bock, *Acts*, 169; Peterson, *Acts*, 174-75; and Cullmann, *Christology of the New Testament*, 73-75. Contra Jones, "Title *Pais* in Luke-Acts," 148-65.

34. Peterson, *Acts*, 185, and Barrett, *Acts*, 1:213.

35. Bock, *Acts*, 341-42; Peterson, *Acts*, 295-96; and Barrett, *Acts*, 1:429.

36. Also important in Luke, especially for his Christology, but less significant for my purposes, is his exclusion of Jesus' explanation of his death as a "ransom for many" (Mark 10:45 [Isa 53:10-12]; cf. Luke 22:22-47) (cf. Bock, *Luke 9:51—24:53*, 1748).

37. Mallen, *Reading and Transformation of Isaiah in Luke-Acts*, 142.

This Isaianic quote specifically foreshadows Jesus' pending crucifixion between two criminals (Luke 23:32, 39–43).[38] Thus, Luke clearly indicates that his crucifixion account is a fulfillment of Isaiah 53:12. Pao and Schnabel's suggestion that Luke's quotation of Isaiah 53:12 at this narrative juncture serves as "the hermeneutical key to the passion narrative" might be an overstatement—but not by much.[39] According to Luke's narrative logic, every OT evocation in Luke's crucifixion scene, including the evocations to the psalmic literature, must be interpreted in the shadow of Luke's quote of Isaiah 53:12 in 22:37. The significance of Luke's reference to this Isaianic text as it relates to his evocations of the psalmic literature at Jesus' crucifixion is discussed in the next section.

Luke, then, follows Mark in characterizing Jesus as Isaiah's Servant, adding a quote of Isaiah 53:12 in 22:37 at a crucial juncture that frames his entire crucifixion account. Next I look at how Luke appropriates Isaiah's Servant in characterizing Jesus' opponents.

Jesus' Opponents as Those of Isaiah's Servant?

Although Luke clearly follows Mark in characterizing Jesus as Isaiah's Servant, his interest in characterizing Jesus' opponents as those of Isaiah's Servant is less clear. Recall that Mark characterizes Jesus' opponents twice as those of the Servant. In Mark 14:65, those gathered before the Sanhedrin "spit" (ἐμπτύω) on Jesus in the same way that the Servant's opponents spit on him (ἐμπτύω; cf. Isa 50:6). Additionally, in Mark 15:19, the soldiers, in a similar way, spit (ἐμπτύω) on Jesus. Although Luke retains similar, albeit truncated, episodes of mocking (cf. Luke 22:63–65; 23:11), he omits the "spitting" of the opponents that would directly link them to Isaiah's Servant.

In spite of omitting these two references to Isaiah's spitting, Luke includes a reference to it in Luke 18:32, a reference in which Jesus predicts the events of the passion: Jesus tells his disciples that the "Gentiles" will "mock him, insult him, spit [ἐμπτυσθήσεται] on him, flog him, and kill him" (par. Mark 10:34). Specifically, this reference predicts and explains the events of the Lukan passion—events that exclude further Isaianic references to spitting. In light of Luke's pervasive interest in Isaiah's Servant, it is impossible to know why he omits allusions to it in the mocking scenes

38. Bock, *Luke 9:51—24:53*, 1748.
39. Pao and Schnabel, "Luke," 399.

of the passion when he apparently shows awareness of it in Luke 18:32.⁴⁰ Whatever the reason, Luke downplays the particular significance of the Servant's opponents as it relates to Jesus' passion opponents.⁴¹

Summary

Luke follows Mark in characterizing Jesus as Isaiah's Servant but downplays Mark's characterization of Jesus' opponents as the Servant's opponents. In appropriating the Servant motif, Luke, independently of Mark, frames his passion narrative with a quote of Isaiah 53:12 in Luke 22:37 ("and he was numbered with the transgressors"). This Isaianic quote proves significant in my next discussion of how Luke appropriates the psalmic literature in characterizing Jesus and Jesus' opponents.

THE PSALMS IN THE PASSION: JESUS AND HIS OPPONENTS AS THOSE OF THE DAVIDIC KING AND LAMENTER?⁴²

The conclusions of the previous two sections indicate a general Lukan awareness of Mark's motif of characterizing Jesus and Jesus' opponents as OT hero and villains. As Luke's Jesus enters Jerusalem, faces conflict with his opponents, and dies, Luke continues to follow Mark with this motif of characterization: Jesus and Jesus' opponents continue to function as OT hero and villains, specifically in relation to the OT Psalms. As I demonstrate here, Luke's portrayal of these psalmic characters, however, differs in narratively and christologically significant ways.

This section, in exploring these Lukan characterizations, directs attention in part back to Ahearne-Kroll's contributions and to my

---

40. Perhaps Luke uses sources other than Mark (cf. Bock, *Luke 9:51—24:53*, 1789-90), sources that omit the spitting motif. This, however, does not fully explain the issue since Luke was aware of, and used extensively, Mark's passion account and since Luke shows awareness of Mark's spitting motif in general (Luke 18:32).

41. Cf. Bock, *Luke 9:51—24:53*, 1790.

42. In the previous two chapters, I separated the discussions of Mark's and Matthew's appropriation of the Psalms into two separate sections—non-lament and lament psalms. In this chapter, however, it is necessary to conflate these two sections because, as demonstrated below, Luke shows no distinct understanding of the psalmic lament in his characterization of Jesus.

advancements of his work discussed in chapter 2.[43] Recall that Ahearne-Kroll argues that Mark characterizes Jesus as the Messianic Davidic king via several quotes and allusions to non-lament Psalms 109 ("Blessed is he who comes in the name of the Lord " and "the Lord said to my Lord") and 117 ("the stone which the builders rejected"). Furthermore, Ahearne-Kroll argues that Mark characterizes Jesus as the psalmic lamenter par excellence via numerous evocations of the psalmic lament in Gethsemane and at the crucifixion. Finally, recall that chapter 2 advances Ahearne-Kroll's work by arguing that Mark characterizes Jesus' opponents as the Davidic psalmic villains, coalescing and crescendoing this motif of characterization in the passion account. In light of Luke's related use of many of these psalms, the comprehensive goal of this section is to test on his gospel Ahearne-Kroll's arguments and the advancements made to them in chapter 2.

More specifically, in this section, I argue that Luke follows Mark in characterizing Jesus as the psalmic Davidic king but does little to characterize him as the psalmic Davidic lamenter. In other words, as stated at the outset of this chapter, there is, at best, a muted voice of the lamenter to be heard in Luke's characterization of Jesus. The predominant OT voice, rather, that is heard most clearly in Luke's passion is that of Isaiah's righteous Suffering Servant. I additionally argue that Luke follows Mark in characterizing Jesus' opponents as those of the psalmic Davidic king but with one major difference. Luke downplays the significance of characterizing Jesus' opponents as those of the Davidic psalmist at the crucifixion.

Three steps are needed to make these points. (1) Delineating Luke's psalmic evocations provides the primary data to be explored in the subsequent two steps: (2) Luke's appropriation of the Psalms in characterizing Jesus, and (3) Luke's appropriation of the Psalms in characterizing Jesus' opponents.

Delineating Luke's Psalmic Evocations

Two sets of Lukan data are delineated in this section. Following the methodology of Ahearne-Kroll and the advancements made to his work in chapters 2 and 3, in this section, I first delineate Luke's uses of Psalms

---

43. The focus here is not to explore Luke's general use of the Psalms, which many have aptly undertaken (see Doble, "Psalms in Luke-Acts," 83–117). The focus, rather, is specifically on how Luke in relation to Mark characterizes Jesus and Jesus' opponents via the psalmic literature.

109 and 117. Second, I delineate Luke's evocations of the psalmic lament. The methodology I use for delineating these Lukan lament psalms is Ahearne-Kroll's concept of simple evocation—allusions that refer to only one OT text (see "Methodology" in chapter 1). As in chapters 2 and 3, I undertake an auxiliary investigation of supplementary data at the end of this section that includes other Lukan allusions to psalmic literature.

The psalmic data discussed in this section, including the "Supplementary Data" at the end of this section, comes from three sources: Pao and Schnabel's commentary on Luke in Beale's and Carson's *Commentary on the New Testament Use of the Old Testament*, the NA^{27}, and Moo's *Old Testament in the Gospel Passion Narratives*. Some methodological caveats are in order concerning the data that comes from Pao and Schnabel's Lukan commentary. Recall from chapter 3 that the same methodology of amassing Matthew's possible psalmic evocations was used in relation to Craig Blomberg's commentary on Matthew in Beale's and Carson's *Commentary on the New Testament Use of the Old Testament*. Pao and Schnabel's approach to Luke's gospel differs from Blomberg's approach to Matthew's gospel in a way pertinent to the discussion below.

Pao and Schnabel, to a significantly greater degree than Blomberg, often list at great length possible OT background passages to respective NT references. For example, in explaining the Gerasene demoniac in Luke 8:26–39, Pao and Schnabel provide general OT background information concerning the connection between impurities in general and the pagan/demonic worship of idols among the Gentiles more specifically. Included in this background information is lament Psalm 24:4 (MT);[44] Pao and Schnabel do not intend to suggest a direct Lukan allusion to or echo of MT Psalm 24:4. Including all such references from Pao and Schnabel is beyond the scope, and is unnecessary for the argument, of this section. The Psalmic texts, then, that Pao and Schnabel include merely as background information, which are not intended to be understood as echoes or allusions, are omitted.[45]

---

44. Pao and Schnabel, "Luke," 308–9. See esp. Pao and Schnabel's discussion of "fasting" in Luke 5:35 ("Luke," 293).

45. These omitted Lukan texts include the following. Psalmic lament: Luke 1:46–55, 78; 3:9; 5:24, 35; 6:36, 43–45; 8:22–25; 26–39; 10:20, 21–22; 11:1–4, 13; 12:20, 22–34, 49–59; 13:34, 35a; 16:15; 18:18–20, 38–39; 20:9–19, 35–36; 21:25–28; 22:39–46, 63–65; 23:18, 25; 24:44–49. Non-lament psalms: Luke 1:32–33, 46–47, 50, 53, 54–55, 68–79, 71, 72, 74–75; 2:11, 19, 34; 3:31; 4:43; 6:20–26, 21, 25, 30; 9:28–36; 11:1–4, 20; 12:12, 28; 13:27, 28–29, 35a; 17:29; 18:1–8; 20:9–19, 47; 21:25, 26, 27, 33b; 22:24–38, 39–46; 23:9–11; 24:46.

Of Heroes and Villains

Luke's Evocations of Psalms 109 and 117

I do not need to discuss at length four of the five Lukan evocations of Psalms 109 and 117, since there is a general consensus that they are marked or unmarked quotations of these respective psalms. These four are evocations are Psalm 117:26 in (1) Luke 13:35 and (2) Luke 19:38 ("Blessed is he who comes in the name of the Lord!"); (3) Psalm 117:22 in Luke 20:17 ("The stone that the builders rejected has become the cornerstone"); and (4) Psalm 109:1 in Luke 20:42–43 ("The Lord said to my Lord, 'Sit at my right hand, until I make your enemies your footstool'").

A fifth evocation, however, requires a few brief comments. Luke 22:69b shares several linguistic parallels with Psalm 109:1:

Psalm 109:1: εἶπεν ὁ κύριος τῷ κυρίῳ μου <u>κάθου ἐκ δεξιῶν</u> μου

Luke 22:69: ἔσται ὁ υἱὸς τοῦ ἀνθρώπου <u>καθήμενος ἐκ δεξιῶν</u> τῆς δυνάμεως τοῦ θεοῦ

Aside from these linguistic parallels, the popularity of Psalm 109 in early Christianity—the most quoted OT verse in the NT[46]—and Luke's broader use of Psalm 109:1 suggests an evocation. Luke quotes Psalm 109:1 (Luke 20:42–43) two chapters earlier, and quotes it again in Acts 2:34–35. In the immediate context of the quote of Psalm 109:1 in Acts 2:34–35, Luke further emphasizes Jesus' exaltation to God's right hand (Acts 2:33). Finally, Luke changes Mark's word order (ἐκ δεξιῶν καθήμενον) by fronting καθήμαι, aligning Luke 22:69 more centrally with Psalm 109:1. Luke 22:69, then, is a simple evocation of Psalm 109:1.[47]

Luke's Lament Evocations

Pao and Schnabel, the NA[27], and Moo note thirteen possible Lukan lament allusions. I suggest that at least four are simple evocations.[48] I delineate these four here while I discuss the other nine at the end of this

---

46. Direct quotes: Matt 22:44; Mark 12:36; Acts 2:34–35; Heb 1:13. Partial quotes and allusions: Matt 26:64; Mark 14:62; Rom 8:34; 1 Cor 15:25; Eph 1:20, 22; Col 3:1; Heb 1:3; 8:1; 10:12–13. For a thorough discussion, see Hay, *Glory at the Right Hand*, 45–46.

47. Cf. Bock, *Luke 9:51—24:53*, 1796–1801, and Nolland, *Luke 18:35—24:53*, 3:1110–11.

48. In light of the lengthier discussions in chapters 2 and 3, which include background explorations into Second Temple literature, it is unnecessary to discuss here these evocations at length.

section as supplementary data.⁴⁹ There is no need to discuss at length two of these four Lukan evocations since most scholars agree that they are marked or unmarked quotations of these respective psalms: (1) Psalm 6:9 in Luke 13:27 ("Depart from me, all you workers of evil"), and (2) Psalm 30:6 in Luke 23:46 ("Father, into your hands I commit my spirit").⁵⁰

Two others, however, require a few brief comments. Scholars widely agree that Luke 23:34 evokes Psalm 21:19 for four reasons. First, there are significant lexical similarities between the texts:

Psalm 21:19: <u>διεμερίσαντο τὰ ἱμάτιά</u> μου ἑαυτοῖς καὶ ἐπὶ τὸν ἱματισμόν μου <u>ἔβαλον κλῆρον</u>

Luke 23:34: <u>διαμεριζόμενοι</u> δὲ <u>τὰ ἱμάτιά</u> αὐτοῦ, <u>ἔβαλον κλῆρον</u>

Second, a suffering person is only described in this way in Psalm 21:9. Third, this detail is not necessary for the progress of the Lukan narrative. Finally, Psalm 21 is widely attested in the Second Temple era (see discussions in chapters 2 and 3).⁵¹

Scholars also widely agree that Luke evokes Psalm 21:8–9 in 23:35 for three reasons. First, there are significant lexical parallels between the texts:

Psalm 21:8–9: ⁸πάντες οἱ <u>θεωροῦντές</u> με <u>ἐξεμυκτύρισάν</u>... ⁹ἤλπισεν ἐπὶ κύριον <u>ῥυσάσθω</u> αὐτὸν <u>σωσάτω</u> αὐτόν ὅτι θέλει αὐτόν

Luke 23:35: ὁ λαὸς <u>θεωρῶν</u>. <u>Ἐξεμυκτήριζον</u>... οἱ ἄρχοντες λέγοντες, ἄλλους <u>ἔσωσεν</u>, <u>σωσάτω</u> ἑαυτόν

---

49. The nine excluded references are Luke 1:35; 2:38; 5:30; 12:10; 13:28; 18:13; 21:33a; 22:42; and 23:9. As noted in the supplementary data below, seven of these are excluded as simple evocations because they allude to more than one OT text. The other two are excluded based on thin linguistic and thematic parallels: (1) Jesus' use of the "the Holy Spirit" (τὸ ἅγιον πνεῦμα) in his statement about blasphemy (Luke 12:10) is similar to David's reference in Ps 50:13: "Do not take your Holy Spirit (τὸ πνεῦμα τὸ ἅγιόν) from me." In light of Luke's pervasive use of the "Holy Spirit" in Luke-Acts (at least fifty times), however, it is dubious to specify a psalmic allusion at this particular juncture. (2) In Luke 18:13, a tax collector prays "God, have mercy on me, a sinner (Ο θεός, ἱλάσθητί μοι τῷ ἁμαρτωλῷ)" in a similar way that David prays in Ps 50:1–3 "Have mercy (λέησόν) on me, O God (ὁ θεός)... blot out my transgressions (ἀνομίαν)." OT characters address God (ὁ θεός) too frequently (cf. Ps 39:9; 59:3) to ensure a linguistic connection specifically between Ps 50:1–3 and Luke 18:13, and the two different terms that Luke uses (ἱλάσθητί... ἁμαρτωλῷ) in place of those in Psalm 50 (λέησόν... ἀνομίαν) decrease the likelihood of a simple evocation.

50. The classification of Psalm 30 as a lament is actually debated. See below.

51. Pao and Schnabel, "Luke," 396 (cf. Nolland, *Luke 18:35—24:53*, 3:1146, and Bock, *Luke 9:51—24:53*, 1850).

Second, the verbs θεωρέω and ἐκμυκτηρίζω appear in the same context only in Psalm 21:8. Third, aside from 23:35, Luke only uses ἐκμυκτηρίζω once (Luke 16:14). Finally, as stated above and as established at length in chapters 2 and 3, Psalm 21 is widely attested in the Second Temple era.[52]

The Psalms in Characterizing Jesus

Jesus as David?

Luke makes clear from the outset of his gospel that Jesus is the Son of David (Luke 1:27, 32; 3:31).[53] Furthermore, Luke, like Mark, evokes Psalms 109 and 117 in various passages to present Jesus as David's heir to the throne. There is debate, however, whether Luke follows Mark in depicting Jesus *as* David. Bovon, for example, argues:

> Luke does not insist on the typology David-Jesus, but rather on the continuity of history and its fulfillment in Christ. More than a new David, Jesus is the descendant (the son) of David, he in whom the promise is fulfilled. . . . Luke prefers to note the ontological difference in the continuity of redemptive history rather than the identity in the contemporaneous nature of the figures.[54]

Rese agrees, arguing that Lukan typology is found only in Acts 7:37 ("This is the Moses who said to the Israelites, 'God will raise up for you a prophet like me from your brothers'").[55] Dupont, suggesting otherwise, contends that Luke appropriates the OT figures Joseph, Moses, David, and possibly Jonah as types of Christ.[56] Bock, agreeing with Dupont by noting examples like Luke's prophet motif (see discussion above), retorts against Rese, "Rese may well have underestimated the nature and the role of typology or OT pattern in his work."[57]

---

52. Pao and Schnabel, "Luke," 397 (cf. Nolland, *Luke 18:35—24:53*, 3:1147, and Bock, *Luke 9:51—24:53*, 1851).

53. Strauss, *Davidic Messiah in Luke-Acts*, 76–125; Leske, "Influence of Isaiah on Christology in Matthew and Luke," 247; and Green, *Theology of the Gospel of Luke*, 55–56.

54. Bovon, *Luke the Theologian*, 104 (cf. pp. 99–106, 117–21).

55. Rese, *Alttestamentliche Motive in der Christologie des Lukas*, 36–42.

56. Dupont, *Salvation of the Gentiles*, 129–59.

57. Bock, *Proclamation from Prophecy and Pattern*, 42, 120–21.

Although not as prominent as in Mark (or Matthew), I agree with Dupont and Bock that Luke portrays Jesus as a new David.[58] Luke appropriates Psalms 109, 117, and, foreshadowing the discussion in the next subsection, Psalm 30 to characterize Jesus as David (see "Supplementary Data" below). Furthermore, I agree with Bovon that Luke's Jesus is more than David,[59] but, as I will establish now, within Luke's narrative logic, I think that Jesus also functions as David.

In Luke 13:35, Jesus quotes Psalm 117:26 to say that Jerusalem "will not see [him] again until [she] says 'Blessed is he who comes in the name of the Lord.'" Independently of Mark, Luke personifies Jerusalem as the worshippers of Psalm 117:26 who praise God for the coming king. Conversely, this implies that Jesus is the personified king of Psalm 117—namely, David. In 19:38 Luke presents a scenario in which the characters of the scene correspond to those of Psalm 117. Herein, Luke appropriates Psalm 117:26 to characterize "the whole crowd of disciples" as those who praise God for Jesus as he enters Jerusalem as king (note Luke's redaction of the quote to include "King"). Also included in this scene are Pharisees who challenge Jesus' kingship (Luke 19:39–40), which parallels the psalmist's opponents who challenge David's kingship (Ps 117:22; cf. Luke 20:17: "The stone the builders rejected"). As Luke characterizes the crowd and the Pharisees as certain participants of Psalm 117, Luke also characterizes Jesus as the central protagonist of Psalm 117 who is honored as king—namely, David. Luke returns to Psalm 117 in Luke 20:17. After telling a parable about tenants who kill a farmer's heir (Luke 20:9–16), Jesus compares himself to this heir via a quote of Psalm 117:22: "The stone the builders rejected has become the capstone." Jesus is the rejected stone of Psalm 117—namely, David.

A few scenes later in Luke 20:42, Jesus quotes Psalm 109:1 ("The Lord said to my Lord . . .") to explain his messianic relationship to David: "David thus calls him Lord, so how is he his son?" (Luke 20:44). In this scene, Luke does not appropriate Psalm 109:1 to characterize Jesus as David but, instead, emphasizes Jesus' role as one greater than David (cf. Acts 2:34–35). Luke's Jesus, however, returns to the same psalmic verse

---

58. Strauss, *Davidic Messiah in Luke-Acts*, 126–29, corrects Voss' erroneous argument that Luke's understanding of Jesus as a "new David" abrogates Jesus' Davidic sonship (*Die Christologie der lukanischen Schriften in Grundzügen*, 68). The two motifs are simply opposite sides of the same coin. Luke presents Jesus both as the genealogical son of David and as a character who lives and behaves like him.

59. See, for example, Luke 20:44: "David calls [the Christ] 'Lord.' How then can he be his son?"

(Ps 109:1) in Luke 22:69, speaking as David to his opponents: "From now on the Son of Man will be seated at the right hand of the mighty God" (cf. Mark 14:62).[60] Luke's Jesus is both more than the David of Psalm 109 (Luke 20:44) and is characterized as the David of Psalm 109 (Luke 22:69).

Foreshadowing the discussion in the next subsection, Luke uses an established early Christian hermeneutic to characterize Jesus as David at the crucifixion. Recall from chapter 2 the discussion of Richard Hays's argument that the NT writers pervasively employ a hermeneutical device that portrays Jesus as a petitioner of the Psalms, providing a matrix for their Christology.[61] In 23:46, Luke uses this hermeneutical device to characterize Jesus as the petitioner of Psalm 30: "Father, into your hands I commit my spirit."[62] In the same way that David trustingly prays to God as he succumbs to the attacks of his opponents, Jesus prays the identical words of David in a similar situation. Luke, then, characterizes Jesus as David by portraying him as the speaker of Psalm 30.[63]

Jesus as the Psalmic Lamenter?

Although Luke characterizes Jesus as *king* David, he does not overtly follow Mark in characterizing Jesus as the *lamenting* David, which, as discussed in the conclusion at chapter's end, has significant narrative implications for Luke's gospel. In chapter 1, I asked the question, "To what degree do Mark and Matthew recognize the lament genre?" I demonstrated there that these two writers understand how the lament functions, and I demonstrated in chapters 2 and 3, via an advancement of Ahearne-Kroll's monograph, that they appropriate it toward certain literary and rhetorical ends. Here, Ahearne-Kroll's thesis that Mark characterizes Jesus as the psalmic lamenter is tested on the Third gospel by

---

60. Note Luke's omission of Mark's allusion to Dan 7:13 ["coming with the clouds of heaven"], perhaps emphasizing the evocation of Ps 109:1.

61. Hays, "Christ Prays the Psalms," 101–8.

62. Contrary to Matthew, Luke does not employ this hermeneutical device in his direct quote of Ps 6:9 in 13:27 ("But he will reply, 'I don't know you. . . . Away from me, all you evildoers"; absent in Mark). In Matthew's version, Jesus is the speaker of the Psalm (Matt 7:23; cf. discussion in chapter 3) while in Luke's version, the speaker is the "house owner" (Luke 13:25).

63. Cf. Doble, who notes that in Luke's passion narrative, the readers "'hear' David's voice" ("Psalms in Luke-Acts," 113).

Luke's Appropriation of the Psalmic Lament?

asking the same question in relation to Luke: "To what degree does Luke recognize the lament genre in characterizing Jesus?"

Contrary to Mark and Matthew, Luke shows no clear awareness of the core elements of the psalmic lament in his Gethsemane and crucifixion accounts.[64] Recall from chapter 1, based on the contributions of Claus Westermann, that the core elements of the psalmic lament consist of a distressful complaint/question/appeal from a petitioner directed toward God (a prayer) in order to bring about change for a real or perceived problem. As discussed in chapters 2 and 3, when these elements occur concurrently with evocations of the psalmic lament genre (e.g., in Mark's and Matthew's Gethsemane and crucifixion accounts), then it is likely that the respective gospel writer understands and appropriates, beyond simple thematic trends (e.g., "wagging heads" and "casting lots for clothing"), the core function of the psalmic lament. Luke omits Mark's characterization of Jesus as the psalmic lamenter; I make this argument by exploring Luke's Gethsemane and crucifixion accounts in relation to those in Mark.

Luke's version of Gethsemane (lit. "Mount of Olives"; Luke 22:39) retains Jesus' prayer in 22:42 ("Father, if you are willing, remove this cup from me"), which essentially contains the core elements of the lament. Jesus, facing a cruel death, is a distraught petitioner who prays to God in order to bring about change for his plight ("take this cup from me").[65] Luke, however, omits at least five other contextual clues that do not indicate a clear intention to characterize Jesus as a psalmic lamenter.[66]

First, Luke omits Mark's evocation of Psalm 41/42 ("why are you grieved O my soul"). Recall from chapter 2 that Mark characterizes Jesus as the lamenter in 14:34 (περίλυπός ἐστιν ἡ ψυχή μου) by placing on Jesus'

---

64. Luke's tax collector in Luke 18:13 (perhaps) laments to God in the language similar to Ps 50:1: "But the tax collector, standing far off, would not even lift up his eyes to heaven, but beat his breast, saying, 'God, be merciful to me, a sinner!'" In light of my focus on Luke's depiction of Jesus, it is beyond the scope of this subsection to explore the implications of this tax collector's prayer.

65. Cf. Eklund, "Lord, Teach Us How to Grieve," 29, 41–44.

66. Based on Jesus' petition in Luke 22:42 ("remove this cup") and on the textually disputed inclusion of Luke 22:43–44 ("and his sweat became like drops of blood"), Eklund argues otherwise—namely, that Jesus appears clearly in Luke's Gethsemane account as a lamenter ("Lord , Teach Us How to Grieve," 28–46). But, if I am right in understanding the following five contextual clues as an indication of Luke's movement away from a portrayal of Jesus as a lamenter, then perhaps Eklund's interpretation of Luke's Gethsemane account has been too much influenced by her reading of Mark's and Matthew's accounts.

lips the words of Psalms 41:6, 12; 42:5 (περίλυπος εἶ ψυχή). Closely related to this, second, is Luke's omission of Mark's threefold prayer refrain (Mark 14:35, 39, 41). Recall again from chapter 2 that the Markan Jesus' threefold prayer refrain is important in linking Jesus to the lamenter of Psalm 41/42. Third, Luke omits Mark's explicit mention of Jesus being handed over to "sinners." Recall from chapter 2 that the presence of sinners in Mark's Gethsemane scene helps substantiate a connection between Jesus and the lamenter.

Fourth, Luke omits the Markan Jesus' posture of despair. In Mark 14:35, Jesus "[falls] to the ground to pray" (Mark 14:35; cf. Matt 26:39: "he fell on his face and prayed"). In Luke 22:41, Jesus "knelt down and prayed," a posture that, Neyrey argues, does not indicate the despair that one finds in Mark and Matthew.[67] Finally, Luke omits Mark's mention of Jesus' deep distress (Mark 14:33: Jesus was "greatly distressed and troubled").[68]

In the crucifixion account, Luke records Jesus' quote of Psalm 30:6 ("Father, into your hands I commit my spirit") and excludes the Markan Jesus' quote of Psalm 21:1 ("My God, my God why have you forsaken me"). Although Psalm 30 *may* be classified as a lament psalm,[69] Luke places a prayer on Jesus' lips that is significantly different in nature than those in Mark's account. Mark's Jesus dies with a petitionary question to God about his plight: "My God my God why have you forsaken me?" Luke's Jesus, on the other hand, dies with a calm transition into the

---

67. Neyrey bases his argument on Luke's favored formula for "kneeling" (θεὶς τὰ γόνατα) that, in Stephen's case in Acts 7:60, indicates a "virtuous and dignified posture in the face of death" (cf. Acts 20:36 and 21:15) (*Passion According to Luke*, 53).

68. Neyrey, *Passion According to Luke*, 50–54 (cf. Neyrey, "Absence of Jesus' Emotions," 153–59). Ostensibly, it appears that if Luke 22:43-44 ("An angel from heaven... strengthened him. And being in agony [ἀγωνίᾳ] he prayed more earnestly; and his sweat became like great drops of blood falling down to the ground"), a difficult textual problem to resolve, is original to Luke, then Luke portrays Jesus in deep grief. Neyrey notes, however, that ἀγωνία denotes courageous resolve instead of grievous fear (Neyrey, *Passion According to Luke*, 58–62). If Eklund and others are right that ἀγωνία, indeed, denotes grief (Eklund, "Lord, Teach Us How to Grieve," 34–35), and setting aside the question of the verse's authenticity, then only an incremental degree of support is added to the argument that Luke intends to portray a lamenting Jesus, a degree of support that, I think, is called into question by these five contextual clues under discussion. For a balanced look at the text-critical issues related to Luke 22:43-44, see Bock, *Luke*, 1763–64, and Brown, *Death of the Messiah*, 1:177–86.

69. See discussion in Craigie, *Psalm 1–50*, 197–98; 251–52.

Father's hands via a prayer of trust.[70] Specifically, Jesus' prayer in Luke does not reflect the core elements of the lament in spite of Luke's awareness of the tradition that understands Jesus' crucifixion on the backdrop of Psalm 21 (Luke 23:34: "They divided up his clothes by casting lots" [cf. Ps 21:19]; and Luke 23:35: "The people stood watching" [cf. Ps 21:8–9]).[71]

Luke, although appropriating themes from what modern scholars call the psalmic lament genre, does not overtly depict Jesus as a lamenter. Thus, it is anachronistic for scholars to speak emphatically of the lament in relation to Luke's Jesus, although commentators frequently do so.[72] In relation to his presentation of Jesus with David, Luke, then, broadly appropriates the Psalms more monolithically. Luke's Jesus is *king* David but there is little indication that he is the *lamenting* David. For the remainder of this chapter, then, I will make no distinction between Luke's use of lament and non-lament psalms.

The Psalms in Characterizing Jesus' Opponents

As Luke follows Mark in characterizing Jesus as the psalmic King David, he also follows Mark in characterizing Jesus' opponents as those of the Davidic psalmist. Luke, however, departs from this Markan characterization in one significant way. Luke downplays Mark's characterization of Jesus' opponents as those of the Davidic psalmist at the crucifixion by excluding the crowd as Jesus' opponents, by omitting some Markan evocations to the Psalms, and by highlighting various participants at the crucifixion who do not oppose Jesus. In other words, whereas Mark presents every participant in close proximity to Jesus' execution in unified opposition to Jesus under the rubric of the psalmic literature, Luke's crucifixion account is less monolithic.

---

70. Bock, *Proclamation from Prophecy and Pattern*, 147. For a discussion of possible Lukan motives in this unique presentation of Jesus' dying words, see ibid., 147–48.

71. Or, perhaps as Eklund argues ("Lord, Teach Us How to Grieve" 55–57), Luke's evocations of Psalm 21 preceded by Jesus' quote of Psalm 30 depicts Jesus as a lamenter turning in trust to God, a common device used by the psalmists. But, in light of the above discussion about Jesus in Gethsemane and given Luke's broader downplaying of the motif at the crucifixion (as discussed here and in the next subsection), it is difficult to ensure that Luke intends to depict Jesus as a lamenter. Thus, I think that one can only, at best, speak of a whisper of the lament in Luke's characterization of Jesus.

72. Campbell, "NT Scholar's Use of OT Lament Terminology," 213–26.

Of Heroes and Villains

Establishing this requires making three points. First, I must demonstrate, via a general overview of Luke's characterization of the religious leaders and the crowd that Luke follows Mark in depicting them as distinct unified character groups with identifiably consistent traits. Second, I show that Luke also follows Mark in characterizing Jesus' opponents and the crowd in relation to the psalmist's opponents. These first two steps provide the foundation for, third, an examination of how Luke downplays in his crucifixion account Mark's characterization of Jesus' opponents as those of the Davidic psalmist.

General Characterization of Jesus' Opponents and the Crowd

In a seminal narrative-critical work on conflict in Luke's gospel, Kingsbury correctly argues that, aside from three foils (Zechariah in Luke 1:5, Jairus in Luke 8:41, and Joseph of Arimathea in Luke 23:50–51),[73] Luke's Pharisees, scribes, chief priests, captains/officers of the temple, elders, rulers, and Sadducees form a unified character group.[74] In the same work, Kingsbury also argues that Luke's crowd similarly forms a unified character group. Luke's formation of these character groups is similar to Mark's narrative portrayal of the same groups. First, I discuss Luke's characterization of the religious leaders, followed by a discussion of the crowd.

Luke introduces the religious leaders in 5:17–26 as those who oppose Jesus' claim to have authority to forgive sin. This opposition remains virtually constant through every major Lukan narrative division.[75] In Jesus' Galilean ministry (Luke 4:14—9:50), the religious leaders oppose

---

73. A few foils also surface in Acts 6:7 (some priests), 15:5 (some Pharisees), and 26:5 (Paul, the Pharisee).

74. Kingsbury, *Conflict in Luke*, 21–22 (cf. Bock, *Luke 1:1—9:50*, 37; contra Brawley, *Luke-Acts and the Jews*, 84–132, who argues that the Sadducees are Jesus' primary opponents, and Moxnes, *Economy of the Kingdom*, 18, who argues that the Pharisees are clearly distinguishable from the Sadducees). For a more detailed narrative-critical summary of the religious leaders in Luke, see Tannehill, *Narrative Unity of Luke-Acts*, 1:167–99. Green calls Kingsbury's monolithic understanding of "the Jews" as a "major failing" (*Theology of the Gospel of Luke*, 69n33). Green's rebuttal to Kingsbury is that Luke, aside from writing negatively about the Jews, also writes positively about *Judaism* (ibid., 71–72, italics added). In discussing Luke's positive presentation, Green subtly shifts his focus away from the Jews proper to the institution of Judaism. Kingsbury's focus, however, is on Luke's characterization of individuals and groups and not on Luke's depiction of Judaism as an institution.

75. On Luke's division into these three major sections, see Bock, *Luke 1:1—9:50*, 44–48.

Jesus' challenge to their Sabbath traditions (Luke 6:1–11) and, as early as Luke 6:11, "discuss with one another what they might do to Jesus." In the subsequent chapter, Jesus, in a conversation with the crowd, reveals that at the Messiah's debut, the religious leaders reject John the Baptist (Luke 7:29–30), Jesus' forerunner. They also challenge Jesus' prophetic ability in relation to a sinful woman (Luke 7:36–50).

The opposition of the religious leaders intensifies in Luke's "travel narrative" (Luke 9:51—19:44). Jesus reveals to his disciples that the religious leaders will reject and kill him (Luke 9:22; cf. Luke 9:44; 12:50; 17:25; 18:31–32). Jesus speaks excoriating woes (Luke 11:33–54) against the religious leaders because of their greed and wickedness (Luke 11:39), love for attention (Luke 11:43), ignorance (Luke 11:44, 52), legalism (Luke 11:46), and for killing prophets (Luke 11:47–51). These woes result in a plot to "catch [Jesus] in something he might say" (Luke 11:54). Sabbath controversies with the religious leaders continue in Luke 13:10–17 and 14:1–4 coupled with opposition for welcoming and eating with "sinners" (Luke 15:1–2). As these controversies unfold, Luke adds indicting qualitative statements about the religious leaders. They are hypocritical (Luke 12:1) and lovers of money (Luke 16:14), but their chief trait, as Powell rightly notes, is self-righteousness (Luke 18:19; cf. 5:32; 7:30; 15:17).[76]

The opposition of the religious leaders climaxes in Luke's Jerusalem narrative (Luke 19:45—24:53). At every turn, the religious leaders question Jesus. The chief priests, scribes, and elders question his authority (Luke 20:1–8) and they send "spies" to question him about taxes (Luke 20:20–26), while the Sadducees question him about marriage at the resurrection (Luke 20:27–39). As a result of Jesus' insightful answers to each challenge, "they no longer dared to ask him any [more] question[s]" (Luke 20:40). Their silence, however, is not surrender. They proceed to arrest, try, and kill Jesus (Luke 22:47–53; 22:63—23:49).

Kingsbury also argues correctly that Luke presents "the crowd/people" (using copiously ὄχλος and λαός interchangeably[77]) as a unified char-

76. Powell, "Religious Leaders in Luke," 95.

77. Compare Luke 6:17 with 6:19; Luke 7:24 with 7:29; Luke 9:12 with 9:13; Luke 18:36 with 18:43; and Luke 23:4 with 23:13. There is, however, a slight Lukan distinction between the terms, as Kingsbury notes: The "crowd" is more vague, often simply denoting a large group of people, while the "people" often possesses a religious coloration and refers to Israel as God's chosen nation (Kingsbury, *Conflict in Luke*, 29, citing Minear, "Jesus' Audiences, According to Luke," 81–87; cf. Kodell, "Luke's Use of Laos, 'People,'" 327, and Tannehill, *Narrative Unity of Luke-Acts*, 1:143). Crowe, "LAOS at the Cross," 81, sees a sharp distinction between the "crowd" and the "people." At the

acter group that collectively forms "Israel."[78] Luke's crowd[79] exhibits two fundamentally contrasting traits.[80] First, they are "well disposed" toward Jesus. Throughout Jesus' ministry, the crowd, in contrast to the religious leaders, flock to Jesus from various regions (Luke 5:15; 6:17; 8:4; 12:1) and exhibit genuine admiration for him by gathering around him (Luke 5:1, 3, 19; 12:1; 19:3), by following him (Luke 7:9, 11; 14:25; 18:36–37; 19:1–3), by marveling at his words (Luke 4:22, 32; 19:48; 21:38), and by occasionally mobbing him in excited expectation of his teachings and healings (Luke 5:1; 8:42, 45).[81]

Although well disposed toward Jesus, Luke's crowd is "without faith in him."[82] They reject Jesus in Nazareth (Luke 4:28–30), and Jesus compares them to ignorant children who play flutes and sing dirges (Luke 7:32). Some of the crowd accuse Jesus of driving out demons by Beelzebub (Luke 11:14–15) and test him by asking for a sign (Luke 11:16). In response to the request for a sign, Jesus calls the crowd a "wicked generation" (Luke 11:29). Jesus also caustically calls them "hypocrites" who know how to interpret the weather but do not know how to interpret the issues of their day (Luke 12:54–59).

Note that Luke predominantly follows Mark in characterizing the religious leaders and the crowd as distinct unified character groups with specific identifiable traits. Recall from chapter 2 that Mark's religious leaders form a unified character group in opposition to Jesus and that

---

crucifixion, however, Luke's crowd and people are identical based on, what Nolland calls, "the inclusion effect" of Luke 23:27 ("a large number of people [λαοῦ] followed him") and Luke 23:48 ("when the crowd [ὄχλοι] who had gathered . . .") (Nolland, *Luke 18:35—24:53*, 3:1159; contra Kodell, "Luke's Use of Laos," 327–43).

78. Kingsbury, *Conflict in Mark*, 28–31. Prior to Kingsbury, many also sought to understand Luke's variegated presentation of the crowd. Jacob Jervell argues that Luke's crowd is divided into the repentant and unrepentant (*Luke and the People of God*, 41–74). Johnson detects a Lukan dramatic pattern (*Literary Function of Possessions in Luke-Acts*, 48–69, 95–126). Joseph B. Tyson sees a Lukan pattern of the crowd that moves from initial acceptance to final rejection ("Jewish Public in Luke-Acts," 574–83). Brawley suggests that Luke's crowd is "fluid and can wear different masks" (*Luke-Acts and the Jews*, 139, 147). J. T. Sanders, concerned more with historical matters, contends that Luke is an anti-Semitic document that completely rejects the Jews (*Jews in Luke-Acts*; cf. Bock's rebuttal of Sanders in *Luke 1:1—9:50*, 38–39).

79. For simplicity, "crowd" is used to refer to Luke's interchangeable use of ὄχλος and λαός.

80. Kingsbury, *Conflict in Mark*, 29.

81. Ibid., 29–30.

82. Ibid., 31.

Luke's Appropriation of the Psalmic Lament?

he characterizes the crowd as simultaneously well disposed, but without faith, in Jesus. As the next discussion demonstrates, Luke also follows Mark in characterizing the religious leaders and the crowd in relation to the psalmic literature.

Jesus' Opponents and the Crowd in Relation to the Psalmic Literature

Luke also follows Mark in appropriating many of the same psalms as Mark does to characterize the crowd and Jesus' opponents. At Jesus' triumphal entry (Luke 19:28-44), Luke follows Mark closely in characterizing the crowd (one time) and Jesus' opponents (two times) in tandem with the psalmic literature. In Luke 19:38, as Jesus enters Jerusalem, the crowd speaks in unison with the worshippers of Psalm 117:26 who celebrate the arrival of the king: "Blessed is the king who comes in the name of the Lord!"[83] As in Mark, Luke presents the crowd positively as those awaiting Jesus' reign. In Luke 20:17, after recounting a parable about tenants killing a farmer's heir, Luke characterizes the scribes and chief priests as the opponents of Psalm 117 by identifying Jesus as the "stone" of Psalm 117:22 (see discussion above) and by identifying the scribes and chief priests as the "builders" who "reject" the stone. Luke indicates clearly in 20:19 the identity of these builders: "[The scribes and chief priests] knew [Jesus] had spoken this parable against them."[84] In 20:42-43, Luke

---

83. Prior to Jesus' triumphal entry in 19:38 Luke characterizes a personified Jerusalem (or perhaps the Pharisees [Luke 13:31]; see Bock, *Proclamation from Prophecy and Pattern*, 118) in 13:35 with the same reference to Ps 117:26. In response to Jesus' grief over Jerusalem, who "kills the prophets" (Luke 13:34), Jesus says, "You will not see me again until you say, 'Blessed is he who comes in the name of the Lord'" (Luke 13:35). Some argue that Luke depicts positively Jerusalem turning in worship to Jesus at the eschaton (Bock, *Luke 9:51—24:53*, 1251, and Nolland, *Luke 9:21—18:34*, 2:742), while others argue that Luke depicts them negatively by comparing them ironically with the crowd who worships with the same psalmic quote in Luke 19:38 (Wagner, "Psalm 118 in Luke-Acts: Tracing a Narrative Thread," 167n44, and Marshall, *Luke*, 577). In the immediate context of Luke 13:35, the reference to Ps 117:26 portrays Jerusalem negatively in light of its juxtaposition to Jesus' description of his obdurate opponents (Luke 13:31-34).

84. Nolland, *Luke 18:35—24:53*, 3:952-53, and Tannehill, *Narrative Unity of Luke-Acts*, 1:192-93. Tannehill argues that Jesus also includes the crowd as ignorant participants of the parable (and presumably as the "builders" of Ps 117:22) based on Luke directing the parable of the tenants to "the people" (Luke 20:9; omitted in Mark and Matthew) (Tannehill, *Narrative Unity of Luke-Acts*, 161). Luke makes clear, however, in 20:19 that Jesus emphasizes the religious leaders as the referent of the psalmic quote (*pace* Schweizer, *Luke*, 304; Klostermann, *Das Lukasevangelium*, 193).

characterizes Jesus' opponents, perhaps specifically the scribes,[85] as the opponents of Psalm 109: Jesus equates them with the psalmist's "enemies" who will be a "footstool for [his] feet."

Luke continues to follow Mark at the crucifixion in characterizing Jesus' opponents and the crowd in tandem with the psalmic literature. In 23:34b, Luke follows Mark 15:34 in characterizing the soldiers, who divide Jesus' clothes "by casting lots," in tandem with David's opponents in Psalm 21:19. In Luke 23:35a, the crowd "watches" Jesus' suffering in the same way many "watched" the Davidic psalmist suffer in Psalm 21:8a. As the crowd watches, the rulers in Luke 23:35 mock Jesus in the same way that the mockers in Psalm 21:8 mock David: "The rulers scoffed at him, saying, 'He saved others; let him save himself, if he is the Christ of God, his Chosen One!'" The soldiers in Luke 23:36–37 join the foray by challenging Jesus' ability to "save."

Jesus' Opponents at the Crucifixion: The Downplaying of a Markan Motif

Although Luke retains the general tenor of Mark's characterization of Jesus' opponents as those of David, he downplays this motif of characterization at Jesus' crucifixion in at least three significant ways: He excludes the crowd[86] as Jesus' opponents at Jesus' death, omits some Markan evocations to the Psalms, and highlights various participants at the crucifixion who do not oppose Jesus.[87] In other words, whereas Mark presents every

---

85. Luke does not directly identify the antecedent of αὐτούς in introducing the psalmic quote in Luke 20:41 ("Then Jesus said to them [αὐτούς]"), but Jesus is probably speaking to the scribes of Luke 20:39 (Bock, *Luke 9:51—24:53*, 1634; *pace* Marshall, *Luke*, 747; contra Nolland, *Luke 18:35—24:53*, 3:972). This possibility is further strengthened in light of Jesus' statements just subsequent to his quote of Ps 109:1: "Beware of the scribes . . ." (Luke 20:46). In spite of the indecipherable referent to Luke's αὐτούς, it is clear that the view Jesus is correcting in quoting Ps 109:1 (the Christ as David's son) is "a view promoted by some of the leadership groups opposed to Jesus" (Nolland, *Luke 18:35—24:53*, 3:970).

86. As Brown notes, the identity of Luke's crowd remains consistent throughout the Jerusalem narrative. Brown bases this on key words that Luke uses interchangeably in three passages (Brown, *Death of the Messiah*, 2:1167).

Luke 23:27: "A large number of people (λαὸς) followed him"

Luke 23:35 "The people (λαὸς) stood watching (θεωρέω)"

Luke 23:48: "When the crowds (ὄχλοι) . . . saw (θεωρέω) what had happened"

87. Prior to the crucifixion, Luke also downplays this motif. Luke omits Mark's evocation of Ps 40:10 ("the one eating with me"; Mark 14:18) at the Last Supper in

participant in close proximity to Jesus' execution in unified opposition to Jesus under the rubric of the psalmic lament, Luke's crucifixion account is less monolithic.[88] This is demonstrated by examining how Luke characterizes in his crucifixion scene the soldiers, the crowd, the rulers, a centurion, and the criminals at Jesus' execution. Note especially in this examination that Luke, unlike Mark, alternates between portraying characters positively and negatively in relation to Jesus' crucifixion.

In 23:34b, Luke follows Mark 15:34 in characterizing the soldiers as the opponents of the Davidic psalmist. Just as the opponents in Psalm 21:19 cast lots for David's clothes, Jesus' opponents do the same thing. Luke, however, departs from Mark 23:35 in the next verse by uniquely altering Mark's characterization of the "passerby" as they relate to Psalm 21. Luke changes Mark's "passerby" to the "crowd" and drops the emphasis on their participation in the mockery. Luke's crowd only "watches" (θεωρῶν; cf. Ps 21:8a) Jesus' crucifixion while Mark's passerby mockingly "wag their heads" and caustically taunt Jesus (Mark 15:29; cf. Ps 21:8b). Before returning to the other characters in Luke's crucifixion scene, a brief digression on how to interpret this Lukan portrayal of the crowd is needed.

There are three predominant interpretations of Luke's crowd in 23:35, who "watch" but do not "wag their heads." They are perhaps outright supporters of Jesus,[89] sympathetic witnesses to him in contrast to the religious leaders,[90] or mockers.[91] It is unlikely that Luke depicts the crowd as outright supporters of Jesus since, as Bock rightly notes, Peter

---

describing Judas' betrayal (Luke 22:21–22) and he omits the appellative "sinners" in the Gethsemane account (Luke 22:39–46). Recall from chapter 2 that Mark evokes Ps 40:10 to characterize Judas in tandem with the psalmic opponents and portrays the "sinners" (Judas, the crowd, chief priests, scribes, and elders) in Gethsemane also as the psalmic opponents. Some see a possible Lukan allusion to Ps 40:10 in Luke 22:21–22 based on thematic similarities (Green, *Luke*, 764–65). With no verbal parallels between the passages, and since Luke does not allude to Psalm 40 elsewhere, it is quite speculative to suggest a Lukan allusion—a suggestion probably based more on a Markan understanding of the events of the Last Supper than on a Lukan understanding of them.

88. The relationship of Luke's crucifixion scene to Mark's is notoriously difficult to navigate (see Carroll, "Luke's Crucifixion Scene," 108n6; Bock, *Luke 9:51—24:53*, 1835–39). Following Carroll, it is assumed here that Luke's most probable source for his crucifixion scene is Mark (Carroll, "Luke's Crucifixion Scene," 108n6).

89. Brown, *Death of the Messiah*, 2:989–90.

90. Nolland, *Luke 18:35–24:53*, 3:1144–45 (cf. Creed, *Luke*, 287). Grundmann suggests that they are curious onlookers (Grundmann, *Das Evangelium nach Lukas*, 433).

91. Marshall, *Luke*, 869.

Of Heroes and Villains

calls for their repentance in Acts 2:22–41.[92] It is also unlikely that Luke depicts the crowd as mockers since the καί, in Luke 23:35, best translated as "but" (ESV) or "and... even" (NIV), does not implicate the crowd in the "scoffing" of the rulers: "The people stood by, watching, but (καί) the rulers scoffed at him."[93] Luke's crowd, then, behaves somewhere on the continuum between mockers and supporters, perhaps as sympathetic witnesses (although Luke places no qualitative description that implies this). Most pertinent for the argument at hand is that Luke's crowd, in contrast to Mark's passerby, does not mock Jesus. Whatever their "watching" indicates (sympathy or otherwise), Luke does not characterize them in Luke 23:35 as outright opponents of Jesus.

As the crowd watches, the rulers in the same verse (Luke 23:35) mock Jesus similarly to those who mock David in Psalm 21:8: "The rulers scoffed at [Jesus], saying, 'He saved others; let him save himself, if he is the Christ of God, his Chosen One!'" In the subsequent verses (Luke 23:36–37), the soldiers join the foray by challenging Jesus' ability to "save." Luke, however, does not capitalize on Mark's evocation of Psalm 68 in describing the soldiers' behavior, dropping Mark's ποτίζω ("give to drink").

> Psalm 68:22: καὶ ἔδωκαν εἰς τὸ βρῶμά μου χολὴν καὶ εἰς τὴν δίψαν μου ἐπότισάν με ὄξος
>
> Mark 15:36: δραμὼν δέ τις [καὶ] γεμίσας σπόγγον ὄξους περιθεὶς καλάμῳ ἐπότιζεν αὐτόν λέγων
>
> Luke 23:36: ὄξος προσφέροντες αὐτῷ

As the scene continues to unfold, a criminal crucified with Jesus also joins the foray in Luke 23:39 by challenging Jesus' ability to "save." This scoffing criminal is juxtaposed with another dying criminal who recognizes Jesus' righteousness and decides to trust in him (Luke 23:39–43). After Jesus dies, two characters respond positively to the events. A centurion "praises God" and proclaims Jesus as a "righteous man" (Luke 23:47). The crowd, who previously joined the religious leaders in condemning Jesus (Luke 23:13–25), "beat their breasts" in mourning about his death (Luke 23:48).[94]

---

92. Bock, *Luke 9:51—24:53*, 1851 (cf. Carroll, "Luke's Crucifixion Scene," 108–10, 111, 196n11).

93. Nolland, *Luke 18:35—24:53*, 3:1147 (citing Marshall, *Luke*, 869). *Pace* Brown, *Death of the Messiah*, 2:990; contra Plummer, *Luke*, 532.

94. The specific spiritual condition of the crowd with respect to this behavior is irrelevant. Whether they repent (Brown, *Death of the Messiah*, 2:1168) or only grieve (Marshall, *Luke*, 877; Bock, *Luke 9:51—24:53*, 1865; Carroll, "Luke's Crucifixion

Luke's Appropriation of the Psalmic Lament?

Luke, then, follows Mark in characterizing the religious leaders and the soldiers in tandem with the opponents of the Davidic psalmist. Unlike Matthew, who expands and emphasizes these Markan characterizations, Luke downplays this motif of characterization by omitting two of Mark's evocations of the psalmic literature: Mark 15:29 (cf. Psalm 21:8b) and 15:36 (cf. Ps 68:22). More significant, however, is how Luke uniquely characterizes the crowd and other characters at the crucifixion by alternating between those who reject and those who accept Jesus. Luke does not characterize the crowd as the psalmist's opponents, and his crucifixion scene does not monolithically portray a unified force of opposition against Jesus. In Mark's crucifixion scene, the psalmic evocations stand out more because they are cast on the backdrop of characters who monolithically oppose Jesus. In Luke's crucifixion scene, the psalmic evocations are less prominent because they are cast on the backdrop of characters who variously respond to Jesus. Luke's downplaying of Mark's appropriation of the psalmic literature to characterize Jesus' opponents is further substantiated by examining the following supplementary data.

Supplementary Data

Recall from the "Supplementary Data" from chapter 2 that Mark exhibits a remarkably consistent pattern in appropriating the psalmic material.[95] Nearly one hundred percent of this Markan data supports the argument that Mark characterizes Jesus and/or Jesus' opponents as the hero and villains of the psalmist. In contrast with Mark's monolithic use of the Psalms, Luke's use of the Psalms is significantly more variegated. This point is made by dividing the following data into three categories: Supplementary data used to characterize Jesus, supplementary data used to characterize Jesus' opponents, and supplementary data: miscellaneous uses.

Supplementary Data Used to Characterize Jesus

- Luke 3:16: In preparing the way for Jesus, John the Baptist says that "one more powerful is coming (ἔρχεται)" (cf. Ps 117:26: ὁ ἐρχόμενος).

Scene," 112), Luke presents them as positive in relation to Jesus.

95. See also the psalmic data discussed in "Mark's Appropriation of Non-Lament Psalms 109 and 117 in Mark 11–12" in chapter 2, footnote 15.

Of Heroes and Villains

- Luke 3:22: A heavenly voice says to Jesus, "You are my Son" (cf. Ps 2:7: υἱός μου εἶ σύ; see also Luke 9:35: Οὗτός ἐστιν ὁ υἱός μου).
- Luke 7:19: John the Baptist's disciples ask Jesus, "Are you the one who is to come (ὁ ἐρχόμενος)?" (Ps 117:26: ὁ ἐρχόμενος).
- Luke 9:22: In predicting his passion, Jesus says that the he must be "rejected (ἀποδοκιμασθῆναι)" (cf. Ps 117:22: ἀπεδοκίμασαν).
- Luke 9:58: Jesus' comparing himself to the birds of the air as the Son of Man is similar to Psalm 8:4–9.
- Luke 17:25: In predicting his passion, Jesus says that he must be "rejected (ἀποδοκιμασθῆναι)" (cf. Ps 117:22: ἀπεδοκίμασαν).
- Luke 22:42: Jesus' submission to God's will (θέλω) parallels the psalmists' in Psalms 39:9 (θέλημά), 142:10 (θέλημά) and MT Psalm 51:12 (רוח נדיבה).
- Luke 23:9: Jesus' silence before Herod is similar to the silence of the psalmists in MT Pss 22:15; 38:14–16; 39:9.

Supplementary Data Used to Characterize Jesus' Opponents

- Luke 5:30: The Pharisees "were complaining (ἐγόγγυζον)" about Jesus eating with sinners. Γογγύζω is the same word used to describe Israel's wilderness "complaining" in Psalms 58:16 and 105:25 (cf. Exod 15:24; 16:7–12; 17:3; Num 11:1; 14:2; Sir 46:7).
- Luke 9:22 and 17:25: In predicting his passion, Jesus says that the he must be "rejected (ἀποδοκιμασθῆναι)" (cf. Ps 117:22: ἀπεδοκίμασαν).

Supplementary Data: Miscellaneous Uses

- Luke 1:25: Elizabeth says concerning her pregnancy, "The Lord has done [this] for me in the days when he looked (ἐπεῖδεν) on me" (cf. Ps 137:6: ἐφορᾷ).
- Luke 1:35: An angel tells Mary that "the Holy Spirit (τὸ πνεῦμα τὸ ἅγιόν)" will come upon her (cf. Ps 50:13: τὸ πνεῦμα τὸ ἅγιόν; see also Isa 32:15; 63:10–11).

- Luke 1:43: Elizabeth says to Mary, "Why is this granted to me that the mother of my Lord (τοῦ κυρίου μου) should come to me? (cf. Ps 109:1: τῷ κυρίῳ μου).

- Luke 1:51: Mary in a song of praise states that God "has scattered (διεσκόρπτισεν) the proud" (cf. Ps 88:11: διεσκόρπισας).

- Luke 1:68: Zechariah praises God for "bringing redemption to his people (λύτρωσιν τῷ λαῷ αὐτοῦ)" (cf. Ps 110:9: λύτρωσιν ἀπέστειλεν τῷ λαῷ αὐτοῦ).

- Luke 1:79: Zechariah says that his son, John the Baptist, will "give light to those who sit in darkness and in the shadow of death (ἐπιφᾶναι τοῖς ἐν σκότει καὶ σκιᾷ θανάτου καθημένοις)" (cf. Ps 106:10: καθημένους ἐν σκότει καὶ σκιᾷ θανάτου; see also Isa 9:2; 42:7; 49:9–10; 59:8–9; Mic 7:8).

- Luke 2:38: "Redemption of Jerusalem (λύτρωσιν ἐν Ἰερουσαλήμ)" (cf. Ps 129:5–8: λύτρωσις ... λυτρώσεται ... Ισραηλ; see also Isa 52:8–10).

- Luke 4:10–11: Satan quotes Psalm 91:11–12 to Jesus in Luke's Temptation Scene.

- Luke 12:10: Jesus says that "anyone who blasphemes against the Holy Spirit (τὸ ἅγιον πνεῦμα) will not be forgiven" (cf. Ps 50:13: τὸ πνεῦμα τὸ ἅγιον).

- Luke 13:28: In explaining judgment in the eschaton, Jesus says that "there will be weeping there, and gnashing of teeth (ὁ κλαυθμὸς καὶ ὁ βρυγμὸς τῶν ὀδόντων)" (cf. Ps 34:16; ἔβρυξαν ἐπ' ἐμὲ τοὺς ὀδόντας αὐτῶν; see also Job 16:9; Ps 36:12; 111:10; Lam 2:16; and the discussion on Matt 8:12 in chapter 3).

- Luke 18:13: A tax collector prays, "God, have mercy on me, a sinner (Ο θεός, ἱλάσθητί μοι τῷ ἁμαρτωλῷ)" (cf. Ps 50:1, 3: ἐλέησόν ... ἀνομίαν).

- Luke 19:44: In predicting the fall of Jerusalem, Jesus says that Jerusalem's enemies "will dash (ἐδαφιοῦσίν) [Jerusalem] to the ground, you and the children (τέκνα) within [her] walls" (cf. Ps 136:9: ἐδαφιεῖ ... νήπια; see also 2 Kings 8:12; Hos 10:14; Nah 3:10).

- Luke 21:25c: In predicting future judgment, Jesus states that "nations will be in anguish ... because of the roaring (ἤχους) of the sea and the waves" (cf. Ps 45:4: ἤχησαν).

Of Heroes and Villains

- Luke 21:33a: In speaking of the eschaton, Jesus says that "heaven and earth will pass away (ὁ οὐρανὸς καὶ ἡ γῆ παρελεύσονται)" (cf. Ps 101:26–27: τὴν γῆν . . . οἱ οὐρανοί αὐτοὶ ἀπολοῦνται; see also Isa 51:6; Jer 4:23–26).

- Luke 22:30b: Jesus tells his disciples that they "will sit on thrones, judging the twelve tribes of Israel (καθήσεσθε ἐπὶ θρόνων τὰς δώδεκα φυλὰς κρίνοντες τοῦ Ἰσραήλ)" (cf. Ps 121:4–5: ἐκεῖ γὰρ ἀνέβησαν αἱ φυλαί φυλαὶ κυρίου . . . ὅτι ἐκεῖ ἐκάθισαν θρόνοι εἰς κρίσιν; see also Dan 7:9; 1 Enoch 62).

The purpose in including this supplementary data is simply to note Luke's variegated appropriation of these possible psalmic allusions. Whereas almost every Markan allusion to psalmic literature characterizes Jesus and/or Jesus' opponents, Luke's pattern is considerably more inconsistent, especially as noted above with his fifteen "Miscellaneous Uses" of the Psalms compared with eleven uses to characterize Jesus and/or Jesus' opponents. This inconsistent pattern, to the degree that these references represent allusions, suggests that Luke downplays these Markan characterizations.

The Psalms in Relation to the Isainic Servant Motif

Before concluding this section on Luke's use of the psalmic literature to characterize Jesus and Jesus' opponents, a brief comparison of Luke's use of the Psalms in relation to his Isaianic Servant motif is needed. This reveals that, contrary to Mark's and Matthew's gospel, conflating Luke's Isaianic Servant motif into his psalmic motif is justified.

Recall from chapter 2 that scholars often myopically interpret Mark's crucifixion scene solely though the lens of Isaiah's Servant and have collapsed Mark's Servant motif indistinguishably into his psalmic lamenter motif, overlooking the unique distinctions and contributions of each. Scholars, as noted above, similarly tend to emphasize Isaiah's Servant in Luke. In Luke, however, this tendency is justified since he does not appropriate the Psalms in ways that contrast so starkly with Isaiah's Servant. Whereas Mark uses the Psalms to portray Jesus responding to God as a lamenter, Luke uses the Psalms to portray Jesus responding to God confidently as, among other things, a suffering and innocent Davidic king who trusts in God up to his final breath (see discussion above). In Luke, there is at best a faint voice (in Gethsemane) of a lamenter given to Jesus that questions God about his plight. This psalmic characterization of Jesus, although contributing a Davidic royal identity to him, differs little from Isaiah's Servant who innocently (Isa 50:5), quietly (Isa 42:2; 53:7), and trustingly (Isa 50:7–8) suffers. Luke, then, appropriates Isaiah's Servant and the Davidic psalms more comparably, utilizing traits that are found in both motifs.

Aside from these interrelated traits, Luke specifies more clearly via his quote of Isaiah 53:12 in 22:37 the hermeneutical trajectory of his crucifixion account: "For I tell you that this Scripture must be fulfilled in me: 'And he was numbered with the transgressors.' For what is written about me has its fulfillment." As noted above, prior to this quotation of Isaiah 53, Luke characterizes Jesus complexly as, among other things, the OT prophet par excellence, Isaiah's Servant, and the king of the Davidic psalms. Without abandoning these characterizations, Luke signals the reader in 22:37 to understand Jesus' pending crucifixion primarily in light of Isaiah 53:12, including the evocations of the psalmic literature. This signal, as Strauss notes, is made clear by the emphasis that Luke places on the Isaianic quote:

> [The quote] is given special prominence in Luke's narrative by its long and emphatic introductory formula, 'that which is written must be fulfilled in me' (τοῦτο τὸ γεγραμμένον δεῖ τελεσθῆναι ἐν ἐμοί), and by its climactic location in the farewell discourse. [Additionally], the repetitious phrase which follows (καὶ γὰρ τὸ περὶ ἐμοῦ τέλος ἔχει) further emphasizes that this Scripture which must be fulfilled in Jesus (δεῖ, v. 37a).[96]

Whereas Mark fades his Servant motif into his lamenter motif at Jesus' death, Luke retains his focus more squarely on Jesus as the Servant in the same narratives.

Luke's quote of Isaiah 53 in 22:37 also implicitly introduces a theme that he more explicitly emphasizes throughout the crucifixion—namely, Jesus' innocence. When Jesus states that he will be "numbered with the transgressors," he implies that he is not a transgressor—that is, he is innocent. Luke subsequently notes Jesus' innocence at least seven times. Pilate, Herod, and a criminal pronounce Jesus innocent six times (Luke 23:4, 14, 15a, 15b, 22, 40; cf. 23:20). After Jesus' trusting death-prayer on the cross, a centurion climactically and conclusively states, "Surely this was a righteous man" (note Luke's replacement of Mark's "Son of God" with "righteous man"). Luke's Jesus dies as an innocent, Suffering Servant.

---

96. Strauss, *Davidic Messiah in Luke-Acts*, 326–27.

Luke, then, does not follow Mark in fading his Isaianic Servant motif into the background at the gospel's end. For Luke, rather, it serves a more prominent position by sharing interrelated traits with his psalmic motif and by framing the crucifixion via a direct quote of Isaiah 53:12 in Luke 22:37.

Summary

In this section, I explore in Luke what Ahearne-Kroll explores in Mark—Luke's appropriation of the psalmic lament in characterizing Jesus. I also explore the advancements made in chapter 2 to Ahearne-Kroll's work—Luke's appropriation of the psalmic literature in characterizing Jesus' opponents. Although Luke follows Mark in characterizing Jesus as the Davidic psalmist, he shows little, if any, interest in characterizing Jesus as the psalmic lamenter. Additionally, Luke downplays the significance of portraying his characters at the crucifixion within a psalmic rubric. Instead of providing the cohesive structure that binds every participant at the crucifixion into a climactic unified force of opposition against Jesus, Luke downplays his appropriation of the psalmic lament in characterizing Jesus' opponents by utilizing fewer lament evocations and by presenting a variegated crucifixion scene that vacillates between characters who scoff, mourn, and repent.

CONCLUSION: NARRATIVE AND RHETORICAL IMPLICATIONS

This chapter answers two questions. First, does Luke follow Mark in understanding and appropriating the psalmic lament to characterize Jesus? Luke, contrary to Matthew, who expands and emphasizes Mark's characterization of Jesus as the Davidic lamenter, does not overtly follow Mark in this characterization of Jesus. With respect to Jesus, there is little to no voice of the psalmic lamenter to be heard in Luke's narrative. Second, to what degree does Luke follow Mark in characterizing Jesus and Jesus' opponents as paradigmatic OT hero and villains? Luke largely follows this Markan motif of characterization (expanding it in relation to his rejected-prophet motif and emphasizing it in relation to Jesus as Isaiah's Servant at the crucifixion); Jesus is the OT paradigmatic OT hero while his opponents are the paradigmatic OT villains. Luke, however, downplays the significance of Jesus' opponents as OT villains at the crucifixion. He downplays it by appropriating fewer psalmic evocations, by portraying the crowd positively, and by vacillating between characters who positively and negatively respond to Jesus. These two conclusions result in the following narrative and rhetorical implications.

Narratively, in muting the voice of a Davidic lamenter, Luke accentuates other character traits of Jesus.[97] Instead of imbibing the lamenter's voice, which is often abrasive and, at times, can appear hopeless and defeated ("Why have you forsaken me?"), Luke's Jesus courageously "commits [his] spirit into [the Father's] hands." This climactic prayer depicts a trusting Davidic messiah who peacefully dies as Isaiah's Servant at the hands of his opponents, inciting praise from a centurion (Luke 23:47) and grief from the crowd (Luke 23:48).

Luke also accentuates the traits of Jesus' opponents in appropriating his OT prophet, Isaianic Servant, and psalmic motifs. Jesus' opponents in Luke have many character traits: They are, among other things, hypocritical (Luke 12:1), lovers of money (Luke 16:14), in a wrong relationship with God (18:9–14), and self-righteousness (Luke 18:19; cf. 5:32; 7:30; 15:17). In light of arguments presented in this chapter, another character trait is added to Jesus' opponents; they are also the paradigmatic OT villains, exhibiting the traits of those who opposed the prophets, Isaiah's Servant, and King David. The crowd, conversely, is not characterized as OT villains. Luke's crowd is fickle. At times they admire Jesus and grieve over his plight while, at other times, they demand his death.

The two conclusions in this chapter also have rhetorical implications concerning Luke's characterization of Jesus' opponents, the crowd, and Jesus. Recall from the methodology in chapter 1 that my specific narrative-rhetorical interest is on Mark Allen Powell's "evaluative point of view."[98] Luke's characterization of Jesus' opponents as OT villains increases the reader's negative evaluative viewpoint toward them. As with Mark, an important standard of judgment for Luke is the Hebrew Scriptures (cf. Luke 24:44: "Everything must be fulfilled that is written about me [Jesus] in the Law of Moses, the Prophets, and the Psalms"). Any Lukan character that does not act in accord with the Scriptures is viewed negatively. Luke's reader understands the religious leaders as bad because the narrator, Jesus,

---

97. Recall from chapter 2 that a character trait is any attribute, either explicitly or implicitly stated, that a narrator uses to distinguish in a relatively enduring way one character from another (Powell, *What Is Narrative Criticism?*, 54).

98. Powell, *What Is Narrative Criticism?*, 24; cf. 53–54, 60–61.

and the Scriptures say they are. Luke appropriates these motifs, then, to provide an evaluative standard against which to place Jesus' opponents in order to substantiate his negative portrayal of them.

Luke's evaluative point of view of the crowd is both positive and negative. With regards to the crowd, Luke sometimes incites the readers to compassion while at other times he incites them to antagonism. While Mark decisively places a negative evaluative assessment on the crowd from Gethsemane onward, Luke continues to offer both positive and negative assessments. After Luke's crowd joins the religious authorities in opposition against Jesus in 23:1–25, the readers are surprised at the crowd's compassionate reaction to Jesus a few moments later at the crucifixion. Whereas Mark directs his reader at gospel's end to judge the crowd negatively, Luke's evaluative point of view of the crowd is less monolithic.

5

Conclusion

THE PSALMIC LAMENT HAS a long history of influence—an influence that intersects the Synoptic Gospels. Although NT scholars have long recognized that the Synoptic writers quote and allude to the lament psalms (usually referring to them as the "psalms of the righteous sufferer"), they only stood in the shadow of Isaiah's Servant until Stephen P. Ahearne-Kroll's 2007 monograph *The Psalms of Lament in Mark's Passion*. Ahearne-Kroll challenges the prevailing assumption that the Isaianic Servant and the psalmic lamenter motifs are indistinguishably unified in Mark's narrative by arguing that Mark characterizes Jesus in his passion as the Davidic lamenter par excellence. Isaiah's Servant, Ahearne-Kroll argues, is present in Mark, but Jesus as the Davidic lamenter receives the narrative emphasis in the passion. Ahearne-Kroll, then, gives a voice to the psalmic lamenter in Mark's narrative. I advance Ahearne-Kroll's work in this book by exploring the psalmic lament motif more broadly in Mark and by extending the investigation to the other two Synoptic Gospels. Now, by way of a quick summary of each chapter and their respective contributions, I am able to chart a path for further research in the field of lament studies in the Synoptics.

SUMMARY AND CONTRIBUTIONS

Chapter 1

Chapter 1 sets the stage for the subsequent three chapters by situating my contributions against the backdrop of previous and current research and by delineating a methodology for the task. In essence, I join the conversation about the psalmic lament that OT scholar Hermann Gunkel began in 1933, that Claus Westermann (and many others in both OT and NT studies) subsequently advanced, and that Ahearne-Kroll introduces as a motif independent from Isaiah's Servant to Markan studies in 2007. In advancing this conversation, chapter 1 establishes that Mark and Matthew understand how the lament functions, which validates the research in the subsequent three chapters. Chapter 1 also frames my exploration of this with an eclectic methodology, which includes narrative, redaction, and rhetorical criticisms within a broader framework of N. T. Wright's and Andreas Köstenberger's "hermeneutical triad" (history, literature, and theology). The method I use to delineate the primary data under investigation is Ahearne-Kroll's concept of "simple evocation"—allusions that refer to one and only one OT text. Adding auxiliary support for the arguments in each respective chapter are investigations into "supplementary data"—possible allusions that do not meet the criteria of "simple evocation." Providing a degree of control to these methodologies is the pursuit of authorial intent within Grant Osborne's "hermeneutical spiral" and N. T. Wright's "critical realism."

Chapter 2

Chapter 2 picks up where Ahearne-Kroll left off, who focuses solely on Mark's appropriation of the psalmic lament to characterize Jesus. Specifically, I advance Ahearne-Kroll's work on Mark's gospel in three ways. First, I demonstrate that Mark appropriates the psalmic literature (Psalms 109 and 117 and the lament psalms) not only to characterize Jesus (*pace* Ahearne-Kroll) but also to characterize Jesus' opponents. Mark appropriates Psalms 109 and 117 to emphasize Jesus' conquest of his enemies while he uses the lament psalms to narratively describe their attacks on Jesus.

Second, whereas Ahearne-Kroll isolates and examines Mark's use of the psalmic lament motif, chapter 2 explores its Markan relation to Isaiah's Servant. I examine these two Markan motifs in tandem since most NT scholars indistinguishably conflate them. I argue that Mark appropriates his psalmic and Servant motifs similarly but not identically in characterizing Jesus; each motif contributes independently to Mark's narrative. Specifically, Isaiah's Servant provides for Mark a messiah who humbly submits to and silently embraces suffering in God's presence in order to die vicariously for others. The psalmic lamenter, conversely, provides for Mark a messiah who in struggling with his plight of suffering experiences God's absence and prays for relief. Neither motif independently provides for Mark the narrative goods to adequately characterize his messiah. Additionally, Mark appropriates Isaiah's Servant motif to characterize Jesus' opponents as those of the Servant.

Third, chapter 2 demonstrates that Mark characterizes Jesus and Jesus' opponents as the paradigmatic OT hero and villains, respectively. Establishing Mark's characterization of Jesus' opponents as OT paradigmatic villains provides a way forward in understanding how Mark demarcates "Jesus' opponents" as a character group. Recall that the debate revolves around which characters to include in a unified group of opposition against Jesus. As argued in chapter 2, Mark's hermeneutic of characterizing Jesus' opponents as paradigmatic OT villains is the unifying force that holds together Mark's concept of Jesus' opposition, allowing simultaneous consistency (the Jewish leaders' monolithic front against Jesus) and modification (e.g., the adding of the crowds, soldiers, and others to Jesus' opposition in the passion). In composing his cast of characters, Mark's overarching concern in characterizing Jesus' opponents is to delineate who aligns with the OT villains in opposition against Jesus.

Fourth, chapter 2 explores narrative and rhetorical implications in relation to Mark's appropriation of the psalmic lament. Narratively, chapter 2 adds another character trait to the Markan Jesus' opponents. Jesus' opponents in Mark are not only mistaken about Jesus, without authority, fearful of people, manipulative, erroneous interpreters of Scripture, mistaken about the correct standards for making decisions, and hypocritical, but, as I demonstrate in chapter 2, they also bear the traits of the enemies of the Davidic psalmist (both King David and the lamenting David) and of Isaiah's Servant. Rhetorically, these characterizations enhance Mark's evaluative point of view of Jesus' opponents. Mark's readers understand Jesus' opponents as bad because the narrator, Jesus, *and* the Scriptures say they are bad.

Chapter 3

Chapters 3 and 4 advance the discussion of the psalmic lament in Mark by testing on Matthew's and Luke's narratives Ahearne-Kroll's arguments and the ancillary advancements made to his work in chapter 2. Specifically, chapter 3 explores how Matthew appropriates the psalmic lament to characterize Jesus and Jesus' opponents interchangeably with, and as the climax to, his characterization of Jesus and Jesus' opponents in tandem with his Isaianic and OT prophet motifs. Whereas Ahearne-Kroll gives a voice to the psalmic lamenter in Mark, in chapter 3 I give a voice to the psalmic lamenter in Matthew via four specific contributions.

First, Matthew follows Mark in characterizing Jesus and Jesus' opponents as paradigmatic OT hero and villains, crescendoing and climaxing these characterizations with his appropriation of the psalmic lament. Matthew, however, expands and emphasizes this technique of characterization, appropriating it more extensively than Mark does. Matthew follows Mark in characterizing Jesus as Isaiah's Servant, as the Davidic psalmic king, and as the Davidic psalmic lamenter, and Matthew follows Mark in characterizing Jesus' opponents as those of Isaiah's Servant, as those of the Davidic psalmic king, and as those of the Davidic psalmic lamenter. With his appropriation of each motif, however, Matthew expands and emphasizes these characterizations of Jesus and Jesus' opponents by adding new quotes, allusions, and evocations to these motifs and/or by altering those that Mark already appropriates. Confirming these expansions and emphases is Matthew's appropriation of a motif independent of Mark—Matthew's "rejected-prophet" motif—wherein Matthew characterizes Jesus and Jesus' opponents as the paradigmatic OT prophet and as the OT prophet's opponents, respectively.

Second, Matthew's characterization of Jesus' opponents as paradigmatic OT villains, as with Mark's gospel, provides a way forward in the debate to understand how Matthew characterizes Jesus' opposition. The debate, in essence, revolves around which characters to include in Matthew's unified portrayal of Jesus' opponents. In chapter 3, I argue that although Matthew unites particular characters (e.g., the scribes and the Pharisees) into single character groups that possess certain consistent character traits, Matthew's OT hermeneutic of characterizing Jesus' opponents as paradigmatic OT villains is the unifying category that provides simultaneous consistency (the Jewish leaders' monolithic front against Jesus) and modification (e.g., the adding of the crowds, soldiers, and others to Jesus' opposition in the passion). In other words, Matthew's guiding rubric in characterizing Jesus' opponents is his OT hermeneutic.

Third, contrary to the current consensus among Synoptic scholars, Matthew does not indistinguishably conflate his Isaianic Servant and psalmic lamenter motifs. Furthermore, Matthew, in relation to Mark, enhances the distinctions between the two motifs. Although Matthew's Isaianic Servant and psalmic lamenter motifs share obvious similarities (e.g., both the Servant and the lamenter face physical and psychological opposition from opponents and both are mocked, beaten, spit upon, and shamelessly killed), they also share distinct attributes: (1) Isaiah's Servant is not a petitioner whereas the central role of the lamenter is that of a petitioner who asks God to change his given plight, (2) in relation to his earthly opponents, Isaiah's Servant humbly submits to and embraces suffering; in relation to God, the lamenter struggles in prayer to remove it, (3) God is consistently present for Isaiah's Servant while he is pervasively absent for the lamenter, and (4) Isaiah's Servant perceives that his death is endowed with purpose; that is, he suffers and dies vicariously for others, while the lamenter does not fully understand his suffering. Each motif, then, contributes independently to Matthew's narrative in unique ways. Neither motif independently provides for Matthew the narrative goods to adequately characterize his messiah.

Fourth, in chapter 3, I explore narrative and rhetorical implications in relation to Matthew's appropriation of the psalmic lament. Narratively, Matthew follows Mark in adding another character trait to Jesus' opponents. Narrative critics have long recognized that Jesus' opponents in Matthew are evil, hypocritical, and spiritually blind. I further argue that they are also the paradigmatic OT villains. Narratively unique to Matthew is his continued characterization of Jesus' opponents in two post-crucifixion scenes, wherein most of Jesus' opponents continue in their opposition against Jesus. Matthew depicts the crowd in these post-crucifixion scenes, however, as possible recipients of repentance.

Rhetorically, Matthew's characterization of Jesus' opponents as paradigmatic OT villains is similar to Mark's rhetorical effect in appropriating the same motif; it enhances Matthew's evaluative point of view of Jesus' opponents. Jesus' opponents are bad because the narrator, Jesus, *and* the Scriptures say that they are bad. Matthew, however, emphasizes Mark's rhetorical effect in characterizing Jesus' opponents as paradigmatic OT villains by depicting these opponents more sinisterly than does Mark.

Chapter 4

Chapter 4 advances the discussion of the psalmic lament in Mark by testing on Luke's narrative Ahearne-Kroll's arguments and the ancillary advancements made to his work in chapter 2. Specifically, chapter 4 explores (1) the degree to which Luke understands and appropriates the psalmic lament to characterize Jesus and (2) the degree to which Luke follows Mark in characterizing Jesus and Jesus' opponents as paradigmatic OT hero and villains.

Concerning the first exploration, I maintain that although Luke follows Mark in appropriating psalmic lament literature, Luke does not overtly characterize Jesus as the Davidic lamenter. In essence, there is little to no indication that Luke, in contrast to Mark and Matthew, reflects in his depiction of Jesus an understanding of the core elements of the psalmic lament discussed in chapter 1. Whereas Ahearne-Kroll, as discussed in chapter 2, gives a voice to the psalmic lamenter in Mark, and chapter 3 gives a voice to the psalmic lamenter in Matthew, chapter 4 demonstrates that at best a muted lamenter's voice with respect to Jesus is heard in Luke. Luke's Jesus is King David but not a lamenting David. Luke, rather, emphasizes in his passion account what many scholars erroneously and myopically ascribe to the passion accounts of Mark and Matthew—Luke focuses on Jesus as Isaiah's righteous sufferer.

Concerning the second exploration, I argue that Luke follows Mark in pervasively characterizing Jesus as the OT paradigmatic hero, his characterization of Jesus as the Davidic lamenter notwithstanding. Luke also generally follows Mark in characterizing Jesus' opponents as paradigmatic OT villains (expanding it in relation to his rejected-prophet motif and emphasizing it in relation to Jesus as Isaiah's Servant at the crucifixion), but Luke omits an important and narratively influential aspect of this motif of characterization. Specifically, Luke downplays the significance of characterizing Jesus' opponents as those of the Davidic psalmist at the crucifixion in several ways. Luke excludes the crowd as Jesus' opponents, omits two Markan evocations of the Psalms, and highlights various participants at the crucifixion who do not oppose Jesus.

FURTHER RESEARCH

Recent dissertations, papers presented at academic societies, and academic and popular books indicate that conversations concerning the influence of the lament on the NT are on the rise (see chapter 1). My arguments advance these conversations, but much more can be said. Within narrative criticism, explorations of characters in the Synoptics who (possibly) lament to Jesus might prove fruitful. For example, characters, especially in Matthew, frequently approach Jesus and address him with the vocative "Lord" and ask him to change their particular plight. Similarly, perhaps Luke, though showing little interest in a lamenting Jesus, might be influenced by the lament in his portrayals of other characters, especially in light of his tax collector who prays to God in the style of a psalmic lamenter: "God, be merciful to me" (Luke 18:13; cf. Ps 50:1: "Have mercy on me, O God") and the blind beggar who twice speaks to Jesus in a similar way: "Jesus, Son of David, have mercy on me . . . Son of David, have mercy on me" (Luke 18:38–39).

On a different methodological note, more might be said about broader christological and theological implications in Mark's and Matthew's appropriation of the psalmic lament. As is well known, the portrait of Jesus in the gospels is quite complex. Mark's Jesus, for example, is, among other things, God's Son and Lord. Matthew includes this Markan portrait of Jesus, but further portrays Jesus as, among other things, Immanuel (God with us) and Teacher. More might be said, for example, about the christological and theological implications of Matthew's Jesus as both Immanuel and lamenter. What does it mean for Matthew's Jesus to be simultaneously a lamenter who experiences God's absence and to be the Immanuel who is "God with us" for his followers (cf. Matt 1:23; 28:20)?

Explorations such as these, and perhaps others, are needed in order to provide a more complete Synoptic appropriation of the psalmic lament—one that will augment their use of it to characterize Jesus as their OT paradigmatic hero and his opponents as the OT paradigmatic villains.

Bibliography

Ahearne-Kroll, Stephen P. "Abandonment and Suffering." In *Septuagint Research: Issues and Challenges in the Study of the Greek Jewish Scriptures*, edited by Wolfgang Kraus and R. Glenn Wooden, 293–309. Atlanta: SBL, 2006.
———. "Challenging the Divine: LXX Psalm 21 in the Passion Narrative of the Gospel of Mark." In *The Trial and Death of Jesus: Essays on the Passion Narrative in Mark*, edited by Geert Van Oyen and Tom Shepherd, 119–48. Dudley: Peeters, 2006.
———. *The Psalms of Lament in Mark's Passion: Jesus' Davidic Suffering*. SNTSMS 142. Cambridge: Cambridge University Press, 2007.
Albertz, M. *Die synoptische Streitgespräche*. Berlin: Trowitzsch und Sohn, 1919.
Allen, Leslie C. *Psalms 101–150*. WBC 21. Waco, TX: Word Books, 1983.
Allison, Dale C. *The New Moses: A Matthean Typology*. Minneapolis: Fortress, 1993.
———. *Studies in Matthew: Interpretation Past and Present*. Grand Rapids: Baker Academic, 2005.
Alsup, John E. "Typology." In *ABD*, edited by David Noel Freedman, 6:682–83. New York: Doubleday, 1992.
Alter, Robert, and Frank Kermode. *The Literary Guide to the Bible*. Cambridge, MA: Harvard University Press, 1987.
Anderson, Janice C. "Gender and Reading." *Semeia* 28 (1983) 3–27.
———. *Matthew's Narrative Web: Over, and Over, and Over Again*. JSNTSup 91. Sheffield: JSOT Press, 1994.
Aune, David. *Revelation 6–16*. WBC 52b. Nashville: Thomas Nelson, 1998.
Baker, David L. "Typology and the Christian Use of the Old Testament." In *The Right Doctrine from the Wrong Texts: Essays on the Use of the Old Testament in the New*, edited by G. K. Beale, 313–30. Grand Rapids: Baker, 1994.
Banks, Robert. *Jesus and the Law in the Synoptic Tradition*. SNTSMS 28. Cambridge: Cambridge University Press, 1975.
Barnet, John A. *Not the Righteous but Sinners: M. M. Bakhtin's Theory of Aesthetics and the Problem of Reader-Character Interaction in Matthew's Gospel*. JSNTSup 246. New York: T & T Clark International, 2003.
Barrett, C. K. "The Background of Mark 10:45." In *New Testament Essays: Studies in Memory of T. W. Manson*, edited by A. J. B. Higgins, 1–18. Manchester: Manchester University Press, 1959.
———. *A Critical and Exegetical Commentary on the Acts of the Apostles*. 2 vols. ICC. Edinburgh: T & T Clark, 1994, 1998.

Bibliography

Bauer, David R. "The Major Characters of Matthew's Story: Their Function and Significance." *Int* 46 (1992) 357–67.

Bautch, Richard. *Developments in Genre between Post-Exilic Penitential Prayers and the Psalms of Communal Lament.* SBL Academia Biblica 7. Atlanta: SBL, 2003.

Beale, G. K., and D. A. Carson, eds. *Commentary on the New Testament Use of the Old Testament.* Grand Rapids: Baker Academic, 2007.

Beare, Francis Wright. *The Gospel According to Matthew.* New York: Harper & Row, 1981.

Beaton, Richard. *Isaiah's Christ in Matthew's Gospel.* SNTSMS 123. Cambridge: Cambridge University Press, 2002.

Begrich, Joachim. "Das priesterliche Heilsorakel." *ZAW* 52 (1934) 81–92.

Bellinger, William H., Jr., and William R. Farmer, eds. *Jesus and the Suffering Servant: Isaiah 53 and Christian Origins.* Harrisburg, PA: Trinity Press International, 1998.

Best, Ernest. *The Temptation and the Passion: The Markan Soteriology.* 2nd ed. Society of New Testament Studies Monograph Series 2. Cambridge: Cambridge University Press, 1990.

Betz, Otto. "Jesus and Isaiah 53." In *Jesus and the Suffering Servant: Isaiah 53 and Christian Origins*, edited by W. H. Bellinger and W. R. Farmer, 70–87. Harrisburg, PA: Trinity Press International, 1998.

Black, C. Clinton. *The Rhetoric of the Gospel: Theological Artistry in the Gospels and Acts.* St. Louis: Chalice, 2001

———. "Rhetorical Criticism." In *Hearing the New Testament: Strategies for Interpretation*, edited by Joel Green, 256–77. Grand Rapids: Eerdmans, 1995.

Black, Matthew. "Servant of the Lord and Son of Man." *SJT* 6 (1953) 1–11.

Blinzler, Josef. *The Trial of Jesus: The Jewish and Roman Proceedings against Jesus Christ Described and Assessed from the Oldest Accounts.* Westminster: Newman, 1959.

Blomberg, Craig. *Matthew.* NAC. Nashville: Broadman, 1992.

———. "Matthew." In *Commentary on the New Testament Use of the Old Testament*, edited by G. K. Beale and D. A. Carson, 1–109. Grand Rapids: Baker Academic, 2007.

Bock, Darrell L. *Acts.* BECNT. Grand Rapids: Baker Academic, 2007.

———. "Jesus as Blasphemer." In *Who Do My Opponents Say I Am?: An Investigation of the Accusations against the Historical Jesus*, edited by Joseph B. Modica and Scot McKnight, 76–94. London: T & T Clark, 2008.

———. *Luke 1:1—9:50.* BECNT. Grand Rapids: Baker Academic, 1994.

———. *Luke 9:51—24:53.* BECNT. Grand Rapids: Baker Academic, 1996.

———. *Proclamation from Prophecy and Pattern: Lucan Old Testament Christology.* JSNTSup 12. Sheffield: JSOT Press, 1987.

Bockmuehl, Markus. *Seeing the Word: Refocusing New Testament Study.* Grand Rapids: Baker Academic, 2006.

Boda, Mark J. "Quotation, Allusion." In *DBCI*, edited by Stanley E. Porter, 296–98. London: Routledge, 2007.

Bolt, Peter G. *The Cross from a Distance: Atonement in Mark's Gospel.* NSBT 18. Downers Grove: InterVarsity, 2004.

Bonnard, Pierre. *L'Évangile selon saint Matthieu.* 2nd ed. Commentaire du Nouveau Testament 1. Neuchâtel: Delachaux et Niestlé, 1970.

Boomershine, Thomas E. "Mark, the Storyteller: A Rhetorical-Critical Investigation of Mark's Passion and Resurrection Narrative." PhD diss., Union Theological Seminary, 1974.
Borg, Marcus J. *Conflict, Holiness and Politics in the Teachings of Jesus.* SBEC 5. New York: Mellen, 1984.
Boring, M. Eugene. *Mark: A Commentary.* Louisville: Westminster Knox, 2006.
Bouzard, Walter C., Jr. *We Have Heard with Our Ears, O God: Sources of the Communal Laments in the Psalms.* SBLDS 159. Atlanta: Scholars, 1997.
Bovon, Francois. *A Commentary on the Gospel of Luke 1:1—9:50.* Hermeneia 38.1. Translated by Christine M. Thomas. Minneapolis: Fortress, 2002.
———. "La figure de Moïse dans l'oeuvre de Luc." In *La Figure de Moïse: Écriture et relectures.* Publications de la Faculté de théologie de l'Université de Genève 17, edited by R. Martin-Archard, 47–65. Geneva: Labor et Fides, 1978.
———. *Luke the Theologian: Fifty-Five Years of Research (1950–2005).* 2nd ed. Waco, TX: Baylor University Press, 2006.
Bowker, John. *Jesus and the Pharisees.* New York: Cambridge University Press, 1973.
Bratcher, Robert G. "Unusual Sinners." *BL* 39 (1988) 335–37.
Brawley, Robert L. *Luke-Acts and the Jews: Conflict, Apology, and Conciliation.* SBLMS 33. Atlanta: Scholars, 1987.
Brooks, James A. *Mark.* NAC 23. Nashville: Broadman, 1991.
Brown, Jeannine K. "Genre Criticism and the Bible." In *Words and the Word: Explorations in Biblical Interpretation and Literary Theory,* edited by D. G. Firth and J. A. Grant, 111–50. Nottingham: Apollos, 2008.
Brown, Raymond E. *The Death of the Messiah.* 2 vols. New York: Doubleday, 1994.
Brownlee, William H. "The Servant of the Lord in the Qumran Scrolls I." *BASOR* 132 (1953) 8–15.
———. "The Servant of the Lord in the Qumran Scrolls II." *BASOR* 135 (1953) 33–38.
Broyles, Craig C. *The Conflict of Faith and Experience in the Psalms: A Form-Critical and Theological Study.* Sheffield: JSOT Press, 1989.
Bruce, F. F. *Biblical Exegesis in the Qumran Texts.* Exegetica 3. The Hague: Van Keulen, 1959.
Brueggemann, Walter. *The Message of the Psalms: A Theological Commentary.* Minneapolis: Augsburg, 1984.
Bultmann, Rudolf. *History of the Synoptic Tradition.* Translated by J. Marsh. Peabody, MA: Hendrickson, 1963.
Burger, Christoph. *Jesus als Davidssohn: Eine Traditionsgeschichtliche Untersuchung.* FRLANT 98. Göttingen: Vandenhoeck & Ruprecht, 1970.
Burnett, Fred W. "Characterization and Reader Construction of Characters in the Gospels." *Semeia* 63 (1993) 3–28.
Buse, S. Ivor. "The Markan Account of the Baptism of Jesus and Isaiah LXIII." *JST* 7 (1956) 74–75.
Cadbury, Henry. *The Making of Luke-Acts.* London: Macmillan, 1927.
Campbell, D. Keith. "Matthew's Hermeneutic of Psalm 22:1 and Jeremiah 31:15: A Window through which to View the Influence of Israel's Lament upon Matthew's Gospel." *Faith and Mission* 24 (2007) 46–58.
———. "NT Scholars' Use of OT Lament Terminology and Its Theological and Interdisciplinary Implications." *BBR* 21 (2011) 213–26.

Bibliography

―――. "The Psalmic Lament in the Synoptic Gospels: Beyond Thematic to Theological Understanding." Paper presented at the annual meeting of the SBL, Atlanta, November 22, 2010.

Cargal, Timothy B. "His Blood Be Upon Us and Upon Our Children: A Matthean Double Entendre?" *New Testament Studies* 37 (1991) 101–12.

Carroll, John T. "Luke's Crucifixion Scene." In *Reimaging the Death of the Lukan Jesus*. Bulletin de bibliographie biblique 73, edited by Dennis D. Sylva, 108–24. Frankfurt: Hain, 1990.

Carroll, John T., and Joel B. Green. *The Death of Jesus in Early Christianity*. Peabody, MA: Hendrickson, 1995.

Carson, D. A. "The Jewish Leaders in Matthew's Gospel: A Reappraisal." *JETS* 25 (1982) 161–74.

―――. *Matthew*. EBC 8. Grand Rapids: Zondervan, 1984.

Carson, D. A., and Douglass Moo. *An Introduction to the New Testament*. Grand Rapids: Zondervan, 2005.

Carter, Warren. *Matthew: Storyteller Interpreter Evangelist*. Peabody, MA: Hendrickson, 1996.

Chilton, Bruce. *A Galilean Rabbi and His Bible: Jesus' Use of the Interpreted Scripture of His Time*. Good News Studies 8. Wilmington, DE: Michael Glazier, Inc., 1984.

Collins, Adela Yarbro. *Mark: A Commentary*. Minneapolis: Fortress, 2007.

―――. "The Appropriation of the Psalms of Individual Lament by Mark." In *Scriptures in the Gospels*, edited by C. Tuckett, 223–41. Leuven: Leuven University Press, 1997.

Conzelmann, Hans. *The Theology of St. Luke*. London: Faber and Faber, 1960.

Cook, Michael J. "Jesus and the Pharisees—The Problem as it Stands Today." *JES* 15 (1978) 441–60.

―――. *Mark's Treatment of the Jewish Leaders*. NTSup 51. Leiden: Brill, 1978.

Cothenet, Edouard. "Les prophètes chrétiens dans l'Évangile selon saint Matthieu." In *L'Évangile selon Matthieu: Rédaction et théologie*, edited by M. Didier, 281–308. BETL 29. Gembloux: Duculot, 1972.

Cotrozzi, Stefano. *Expect the Unexpected: Aspects of Pragmatic Foregrounding in Old Testament Narratives*. LHBOTS 510. New York: T & T Clark, 2010.

Cousland, J. R. C. *The Crowds in the Gospel of Matthew*. NTSup 102. Boston: Brill, 2002.

Craigie, Peter C. *Psalm 1–50*. WBC 19. Waco, TX: Word Books, 1983.

Creed, John Martin. *The Gospel According to St. Luke: The Greek Text with Introduction, Notes, and Indices*. London: Macmillan, 1930.

Crisler, Channing L. "Caring for Creation by Hearing Its Lament: The Use of Old Testament Lament Language in New Testament Texts." Paper presented at the annual meeting of the the Evangelical Theological Society, Milwaukie, WI, November 16, 2012.

―――. "The 'I' Who Laments: Understanding the Enigmatic 'I' of Romans 7:7–25 in Light of Old Testament Lament Language." Paper presented at the annual meeting of the Evangelical Theological Society, Milwaukie, WI, November 15, 2012.

―――. "Lament in Romans: Promise, Suffering, and the Cry of Distress." PhD diss., The Southern Baptist Theological Seminary, 2012.

―――. "Paul's Use of Lament in Romans." Paper presented at the annual meeting of the Evangelical Theological Society, Atlanta, November 17, 2010.

Crowe, Jerome. "The LAOS at the Cross: Luke's Crucifixion Scene." In *The Language of the Cross*, edited by Aelred Lacomara, 77–90. Chicago: Franciscan Herald, 1977.
Cullmann, Oscar. *The Christology of the New Testament*. Translated by S. C. Guthrie and C. A. M. Hall. Philadelphia: Westminster, 1963.
Culpepper, R. Alan. *Anatomy of the Fourth Gospel: A Study in Literary Design*. Philadelphia: Fortress, 1983.
———. *Mark*. SHBC. Macon, GA: Smyth & Helwys, 2007.
Dahl, Nils Alstrup. "The Passion Narrative in Matthew." In *Interpretation of Matthew*, edited by Graham N. Stanton, 53–67. Edinburgh: T & T Clark, 1995.
Daniel, Constantin. "'Faux prophètes': Surnom des Esséniens dans le sermon sur la montagne." *Revue de Qumran* 7 (1969) 45–79.
Davies, W. D. and Dale Allison. *A Critical and Exegetical Commentary on the Gospel According to Saint Matthew*. 3 vols. ICC 1–3. Edinburgh: T & T Clark, 1988 to 1997.
Day, John. *Psalms*. OTG. Sheffield: Sheffield Academic, 1990.
Derrida, Jacques. *Of Grammatology*. Translated by G. C. Spivak. Baltimore: Johns Hopkins University Press, 1997.
Detweiler, Robert, ed. "Derrida and Biblical Studies." *Semeia* 23 (1982) 1–97.
———. "Reader-Response Approaches to Biblical and Secular Texts." *Semeia* 31 (1985) 1–230.
Dewey, Joanna. "The Literary Structure of the Controversy Narratives in Mark." *JBL* 92 (1973) 394–401.
———. *Markan Public Debate: Literary Technique, Concentric Structure, and Theology in Mark 2:1—3:6*. SBLDS 48. Chicago: Scholars, 1980.
Dhanaraj, Dharmakkan. *Theological Significance of the Motif of Enemies in Selected Psalms of Individual Lament*. Glückstadt: J. J. Augustin, 1992.
Dibelius, Martin. *From Tradition to Gospel*. Cambridge: James Clarke, 1971.
Dobbs-Allsopp, F. W. "Darwinism, Genre Theory, and City Laments." *JAOS* 120 (2000) 625–30.
Doble, Peter. "The Psalms in Luke-Acts." In *The Psalms in the New Testament*, edited by Steve Moyise and Maarten J. J. Menken, 83–117. New York: T & T Clark International, 2004.
Dodd, C. H. *According to the Scriptures*. London: James Nisbet, 1952.
———. *Historical Tradition in the Fourth Gospel*. Cambridge: Cambridge University Press, 1963.
Donahue, John R., and Daniel J. Harrington. *The Gospel of Mark*. SP 2. Collegeville, MN: Liturgical, 2002.
Douthwaite, John. *Towards a Linguistic Theory of Foregrounding*. Alessandria, IT: Edizioni dell'Orso, 2000.
Doyle, B. Rod. "A Concern of the Evangelist: Pharisees in Matthew 12." *ABR* 34 (1986) 17–34.
Dry, Helen Aristar. "Foregrounding: An Assessment." In *Language in Context: Essays for Robert E. Longacre*, edited by Shin Ja J. Hwang and William R. Merrifield, 435–50. Dallas: Summer Institute of Linguistics and University of Texas at Arlington, 1992.
Duling, Dennis C. "Matthew's Plurisignificant 'Son of David' in Social Science Perspective: Kinship, Kingship, Magic, and Miracle." *BTB* 22 (1992) 99–116.

Bibliography

———. "The Therapeutic Son of David: An Element in Matthew's Christological Apologetic." *NTS* 24 (1978) 392–409.
Duhm, D. B. *Das Buch Jesaja*. Handkommentar zum Alten Testament 3.1. Göttingen: Vandenhoeck & Ruprecht, 1892.
Dunn, James D. G. *Jesus Remembered*. Grand Rapids: Eerdmans, 2003.
Dupont, Jacques. *The Salvation of the Gentiles: Essays on the Acts of the Apostles*. New York: Paulist Press, 1979.
Eco, Umberto. *The Limits of Interpretation*. Bloomington: Indiana University Press, 1990.
Edwards, James R. *The Gospel According to Mark*. PNTC. Grand Rapids: Eerdmans, 2002.
———. "The Servant of the Lord and the Gospel of Mark." *SBJT* 8 (2004) 36–49.
Efroymson, David P. "Jesus: Opposition and Opponents." In *Within Context: Essays on Jews and Judaism in the New Testament*, edited by D. Efroymson et al., 85–103. Collegeville, MN: Liturgical Press, 1993.
Eklund, Rebekah Ann. "Lord, Teach Us How to Grieve: Jesus' Laments and Christian Hope." ThD diss., Duke Divinity School, 2012.
Elbogen, Ismar. *Der jüdische Gottesdienst in seiner geschichtlichen Entwicklung*. Leipzig: Fock, 1913.
Evans, C. F. *Saint Luke*. TPINTC. Philadelphia: Trinity Press International, 1990.
Evans, Craig A. *Mark 8:27—16:20*. WBC 34b. Nashville: Thomas Nelson, 2001.
———. "Praise and Prophecy in the Psalter and in the New Testament." In *The Book of Psalms: Composition and Reception*, edited by Peter W. Flint and Patrick D. Miller, 551–79. Boston: Brill, 2005.
Feiler, Paul Frederick. "Jesus the Prophet: The Lucan Portrayal of Jesus as the Prophet Like Moses." PhD diss., Princeton Theological Seminary, 1986.
Ferris, Paul Wayne., Jr. *The Genre of Communal Lament in the Bible and the Ancient Near East*. Atlanta: Scholars, 1992.
Fløysvik, Ingvar. *When God Becomes My Enemy: The Theology of the Complaint Psalms*. St. Louis: Concordia, 1997.
Forster, E. M. *Aspects of the Novel*. New York: Harcourt, Brace, 1954.
Foster, Paul. "The Use of Zechariah in Matthew's Gospel." In *The Book of Zechariah and Its Influence*, edited by Christopher Tuckett, 65–85. Burlington, VT: Ashgate, 2003.
Fowler, Robert M. *Let the Reader Understand: Reader-Response Criticism and the Gospel of Mark*. Bloomington: Indiana University Press, 1988.
France, R. T. *The Gospel of Mark: A Commentary on the Greek Text*. NIGTC. Grand Rapids: Eerdmans, 2002.
———. *Jesus and the Old Testament: His Application of the Old Testament Passages to Himself and His Mission*. London: Tyndale, 1971.
———. "Matthew and Jerusalem." In *Built Upon the Rock: Studies in the Gospel of Matthew*, edited by Daniel M. Gurtner and John Nolland, 108–27. Grand Rapids: Eerdmans, 2008.
Franklin, Eric. *Christ the Lord: A Study in the Purpose and Theology of Luke-Acts*. Philadelphia: Westminster, 1975.
Frei, Hans W. *The Eclipse of Biblical Narrative: A Study in Eighteenth and Nineteenth Century Hermeneutics*. New Haven, CT: Yale University Press, 1974.

Friedrich, Gerhard. "προφήτης." In *TDNT*, vol. 6, edited by G. Friedrich, 781–861. Grand Rapids: Eerdmans, 1980.
Gerhardsson, Birger. "Gottes Sohn als Diener Gottes: Messias, Agapé und Himmelscherrschaft nach dem Matthäusevangelium." *ST* 27 (1973) 73–106.
Gerstenberger, Erhard S. *Psalms, Part I, with an Introduction of Cultic Poetry.* FOTL 14. Grand Rapids: Eerdmans, 1988.
Gibbs, James M. "Purpose and Pattern in Matthew's Use of the Title 'Son of David.'" *NTS* 10 (1963/64) 446–62.
Gillingham, Susan. Review of *The Psalms of Lament in Mark's Passion Narrative*, by Stephen P. Ahearne-Kroll. *JSOT* 32 (2008) 199.
Gils, Félix. *Jésus prophète d'après les Évangiles synoptiques.* Orientalia et Biblica Lovaniensia 2. Leuven: Publications Universitaires, 1957.
Gnilka, Joachim. *Das Evangelium nach Markus.* EKKNT 2. 2 vols. Zurich: Benziger Verlag, 1978–79.
Goppelt, Leonhard. *Theology of the New Testament.* Vol. 1, *The Ministry of Jesus in its Theological Significance.* Translated by J. Alsup. Grand Rapids: Eerdmans, 1981.
Gourgues, Michel. *À la droite de Dieu: Résurrection de Jésus et actualization du Psaume 110,1 dans le Nouveau Testament.* Études Bibliques. Paris: Gabalda, 1978.
Green, Joel B. "The Death of Jesus, God's Servant." In *Reimaging the Death of the Lukan Jesus*, edited by Dennis D. Sylva, 1–28. BBB 73. Frankfurt: Hain, 1990.
———. *The Gospel of Luke.* NICNT. Grand Rapids: Eerdmans, 1997.
———. *The Theology of the Gospel of Luke.* NTT. Cambridge: Cambridge University Press, 1995.
Greene, Glenn Roger. "The Portrayal of Jesus as Prophet in Luke-Acts." PhD diss., The Southern Baptist Theological Seminary, 1975.
Grindel, John. "Matthew 12:18–21." *CBQ* 29 (1967) 110–15.
Grogen, Geoffrey W. "The Light and the Stone: A Christological Study in Luke and Isaiah." In *Christ the Lord: Studies in Christology Presented to Donald Guthrie*, edited by H. H. Rowdon, 151–67. Leicester: InterVarsity, 1982.
Grundmann, Walter. *Das Evangelium nach Lukas.* THNT. Berlin: Evangelische Verlagsanstalt, 1966.
———. *Das Evangelium nach Markus.* THNT 2. 2nd ed. Berlin: Evangelische Verlag, 1965.
Guelich, Robert A. "'The Beginning of the Gospel': Mark 1:1–15." *BR* 27 (1982) 5–15.
———. *Mark 1—8:62.* WBC 34a. Dallas: Word, 1989.
Gundry, Robert H. *Mark: A Commentary on His Apology for the Cross.* Grand Rapids: Eerdmans, 1993.
———. *Matthew: A Commentary on His Handbook for a Mixed Church under Persecution.* 2nd ed. Grand Rapids: Eerdmans, 1994.
———. *Matthew: A Commentary on His Literary and Theological Art.* Grand Rapids: Eerdmans, 1982.
———. *The Use of the Old Testament in St. Matthew's Gospel with Special Reference to the Messianic Hope.* SNT 18. Leiden: Brill, 1967.
Gunkel, Hermann and Joachim Begrich. *Introduction to Psalms: The Genres of the Religious Lyric of Israel.* Translated by James D. Nogalski. Macon, GA: Mercer University Press, 1998. Originally published 1933 by Vandenhoeck & Ruprecht as *Einleitung in die Psalmen: Die Gattungen der religiösen Lyrik Israels.*
Hagner, Donald A. *Matthew 1–13.* WBC 33a. Dallas: Word, 1993.

Bibliography

———. *Matthew 14–28*. WBC 33b. Dallas: Word, 1995.
Hahn, Ferdinand. *The Titles of Jesus in Christology: Their History in Early Christianity*. Translated by H. Knight and G. Ogg. London: Lutterworth, 1969.
Ham, Clay Alan. *The Coming King and the Rejected Shepherd: Matthew's Reading of Zechariah's Messianic Hope*. Sheffield: Sheffield Phoenix, 2005.
Hanson, James S. *The Endangered Promises: Conflict in Mark*. SBLDS 171. Atlanta: SBL, 2000.
Harasta, Eva, and Brian Brock. *Evoking Lament: A Theological Discussion*. London: T & T Clark International, 2009.
Hare, Douglas R. A. "Current Trends in Matthean Scholarship." *WW* 18 (1998) 405–10.
———. "The Rejection of the Jews in the Synoptic Gospels and Acts." In *Anti Semitism and the Foundations of Christianity*, edited by Alan T. Davies, 27–47. New York: Paulist, 1979.
Harrington, Daniel J. *The Gospel of Mark*. Sacra Pagina. Collegeville, MN: Liturgical, 1991.
———. "What and Why did Jesus Suffer According to Mark?" *CS* 34 (1995) 32–41.
Harrington, Jay M. *The Lukan Passion Narrative: The Markan Material in Luke 22,54—23,25: A Historical Survey: 1891–1997*. NTTS 30. Boston: Brill, 2000.
Hashimoto, Shigeo. "The Function of the Old Testament Quotations and Allusions in the Marcan Passion Narrative." ThD diss., Princeton Theological Seminary, 1970.
Hatina, Thomas R., ed. *Biblical Interpretation in Early Christian Gospels*. Vol. 2, *The Gospel of Matthew*. LNTS 310. New York: T & T Clark International, 2008.
———. "Embedded Scripture Texts and the Plurality of Meaning: The Announcement of the 'Voice From Heaven' in Mark 1.11 as a Case Study." In *Biblical Interpretation in Early Christian Gospels*. Vol. 1, *The Gospel of Mark*, edited by Thomas R. Hatina, 8–17. LNTS 304. New York: T & T Clark International, 2006.
Hay, David M. *Glory at the Right Hand: Psalm 110 in Early Christianity*. SBLMS 18. Nashville: Abingdon, 1973.
Hays, Richard B. "Christ Prays the Psalms: Israel's Psalter as Matrix of Early Christology." In *The Conversion of the Imagination: Paul as Interpreter of Israel's Scripture*, 101–8. Grand Rapids: Eerdmans, 1993. Originally published as "Christ Prays the Psalms: Paul's Use of Early Christian Exegetical Convention." In *The Future of Christology: Essays in Honor of Leander Keck*, edited by Abraham J. Malherbe and Wayne E. Meeks, 122–36. Minneapolis: Fortress, 1993.
Heimerdinger, Jean-Marc. *Topic, Focus and Foreground in Ancient Hebrew Narratives*. JSOT 295. Sheffield: Sheffield Academic, 1999.
Hengel, Martin. *The Atonement: The Origin of the Doctrine in the New Testament*. Translated by J. Bowden. Philadelphia: Fortress, 1981.
Hill, David. "False Prophets and Charismatics: Structure and Interpretation in Matthew 7:15–23." *Biblica* 57 (1976) 327–48.
Holladay, William Lee. *The Psalms Through Three Thousand Years: Prayerbook of a Cloud of Witnesses*. Minneapolis: Fortress, 1993.
Hooker, Morna. "Did the Use of Isaiah 53 to Interpret His Mission Begin with Jesus." In *Jesus and the Suffering Servant: Isaiah 53 and Christian Origins*, edited by W. H. Bellinger and W. R. Farmer, 88–103. Harrisburg, PA: Trinity Press International, 1998.
———. *The Gospel According to Saint Mark*. BNTC. London: A & C Black, 1991. Reprint of 1997 edition by Hendrickson.

———. *Jesus and the Servant: The Influence of the Servant Concept of Deutero-Isaiah in the New Testament.* London: SPCK, 1959.
Howell, David B. *Matthew's Inclusive Story: A Study in the Rhetoric of the First Gospel.* JSNTSup 42. Sheffield: Sheffield Academic, 1990.
Huizenga, Leroy A. "The Incarnation of the Servant: The 'Suffering Servant' and Matthean Christology." *HBT* 27 (2005) 25–58.
———. *The New Isaac: Tradition and Intertextuality in the Gospel of Matthew.* SupNT 131. Boston: Brill, 2009.
Hultgren, Arland. *Jesus and His Adversaries: The Form and Function of the Conflict Stories in the Synoptic Tradition.* Minneapolis: Augsburg, 1979.
Hummel, Reinhard. *Die Auseinandersetuzung zwischen Kirche und Judentum im Matthäusevangelium.* BET 33. Munich: Kaiser, 1963.
Hurtado, Larry W. *Mark.* NIBC. Peabody, MA: Hendrickson, 1989.
Jeremias, Joachim. *New Testament Theology: The Proclamation of Jesus.* New York: Charles Scribner's Sons, 1971.
———. "Παῖς θεοῦ." In *Theological Dictionary of the New Testament*, vol. 5, edited by G. Friedrich, 677–717. Grand Rapids: Eerdmans, 1979.
———. Review of *Jesus and the Servant: The Influence of the Servant Concept of Deutero-Isaiah in the New Testament*, by Morna D. Hooker. *JTS* 11 (1960) 140–44.
Jervell, Jacob. *Luke and the People of God.* Minneapolis: Augsburg, 1972.
Johnson, Luke Timothy. *The Acts of the Apostles.* SP 5. Collegeville, MN: Liturgical, 1992.
———. "The Christology of Luke-Acts." In *Who Do You Say that I Am? Essays on Christology*, edited by Mark Allen Powell and David R. Bauer, 49–65. Louisville: Westminster John Knox, 1999.
———. *The Literary Function of Possessions in Luke-Acts.* SBLDS 39. Missoula, MT: Scholars, 1977.
Jones, Donald L. "The Title *Pais* in Luke-Acts." In *SBL 1982 Seminar Papers.* SBL Seminar Papers 21, 217–26. Chico, CA: Scholars, 1982.
Juel, Donald. *Messianic Exegesis: Christological Interpretation of the Old Testament in Early Christianity.* Philadelphia: Fortress, 1988.
Kähler, Martin. *The So-Called Historical Jesus and the Historic, Biblical Christ.* Philadelphia: Fortress, 1964.
Karris, Robert J. *Luke: Artist and Theologian; Luke's Passion Account as Literature.* New York: Paulist, 1985.
Käser, Walter. "Exegetische und Theologische Erwägungen zur Seligpreisung der Kinderlosen." *ZNW* 54 (1963) 240–54.
Kee, Howard Clark. "The Function of Scriptural Quotations and Allusions in Mark 11–16." In *Jesus und Paulus*, edited by E. Earle Ellis and Erich Grässer, 165–83. Göttingen: Vandenhoeck & Ruprecht, 1975.
Keener, Craig. *A Commentary on the Gospel of Matthew.* Grand Rapids: Eerdmans, 1999.
Keith, Chris, and Larry Hurtado, eds. *Jesus Among Friends and Enemies: A Historical and Literary Introduction to Jesus in the Gospels.* Grand Rapids: Baker Academic, 2012.
Kelber, Werner H. "Mark 14:32–42: Gethsemane: Passion Christology and Discipleship Failure." *ZNW* 63 (1972) 166–87.
———. *Mark's Story of Jesus.* Philadelphia: Fortress, 1979.

Bibliography

Kingsbury, Jack Dean. *The Christology of Mark's Gospel*. Philadelphia: Fortress, 1983.
———. *Conflict in Luke: Jesus, Authorities, Disciples*. Minneapolis: Fortress, 1991.
———. *Conflict in Mark: Jesus, Authorities, Disciples*. Minneapolis: Fortress, 1989.
———. "The Developing Conflict between Jesus and the Jewish Leaders in Matthew's Gospel: A Literary-Critical Study." *CBQ* 49 (1987) 57–73. Reprinted from *The Interpretation of Matthew*, edited by Graham N. Stanton, 179–97. Edinburgh: T & T Clark, 1995.
———. "Jesus as the 'Prophetic Messiah' in Luke's Gospel." In *The Future of Christology: Essays in Honor of Leander E. Keck*, edited by Abraham J. Malherbe and Wayne A. Meeks, 29–42. Minneapolis: Fortress, 1993.
———. *Matthew as Story*. Philadelphia: Fortress, 1986.
———. "The Religious Authorities in the Gospel of Mark." *NTS* 36 (1990) 42–65.
———. "The Significance of the Cross within Mark's Story." *Int* 47 (1993) 370–79.
———. "The Title 'Son of David' in Matthew's Gospel." *JBL* 95 (1976) 591–602.
Klostermann, Erich. *Das Lukasevangelium*. Tübingen: Mohr Siebeck, 1929.
———. *Das Markusevangelium erklärt*. 4th ed. HNT 3. Tübingen: Mohr Siebeck, 1950.
Knowles, Michael. *Jeremiah in Matthew's Gospel: The Rejected Prophet Motif in Matthean Redaction*. Sheffield: Sheffield Academic, 1993.
Kodell, Jerome. "Luke's use of *Laos*, 'People,' Especially in the Jerusalem Narrative (Lk 19,28–24,53)." *CBQ* 31 (1967) 327–43.
Koskenniemi, Erkki, et al. "Wine Mixed with Myrrh (Mark 15.23) and *Crurifragium* (John 19.31–32): Two Details of the Passion Narratives." *JSNT* 27 (2005) 379–86.
Köstenberger, Andreas J., and Richard Patterson. *Invitation to Biblical Interpretation: Exploring the Hermeneutical Triad of History, Literature, and Theology*. ITSS. Grand Rapids: Kregel, 2011.
Ladd, George Eldon. *A Theology of the New Testament*. Rev. ed. Grand Rapids: Eerdmans, 1974.
Lagrange, Marie-Joseph. *Évangile selon Saint Marc*. Études Bibliques. Paris: Gabalda, 1920.
———. *L'Évangile selon Saint Matthieu*. Paris: Lecoffre, 1948.
Lane, William L. *The Gospel According to Mark: The English Text with Introduction, Exposition, and Notes*. Grand Rapids: Eerdmans, 1974.
Le Donne, Anthony. "The Jewish Leaders." In *Jesus Among Friends and Enemies: A Historical and Literary Introduction to Jesus in the Gospels*, edited by Chris Keith and Larry W. Hurtado, 199–217. Grand Rapids: Baker Academic, 2012.
Lee, Nancy C. *Lyrics of Lament: From Tragedy to Transformation*. Minneapolis: Fortress, 2010.
Leske, Adrian. "The Influence of Isaiah on Christology in the Gospels of Matthew and Luke." In *Crises in Christology: Essays in Quest of Resolution*, edited by William R. Farmer, 241–69. Livonia, MI: Dove, 1995.
———. "Isaiah and Matthew: The Prophetic Influence in the First Gospel: A Report of Current Research." In *Jesus and the Suffering Servant: Isaiah 53 and Christian Origins*, edited by W. H. Bellinger Jr. and W. R. Farmer, 152–69. Harrisburg, PA: Trinity, 1998.
Lindars, Barnabas. *Jesus Son of Man: A Fresh Examination of the Son of Man Sayings*. Grand Rapids: Eerdmans, 1984.
———. *New Testament Apologetic: The Doctrinal Significance of the Old Testament Quotations*. Philadelphia: Westminster, 1961.

Linnemann, Eta. *Studien zur Passionsgeschichte*. FRLANT 102. Göttingen: Vandenhoeck & Ruprecht, 1970.
Loader, W. R. G. "Christ at the Right Hand—Ps. CX in the New Testament." *NTS* 24 (1978) 199–217.
Lührmann, Dieter. *Das Markusevangelium*. HNT 3. Tübingen: Mohr Siebeck, 1987.
———. "Die Pharisäer und die Schriftgelehrten im Markusevangelium." *Zeitschrift für die neutestamentliche Wissenschaft und die Kunde der älteren Kirche* 78 (1987) 169–85.
Luz, Ulrich. *Matthew: A Commentary*. Translated by W. C. Linss. 3 vols. Minneapolis: Augsburg, 1989–2005.
———. *The Theology of the Gospel of Matthew*. Translated by J. Bradford Robinson. Cambridge: Cambridge University Press, 1995.
Malbon, Elizabeth Struthers. *In the Company of Jesus: Characters in Mark's Gospel*. Translated by Marie-Raphaël de Hemptinne. Louisville: Westminster John Knox, 2000.
———. *Mark's Jesus: Characterization as Narrative Christology*. Waco, TX: Baylor University Press, 2009.
Mallen, Peter. *The Reading and Transformation of Isaiah in Luke-Acts*. LNTS 367. New York: T & T Clark, 2008.
Mandolfo, Carleen. *God in the Dock: Dialogic Tension in the Psalms of Lament*. London: Sheffield Academic, 2002.
Marcus, Joel. *Mark 8–16: A New Translation with Introduction and Commentary*. AYB 27a. New Haven, CT: Yale University Press, 2009.
———. "The Old Testament and the Death of Jesus: The Role of Scripture in the Gospel Passion Narratives." In *The Death of Jesus in Early Christianity*, edited by John T. Carroll and Joel B. Green, 205–33. Peabody, MA: Hendrickson, 1995.
———. Review of *Isaiah's New Exodus in Mark*, by Rikki E. Watts. *JTS* 50 (1999) 222–25.
———. *The Way of the Lord: Christological Exegesis of the Old Testament in the Gospel of Mark*. Louisville: Westminster/John Knox, 1992.
Marshall, I. Howard. *The Gospel of Luke*. NIGTC. Grand Rapids: Eerdmans, 1978.
———. "Son of God or Servant of Yahweh: A Reconsideration of Mark 1:11." *NTS* 15 (1969) 326–36.
Martín-Asensio, Gustavo. *Transitivity-Based Foregrounding in the Acts of the Apostles: A Functional-Grammatical Approach to the Lukan Perspective*. JSNTSup 202. SNTG 8. Sheffield: Sheffield Academic, 2000.
Matera, Frank J. *The Kingship of Jesus: Composition and Theology in Mark 15*. SBLDS 66. Chico, CA: Scholars, 1982.
———. "The Prologue as the Interpretive Key to Mark's Gospel." *JSNT* 34 (1988) 3–20.
Maurer, Christian. "Knecht Gottes und Sohn Gottes im Passionsbericht des Markusevangeliums." *Zeitschrift für Theologie und Kirche* 50 (1953) 1–38.
McCaffrey, U. P. "Psalm Quotations in the Passion Narratives of the Gospels." In *The Relationship between the Old and New Testament*, 73–89. Bloemfontein: New Testament Society of South Africa, 1981.
McKnight, Scot, and Joseph B. Modica, eds. *Who Do My Opponents Say that I Am? An Investigation of the Accusations against Jesus*. LNTS 327. New York: T & T Clark, 2008.
Meier, John P. "John the Baptist in Matthew's Gospel." *JBL* 99 (1980) 383–405.

Bibliography

———. *Matthew*. New Testament Message. Wilmington, DE: Glazier, 1980.
———. *The Vision of Matthew: Christ, Church, and Morality in the First Gospel*. New York: Paulist, 1979.
Menken, Martinus J. J. *Matthew's Bible: The Old Testament Text of the Evangelist*. BETL 173. Leuven: Leuven University Press, 2004.
Merkel, Helmut. "The Opposition between Jesus and Judaism." In *Jesus and the Politics of His Day*, edited by E. Bammel and C. F. D. Moule, 129–44. Cambridge: Cambridge University Press, 1984.
Meyer, Ben F. *Critical Realism and the New Testament*. PTMS 17. Allison Park, PA: Pickwick Publications, 1989.
Miller, Patrick D. "Prayer as Persuasion: The Rhetoric and Intention of Prayer." *WW* 13 (1993) 356–62.
———. *They Cried to the Lord: The Form and Theology of Biblical Prayer*. Minneapolis: Fortress, 1994.
Minear, Paul. "The Disciples and the Crowds in the Gospel of Matthew." *ATR* 3 (1974) 28–44.
———. "Jesus' Audiences, According to Luke." *NovT* 16 (1974) 81–109.
Moessner, David P. *Lord of the Banquet: The Literary and Theological Significance of the Lukan Travel Narrative*. Minneapolis: Fortress, 1989.
Moffitt, David. "Righteous Bloodshed, Matthew's Passion Narrative, and the Temple's Destruction: Lamentations as a Matthean Intertext." *JBL* 125 (2006) 299–320.
Moloney, Francis J. *The Gospel of Mark: A Commentary*. Peabody, MA: Hendrickson, 2002.
———. "The Markan Story." *WW* 26 (2006) 5–13.
Moo, Douglas J. *The Old Testament in the Gospel Passion Narratives*. Sheffield: Almond, 1983.
Morrow, William S. *Protest against God: The Eclipse of a Biblical Tradition*. Sheffield: Sheffield Phoenix, 2007.
Moulder, W. J. "The Old Testament Background and the Interpretation of Mark x.45." *NTS* 24 (1977/78) 120–27.
Mowinckel, Sigmund. *The Psalms in Israel's Worship*. Translated by D. R. Ap-Thomas. 2 vols. Nashville: Abingdon, 1962. Originally published in 1951 by Aschehoug as *Offersang og Sangoffer*.
Moyise, Steve, and Maarten J. J. Menken, eds. *The Psalms in the New Testament*. New York: T & T Clark, 2004.
Moxnes, Halvor. *The Economy of the Kingdom: Social Conflict and Economic Relations in Luke's Gospel*. Philadelphia: Fortress, 1988.
Moyise, Steve. *The Old Testament in the New: An Introduction*. T & T Clark Approaches to Biblical Studies. New York: T & T Clark International, 2001.
Mulholland, Moston R. "The Markan Opponents of Jesus." *HTR* 71 (1978) 166.
Neyrey, Jerome. "The Absence of Jesus' Emotions: The Lucan Redaction of Lk 22, 39–46." *Biblica* 61 (1980) 153–71.
———. *The Passion According to Luke: A Redaction Study of Luke's Soteriology*. Theological Inquires. New York: Paulist, 1985.
———. "The Thematic Use of Isaiah 42, 1–4 in Matthew 12." *Biblica* 63 (1982) 457–73.
Nickelsburg, George W. E. "The Genre and Function of the Markan Passion Narrative." *HTR* 73 (1980) 153–84.

Nolan, B. M. *The Royal Son of God: The Christology of Matthew 1–2 in the Setting of the Gospel*. OBO 23. Fribourg: Éditions Universitaires, 1979.

Nolland, John. *The Gospel According to Matthew*. NIGTC. Grand Rapids: Eerdmans, 2005.

———. "The King as Shepherd: The Role of Deutero-Zechariah in Matthew." In *Biblical Interpretation in Early Christian Gospels. Volume 2: The Gospel of Matthew*, edited by Thomas Hatina, 133–46. LNTS 310. New York: T & T Clark International, 2008.

———. *Luke*. 3 vols. WBC 35. Dallas: Word Books, 1989–93.

Novakovic, Lidija. "Matthew's Atomistic Use of Scripture: Messianic Interpretation of Isaiah 53:4 in Matthew 8:17." In *Biblical Interpretation in Early Christian Gospels. Volume 2: The Gospel of Matthew*, edited by Thomas Hatina, 147–62. LNTS 310. New York: T & T Clark International, 2008.

———. *Messiah, the Healer of the Sick: A Study of Jesus as the Son of David in the Gospel of Matthew*. Tübingen: Mohr Siebeck, 2003.

Novello, Henry L. "Jesus' Cry of Lament: Towards a True Apophaticism." *ITQ* 78 (2013) 38–60.

O'Brien, Kelli S. *The Use of Scripture in the Markan Passion Narrative*. LNTS 384. New York: T & T Clark International, 2010.

O'Day, Gail R. "The Citation of Scripture as a Key to Characterization in Acts." In *Scripture and Traditions: Essays on Early Judaism and Christianity in Honor of Carl R. Holladay*, edited by Patrick Gray and Gail R. O'Day, 207–21. Boston: Brill, 2008.

Öhler, Markus. "To Mourn, Weep, Lament and Groan: On the Heterogeneity of the New Testament's Statements on Lament." In *Evoking Lament: A Theological Discussion*, edited by Eva Harasta and Brian Brock, 150–65. London: T & T Clark International, 2009.

O'Leary, Anne M. *Matthew's Judaization of Mark: Examined in the Context of the Use of Sources in Graeco-Roman Antiquity*. LNTS 323. New York: T & T Clark, 2006.

Osborne, Grant R. *The Hermeneutical Spiral*. Downers Grove: InterVarsity, 1991.

Page, Sydney H. T. "The Suffering Servant Between the Testaments." *NTS* 31 (1985) 481–97.

Pannenberg, Wolfhart. *Jesus—God and Man*. Translated by L. Wilkins and D. Priebe. Philadelphia: Westminster, 1977.

Pao, David W., and Eckhard J. Schnabel. "Luke." In *Commentary on the New Testament Use of the Old Testament*, edited by G. K. Beale and D. A. Carson, 251–414. Grand Rapids: Baker Academic, 2007.

Patte, Daniel. *Structural Exegesis for New Testament Critics*. GBS. Minneapolis: Fortress, 1989.

Patten, Rebecca. "The Thaumaturgical Element in the Gospel of Mark." PhD diss., Drew University, 1976.

Pennington, Jonathan T. "Refractions of Daniel in the Gospel of Matthew." In *Early Christian Literature and Intertextuality. Vol. 1, Thematic Studies*, 65–86. LNTS 391. London: T & T Clark, 2009.

Perkins, Pheme. *The Gospel of Mark: Introduction, Commentary, and Reflections*. NIB 8. Nashville: Abingdon, 1995.

Perrin, Norman. *Rediscovering the Teaching of Jesus*. London: SCM, 1977.

———. *What is Redaction Criticism?* GBS. Philadelphia: Fortress, 1969.

Pesch, Rudolf. *Die Apostelgeschichte (Apg 1–12)*. EKKNT 5:1. Zurich: Benziger, 1986.

Bibliography

———. *Das Markusevangelium: Kommentar zu Kap. 8,27—16,20.* HTKNT 2.2. Freiburg: Herder, 1980.
Petersen, Norman R. "'Point of View' in Mark's Narrative." *Semeia* 12 (1978) 97–121.
Peterson, David. *The Acts of the Apostles.* PNTC. Grand Rapids: Eerdmans, 2009.
Plummer, Alfred. *A Critical and Exegetical Commentary on the Gospel According to Saint Luke.* Grand Rapids: Eerdmans, 1951.
———. *An Exegetical Commentary on the Gospel According to St. Matthew.* Grand Rapids: Eerdmans, 1953.
Polhill, John B. *Acts.* NAC 26. Nashville: Broadman, 1992.
Powell, Mark Allen. "The Religious Leaders in Luke: A Literary-Critical Study." *JBL* 109 (1990) 93–110.
———. "The Religious Leaders in Matthew: A Literary-Critical Approach." PhD diss., Union Theological Seminary in Virginia, 1988.
———. *What Is Narrative Criticism.* Minneapolis: Fortress, 1990.
Rese, Martin. *Alttestamentliche Motive in der Christologie des Lukas.* SNT 1. Gütersloh: Gütersloher Verlagshaus Gerd Mohn, 1969.
Resseguie, James L. "Reader-Response and the Synoptic Gospels," *JAAR* 52 (1984) 307–34.
Rhoads, David. "Losing Life for Others in the Face of Death: Mark's Standards of Judgment." *Int* 47 (1993) 358–69.
———. "Narrative Criticism and the Gospel of Mark." *JAAR* 50 (1982) 411–34.
———. *Reading Mark: Engaging the Gospel.* Minneapolis: Fortress, 2004.
Rhoads, David, et al. *Mark as Story: An Introduction to the Narrative of a Gospel.* 3rd ed. Minneapolis: Fortress, 2012.
Rindge, Matthew S. "Reconfiguring the Akedah and Recasting God: Lament and Divine Abandonment in Mark." *JBL* 131 (2012) 755–74.
———. "Theological, Religious, and Sociopolitical Aspects of Lament: Fight Club, Lament Psalms, and Mark 15:34." Paper presented at the annual meeting of the SBL, San Francisco, November 19, 2011.
Rodgers, P. "Mark 15:28." *EQ* 61 (1989) 81–84.
Rowe, C. Kavin. *Early Narrative Christology: The Lord in the Gospel of Luke.* BZNW 139. New York: Walter de Gruyter, 2006.
Ruppert, Lothar. *Jesus als der leidende Gerechte? Der Weg Jesu im Lichte eines alt- und zwischentestamentlichen Motivs.* SGUA 59. Stuttgart: Katholisches Bibelwerk, 1972.
———. *Der leidende Gerechte: Eine motivgeschichtliche Untersuchung zum Alten Testament und zwischentestamentlichen Judentum.* FB 5. Würzburg: Echter Verlag, 1972.
Saldarini, Anthony J. *Matthew's Christian-Jewish Community.* Chicago: University of Chicago, 1994.
———. "The Social Class of the Pharisees in Mark." In *The Social World of Formative Christianity and Judaism: Essays in Tribute to Howard Clark Kee,* edited by J. Neusner and Peder Borgen, 69–77. Philadelphia: Fortress, 1988.
Sanders, J. T. *The Jews in Luke-Acts.* Philadelphia: Fortress, 1987.
Sandmel, Samuel. "Parallelomania." *JBL* 81 (1962) 1–13.
Saunders, S. P. "'No One Dared Ask Him Anything More': Contextual Readings of the Controversy Stories in Matthew." PhD diss., Princeton Theological Seminary, 1990.

Bibliography

Schneck, Richard. *Isaiah in the Gospel of Mark, I–VII*. BIBAL Dissertation Series 1. Vallejo, CA: BIBAL Press, 1994.
Schnider, Franz. *Jesus der Prophet*. OBO 2. Göttingen: Vandenhoeck & Ruprecht, 1973.
Schweizer, Eduard. *The Good News According to Luke*. Translated by D. E. Green. Atlanta: John Knox, 1984.
———. *The Good News According to Matthew*. Translated by David E. Green. Atlanta: John Knox, 1975.
Seccombe, David. "Luke and Isaiah." In *The Right Doctrine from the Wrong Texts: Essays on the Use of the Old Testament in the New*, edited by G. K. Beale, 248–56. Grand Rapids: Baker, 1994.
Senior, Donald. "The Lure of the Formula Quotations: Re-assessing Matthew's Use of the Old Testament with the Passion Narrative as a Test Case." In *The Scriptures in the Gospels*, edited by C. M. Tuckett, 89–115. BETL 131. Leuven: Leuven University Press, 1997.
———. *The Passion Narrative According to Matthew: A Redactional Study*. BETL 39. Leuven: Leuven University Press, 1975.
———. *The Passion of Jesus in the Gospel of Mark*. Passion Series 2. Wilmington, DE: Michael Glazier, 1984.
Shires, H. M. *Finding the Old Testament in the New*. Philadelphia: Westminster, 1974.
Sim, David C. "The 'Confession' of the Soldiers in Matthew 27.54." *HeyJ* 34 (1993) 401–24.
Simmons, William. "The Apostle Paul and Lament: Godly Sorrow as a Pedagogical Tool." Paper presented at the annual meeting of the SBL, Atlanta, November 18, 2010.
Skaggs, Rebecca. "The Apocalypse of John: A Lament?" Paper presented at the annual meeting of the SBL, Atlanta, November 22, 2010.
Smith, Stephen H. *A Lion with Wings: A Narrative-Critical Approach to Mark's Gospel*. Sheffield: Sheffield Academic, 1996.
———. "The Role of Jesus' Opponents in the Markan Drama." *NTS* 35 (1989) 161–82.
Stamps, Dennis L. "Rhetorical Criticism of the New Testament: Ancient and Modern Evaluations of Argumentation." In *Approaches to New Testament Study*, edited by Stanley E. Porter and David Tombs, 129–69. JSNTSup 120. Sheffield: Sheffield Academic, 1995.
Stanton, Graham. *A Gospel for a New People: Studies in Matthew*. Edinburgh: T & T Clark, 1992.
Stein, Robert H. *Mark*. BECNT. Grand Rapids: Baker Academic, 2008.
Strauss, Mark L. *The Davidic Messiah in Luke-Acts: The Promise and its Fulfillment in Lukan Christology*. JSNTSup 110. Sheffield: Sheffield Academic, 1995.
Strecker, Georg. *Der Weg der Gerichtigkeit: Untersuchungen zur Theologie des Matthäus*. FRLANT 82. Göttingen: Vandenhoeck & Ruprecht, 1962.
Stuckenbruck, Loren T. "Satan and Demons." In *Jesus Among Friends and Enemies: A Historical and Literary Introduction to Jesus in the Gospels*, edited by Chris Keith and Larry W. Hurtado, 173–97. Grand Rapids: Baker Academic, 2012.
Stuhlmacher, Peter. "Der messianische Gottesknecht." *JBT* 8 (1993) 131–54.
Subramanian, J. Samuel. *The Synoptic Gospels and the Psalms as Prophecy*. LNTS 351. New York: T & T Clark, 2007.
Suhl, Alfred. "Der Davidssohn im Matthäus-Evangelium." *ZNW* 59 (1968) 57–81.

Bibliography

———. *Die Funktion der alttestamentlichen Zitate und Anspielungen im Markusevangelium*. Gütersloh: Gütersloher Verlagshaus Gerd Mohn, 1965.
Tannehill, Robert C. "The Disciples in Mark: The Function of a Narrative Role." In *The Interpretation of Mark*, edited by W. Telford, 134–57. IRT 7. Philadelphia: Fortress, 1985.
———. "The Gospel of Mark as Narrative Christology." *Semeia* 16 (1979) 57–95.
———. *The Narrative Unity of Luke-Acts: A Literary Interpretation*. 2 vols. Philadelphia: Fortress, 1986.
Tate, W. Randolph. *Interpreting the Bible: A Handbook of Terms and Methods*. Peabody, MA: Hendrickson, 2006.
Taylor, Vincent. *The Gospel According to St. Mark*. London: Macmillan, 1952.
Thielman, Frank. *Theology of the New Testament: A Canonical and Synthetic Approach*. Grand Rapids: Zondervan, 2005.
Thiselton, Anthony C. *New Horizons in Hermeneutics: The Theory and Practice of Transforming Biblical Reading*. Grand Rapids: Zondervan, 1992.
Tilborg, Sjef Van. *The Jewish Leaders in Matthew*. Leiden: Brill, 1972.
Tolbert, Mary Ann. "How the Gospel of Mark Builds Character." *Int* 47 (1993) 347–57.
Torrey, C. C. "The Influence of Second Isaiah in the Gospels and Acts." *JBL* 48 (1929) 24–36.
Turner, David L. *Matthew*. BECNT. Grand Rapids: Baker Academic, 2008.
Tyson, Joseph B. *Luke-Acts and the Jewish People: Eight Critical Perspectives*. Minneapolis: Augsburg, 1988.
Unger, Christoph. *Genre, Relevance and Global Coherence: The Pragmatics of Discourse Type*. PSPLC. New York: Palgrave MacMillan, 2006.
Uspensky, Boris. *A Poetics of Composition*. Berkeley: University of California, 1973.
Vanhoozer, Kevin. *Is There a Meaning in this Text? The Bible, The Reader, and the Morality of Literary Knowledge*. Grand Rapids: Zondervan, 1998.
Vorster, Willem S. "The Function of the Use of the Old Testament in Mark." *Neotestamentica* 14 (1980) 62–72.
Voss, Gerhard J. *Die Christologie der lukanischen Schriften in Grundzügen*. Paris: Desclée de Brouwer, 1965.
Wagner, J. Ross. "Psalm 118 in Luke-Acts: Tracing a Narrative Thread." In *Early Christian Interpretation of the Scriptures of Israel: Investigations and Proposals*, edited by Craig A. Evans and James A. Sanders, 154–78. JSNTSup 148. Sheffield: Sheffield Academic, 1997.
Wallace, Daniel B. *Greek Grammar Beyond the Basics: An Exegetical Syntax of the New Testament with Scripture, Subject, and Greek Word Indexes*. Grand Rapids: Zondervan, 1996.
Watts, Rikki E. *Isaiah's New Exodus and Mark*. WUNT 88. Tübingen: Mohr Siebeck, 1997.
———. "The Lord's House and David's Lord: The Psalms and Mark's Perspective on Jesus and the Temple." *BibInt* 15 (2007) 307–22.
———. "The Psalms in Mark's Gospel." In *The Psalms in the New Testament*, edited by Steve Moyise and Maarten J. J. Menken, 25–45. New York: T & T Clark International, 2004.
———. Review of *The Psalms of Lament in Mark's Passion Narrative*, by Stephen P. Ahearne-Kroll. *JETS* 52 (2009) 159–62.

———. Review of *The Psalms of Lament in Mark's Passion Narrative*, by Stephen P. Ahearne-Kroll. *TS* 70 (2009) 500–501.

Weaver, Dorothy J. *Matthew's Missionary Discourse: A Literary Critical Analysis.* JSNTSup 38. Sheffield: JSOT Press, 1994.

Webb, Geoff R. *Mark at the Threshold: Applying Bakhtinian Categories to Markan Characterisation.* Biblical Interpretation Series 95. Boston: Brill, 2008.

Weber, Joseph C. "Jesus' Opponents in the Gospel of Mark." *Journal of Bible and Religion* 34 (1966) 214–22.

Weeden, Theodore J. "The Conflict between Mark and His Opponents over Kingdom Theology." In *Society of Biblical Literature 1973 Seminar Papers*, 203–41. Society of Biblical Literature Seminar Papers 2. Missoula, MT: Scholars, 1973.

———. *Mark: Traditions in Conflict.* Philadelphia: Fortress, 1971.

Westermann, Claus. *Praise and Lament in the Psalms.* Translated by Keith R. Crim and Richard N. Soulen. Atlanta: John Knox, 1981.

———. *The Praise of God in the Psalms.* Translated by Keith R. Crim. Richmond, VA: John Knox, 1965.

———. "The Role of the Lament in the Theology of the Old Testament." *Int* 28 (1974) 20–38.

Wiarda, Timothy. *Interpreting Gospel Narratives: Scenes, People, and Theology.* Nashville: Broadman and Holman Academic, 2010.

Williams, Joel F. *Other Followers of Jesus: Minor Characters as Major Figures in Mark's Gospel.* JSNTSup 102. Sheffield: Sheffield Academic, 1994.

Winkle, Ross E. "The Jeremiah Model for Jesus in the Temple." *AUSS* 24 (1986) 155–72.

Witherington, Ben. *The Gospel of Mark: A Socio-Rhetorical Commentary.* Grand Rapids: Eerdmans, 2001.

———. *New Testament Rhetoric: An Introductory Guide to the Art of Persuasion in and of the New Testament.* Eugene, OR: Cascade Books, 2009.

Wright, N. T. *The New Testament and the People of God.* Minneapolis: Fortress, 1992.

Of Heroes and Villains

www.ingramcontent.com/pod-product-compliance
Lightning Source LLC
Chambersburg PA
CBHW062036220426
43662CB00010B/1525